THE LIFE OF GOVERNOR LOUIS KOSSUTH WITH HIS PUBLIC SPEECHES IN THE UNITED STATES,

AND A BRIEF HISTORY OF THE HUNGARIAN WAR OF INDEPENDENCE

Osiris Kiadó • Budapest, 2001

First published in New York, 1852

Illustrations courtesy of the Hungarian National Museum
Selected by Katalin Jalsovszky

Published under the auspices of the Embassy of Hungary
in Washington, D. C. in honor of the 150th anniversary
of Governor-President Louis Kossuth's visit to the United States.

Introductory Remarks

By the arrival of Governor Kossuth in this country, and his soul-stirring speeches, an intense interest has been excited, throughout the length and breadth of the land, in behalf of poor, oppressed, down-trodden Hungary, and in reference to the fate of republicanism across the Atlantic. The present tendency seems to be in favor of Absolutism; but a few days may change the whole face of things. There is a vast volcano under the European continent, continually gathering force by the superincumbent weight which now confines its subterranean, rumbling fires. It already shakes the continent and the world; and the time is not far distant, we believe, when its scorching, thundering flames will burst forth, and scatter the thrones of despotism to the winds of heaven. Freedom and tyranny are approaching each other in battle array, and before we are aware, the clash of arms will strike upon the ear, and the bulwarks of oppression will fall. The great Kossuth we believe is to be the leader in this tremendous battle of the world. He has been received in this country in the most enthusiastic manner and his speeches have convulsed the nation and astonished the world. There is probably no man living who possesses such a knowledge of diplomacy, law and the history of nations as Kossuth, and there is the greatest eagerness to have his life and speeches in a permanent form. The following work contains a faithful and graphic account of the life of the distinguished Magyar and his achievements, with a thorough though brief history of the Hungarian War of Independence, by an officer of the army.

Contents

Life of Governor Louis Kossuth

This distinguished General was born at Monok, in Zemplin, one of the northern counties of Hungary, on the 27th of April, 1806. His father was in the Austrian army during the wars against Napoleon; his mother is a woman of extraordinary force of mind and character. When a boy, he was remarkable for the winning gentleness of his disposition, and for an earnest enthusiasm, which gave promise of eminence. A young clergyman, attracted by the character of the boy, took upon himself the office of his tutor. His father died, his tutor was translated to another post, and the walls of his prison-house seemed again to close upon him; but, by the aid of members of his family, he was enabled to attend such schools as the district furnished. He was taught the Latin language, and through that door he was introduced into the broad domains of history, where he could range at will through the immortal past.

During the wars which occurred in Austria from 1527 to 1715, seventeen of the family of Kossuth had been attainted for high treason against Austria. The last, most desperate, and decisively unsuccessful struggle was that waged by Rakozky, at the beginning of the last century. Kossuth pored over the chronicles and annals which narrate the incidents of this contest, till he was master of all the minutest details.

When just entering upon manhood, he made his way to Pest, the capital, to study the legal profession. He entered the office of a notary, and began gradually to make himself known by his liberal opinions, and the fervid eloquence with which he set forth and maintained them.

Kossuth, having completed his legal studies, and finding no favorable opening in the capital, returned in 1830 to his native district, and commenced the practice of the law, with marked success. He also began to make his way toward public life, by his intelligent action in the local assemblies. In a new Diet assembled in 1832 he received a commission as the representative, in the Diet, of a magnate who was absent.

He early made himself known as a debater, and gradually won his way upward and became associated with the leading men of the Liberal party, many of whom were among the proudest and richest of the Hungarian magnates. He soon undertook to publish a report of the details and proceedings of the Diet. This attempt was opposed by the Palatine, and a law hunted up which forbade the "printing and publishing" of these reports. He for a while evaded the law by having is sheet lithographed. Finally the lithographic press was seized by Government. Kossuth, determined not to be baffled, still issued his journal, every copy being written out by scribes, of whom he employed a large number.

To avoid seizure at the post-office, they were circulated through the local authorities, who were almost invariably on the liberal side. He attended the meetings of the Diet, the conferences of the deputies, edited his paper, read almost all new works on politics and political economy, and studied French and English for the sake of reading the debates in the French Chambers and the British Parliament, allowing himself but three hours' sleep in the twenty-four. His periodical penetrated into every part of the kingdom, and the young writer boldly put himself against Metternich and the whole Austrian Cabinet.

Kossuth, though twice admonished by Government, still continued his journal. He was aware that his course was a perilous one. He was once found walking in deep thought in the fortress of Buda, and in reply to a question as to the subject of his meditations, he said, "I was looking at the casemates, for fear that I shall soon be quartered there." Government finally determined to use arguments more cogent than discussion could furnish. Concerning Kossuth, to use the words of an Austrian partisan, it happened that as he was promenading, May 4th, 1837, in the vicinity of Buda, he was seized by the myrmidons of the law and confined in the lower walls of the fortress, there to consider in darkness and solitude how dangerous it is to defy a powerful government, and to swerve from the path of law and of prudence.

He became at once in the popular mind a martyr. Liberal subscriptions were raised through the country for the benefit of his mother and sisters, whom he had supported by his exertions, and who were now left without protection. Wesselenyi, the leader of the liberal party, who was also imprisoned, became blind in prison; Lovassi, an intimate friend of Kossuth, lost his reason; and Kossuth himself, as was certified by his physicians, was in great danger of falling a victim to a serious disease. The rigor of his confinement was mitigated; he was allowed books, newspapers and writing materials, and suffered to walk daily upon the bastions of the fortress, in charge of an officer. Among those who were inspired with admiration for his political efforts, and with sympathy for his fate, was Teresa Mezlenyi, the young daughter of a nobleman. She sent him books, and corresponded with him during his imprisonment, and they were married in 1841, soon after his liberation.

Kossuth's connection with Wesselenyi procured for him a degree of influence among the higher magnates, which he could probably in no other way have attained.

In the second year of his imprisonment, Austria again needed Hungarian assistance. A demand was made upon the Hungarian Diet for an additional levy of 18,000 troops. A large body of delegates was chosen, pledged to oppose this grant except upon condition of certain concessions, among which was a general amnesty, with a special reference to the cases of Wesselenyi and Kossuth. The most sagacious of the conservative party advised Government to liberate all the prisoners, with the exception of Kossuth; but Metternich and the Cabinet grew alarmed at the struggle, and were eager to obtain the grant of men, and to close the refractory Diet. In 1840 a royal rescript suddenly made its appearance, granting the amnesty, accompanied also with conciliatory remarks, and the demands of the Government for men and money were at once complied with.

Kossuth was released from prison in 1840, after an incarceration of three years, bearing in his debilitated frame, his pallid face, and glassy eyes, traces of severe sufferings, both of mind and body. He repaired for a time to a watering-place among the mountains to recruit his shattered health. Abundant subscriptions had been made for his benefit and that of his family, and he now stood on an equality with the proudest magnates. He mingled little with the society at the watering-place, but preferred, as his health improved, to wander among forest-clad hills and lonely valleys. Sometimes a chord would be casually struck which awoke deeper feelings, then his rare eloquence would burst forth with the fearful earnestness of conviction, and he hurled forth sentences instinct with life and passion. The wife of the Lord-Lieutenant, the daughter of a great magnate, was attracted by his appearance, and desired this companion of Kossuth to introduce him to her house. When the desire was made known to Kossuth, the mysterious and nervous expression passed over his face, which characterizes it when excited. "No," he exclaimed, "I will not go to that woman's house; her father subscribed four-pence to buy a rope to hang me with!"

Soon after his liberation, he became principal editor of the Pesth Gazette *(Pesthi Hirlap)*.

His name as editor was sufficient to electrify the country; and he stood forth as the advocate of the rights of the lower and middle classes, against the inordinate privileges enjoyed by the magnates. But when he went to the extent of demanding that the house-tax should be paid by all classes in the community, not even excepting the highest nobility, a party was raised up against him among the nobles, who established a paper to combat so disorganizing a doctrine. This party, backed by the influence of Government, succeeded is defeating the election of Kossuth as member from Pesth, for the Diet of 1843.

He was not altogether without support among the higher nobles. Among his supporters at this period was Count Louis Batthyanyi, one of the most considerable of the Magyar magnates, subsequently President of the Hungarian Ministry, and the most illustrious martyr of the Hungarian cause.

Kossuth was elected a member of the Diet, and no sooner took his seat than the foremost place was at once conceded to him. At the opening of the session he moved an address to the king, concluding with the petition that "liberal institutions, similar to those of the Hungarian Constitution, might be accorded to all the hereditary states, that thus might be created a united Austrian monarchy, based upon broad constitutional principles." During the early months of the session, he showed himself a most accomplished parliarmentary orator and debater, and carried on a series of attacks upon the policy of the Austrian Cabinet; which for skill and power have few parallels in the annals of parliamentary warfare. Some of his speeches are marked by a stringency of logic worthy of Webster or Calhoun – but it was what all eloquence of a high order must ever be – "Logic red hot." The next day after the news of the French Revolution of February, 1848, reached Vienna Kossuth delivered his famous speech on the finances and state of the monarchy concluding with a proposed "Address to the Throne," urging a series of reformatory measures. Among the foremost of these was the emancipation of the country from feudal burdens – the proprietors of the soil to be indemnified by the state; equalizing taxation; a faithful administration of the revenue be satisfactorily guaranteed; the development of the representative system; and the establishment of a government representing the voice of, and responsible to the nation. The speech produced an effect almost without parallel in the annals of debate. Not a word was uttered in reply, and the motion was unanimously carried. On the 13th of March took place the revolution in Vienna, which overthrew the Metternich Cabinet. On the 15th, the Constitution, granted by the Emperor to all the nations within the Empire, was solemnly proclaimed, amidst the wildest transports of joy. Henceforth there were to be no more Germans or Sclavonians, Magyars or Italians; strangers embraced and kissed each other in the streets, for all the heterogeneous races of the Empire were now brothers.

Among the demands made by the Hungarian Diet, was that of a separate and responsible Ministry for Hungary. The Palatine, Archduke Stephen; to whom the conduct of affairs in Hungary had been intrusted, persuaded the Emperor to accede to this demand, and on the following day Batthyanyi, who with Kossuth and a deputation of delegates of the Diet was in Vienna, was named President of the Hungarian Ministry. It was, however, understood that Kossuth was the life and soul of the new Ministry.

Kossuth assumed the department of Finance, then as long before and now, the post of difficulty under Austrian administration. The Diet meanwhile went on to consummate the series of reforms which Kossuth had so long and steadfastly advocated. The remnants of feudalism were swept away – the landed proprietors being indemnified by the state for the loss they sustained. The civil and political rights which had heretofore been in the exclusive possession of the nobles, were extended to the burghers and the peasants. A new electoral law was framed, according the right of suffrage, to every possessor of property to the amount of about one hundred and fifty dollars. The whole series of bills received the royal signature on the 11th of April, the Diet having previously adjourned to meet on the 2nd of July.

Up to this time there had been indeed a vigorous and decided opposition, but no insurrection. The true cause of the Hungarian war was the hostility of the Austrian Government to the whole series of reformatory measures which had been effected through the instrumentality of Kossuth; but its immediate occasion was the jealousy which sprung up among the Serbian and Croatian dependencies of Hungary against the Hungarian Ministry. This soon broke out into an open revolt, headed by Baron Jellachich; who had just been appointed Ban or Lord of Croatia. The Emperor had solemnly sanctioned the action of the Diet, and did as solemnly denounce the proceedings of Jellachich. On the 29th of May the Ban was summoned to present himself at Innspruck, to answer for his conduct; and as he did not make his appearance, an Imperial manifesto was issued on the 10th of June, depriving him of all his dignities, and commanding the authorities at once to break off all intercourse with him. He, however, still continued his operations, and levied an army for the invasion of Hungary, and a fierce and bloody war of races broke out, marked on both sides by the most fearful atrocities.

The Hungarian Diet was opened on the 5th of July, when the Palatine, Archduke Stephen, in the name of the king, solemnly denounced the conduct of the insurgent Croats. A few days after, Kossuth, in a speech in the Diet, set forth the perilous state of affairs, and concluded by asking for authority to raise an army of 200,000 men, and a large amount of money. These proposals were adopted by acclamation, the enthusiasm in the Diet rendering any debate impossible and superfluous.

The Austrian Cabinet began openly to display its hostility to the Hungarian movements. Jellachich repaired to Innspruck, and was openly acknowledged by the court, and the decree of deposition was revoked. Early in September, Austria and Hungary stood in an attitude of undisguised hostility. On the 5th of that month Kossuth, though enfeebled by illness, was carried to the hall of the Diet where he delivered a speech; declaring that so formidable were the dangers that surrounded the nation, that the Ministers might soon be forced to call upon the Diet to name a Dictator, clothed with unlimited powers, to save the country; but before taking this final step, they would recommend a last appeal to the Imperial government. A large deputation was thereupon dispatched to the Emperor, to lay before him the demands of the Hungarian nation. No satisfactory answer was returned, and the deputation left the Imperial presence in silence. On their return, they plucked from their caps the plumes of the united colors of Austria and Hungary, and replaced them with red feathers, and hoisted a flag of the same color on the steamer which conveyed them to Pesth. Their report produced the most intense agitation in the Diet and the capital, but it was finally resolved to make one more attempt for a pacific settlement of the question. In order that no obstacle might be interposed by their presence, Kossuth and his colleagues resigned, and a new Ministry was appointed. A deputation was sent to the National Assembly at Vienna, which refused to receive it. Jellachich had in the meantime entered Hungary with a large army, not as yet, however, openly sanctioned by Imperial authority. The Diet seeing the imminent peril of the country, conferred dictatorial powers upon Kossuth. The Palatine resigned his post, and left the kingdom. The Emperor appointed Count Lemberg to take the entire command of the Hungarian army. The Diet declared the appointment illegal, and the Count, arriving at Pesth without escort, was slain in the streets of the capital by the populace, in a sudden outbreak. The Emperor forthwith placed the kingdom under martial law, giving the supreme civil and military power to Jellachich. The Diet at once revolted, declared itself permanent, and appointed Kossuth Governor, and President of the Committee of Safety.

Then followed the fierce war, which we shall soon describe.

The chronology of the Hungarian struggle may be thus stated: On the 9th of September, 1848, Jellachich crossed the Drave and invaded Hungary; he was driven back, at the close of that month, toward Vienna. In October, Windischgratz advanced into Hungary, and took possession of Pesth, the capital. On the 14th of April, 1849, the Decalaration of Hungarian Independence was promulgated. At the close of that month, the Austrians were driven out at every point, and the issue of the contest, as between Hungary and Austria, was settled. On the 1st of May the Russian intervention was announced. On the 11th of August Kossuth resigned his dictatorship into the hands of Görgey, who, two days after, in effect closed the war by surrending to the Russians.

The Hungarian war lasted a little more than eleven months, during which time there was but one ruling and directing spirit – and that was Kossuth.

Early in January it was found advisable to remove the seat of government from Pesth to the town of Debreczin, in the interior. Pesth was altogether indefensible, and the Austrian army were close upon it; but here the Hungarians had collected a vast amount of stores and ammunition, the preservation of which was of the utmost importance. In saving these the administrative power of Kossuth was strikingly manifested. For three days and three nights he labored uninterruptedly in superintending the removal, which was successfully effected. From the heaviest locomotive engine down to a shot-belt, all the stores were packed up and carried away, so that when the Austrians took possession of Pesth, they only gained the eclat of occupying the Hungarian capital, without acquiring the least solid advantage.

Debreczin was the scene where Kossuth displayed his transcendent abilities as an administrator, a statesman, and an orator. The population of the town was about 50,000, which was at once almost doubled, so that every one was forced to put up with such accomodations as he could find, and occupy the least possible amount of space. Kossuth himself occupied the Town Hall. On the first floor was a spacious anteroom, constantly filled with persons waiting for an interview, which was necessarily a matter of delay, as each one was admitted in his turn; the only exception being in cases where public business required an immediate audience.

This anteroom opened into two spacious apartments, in one of which the secretaries of the Governor were always at work. Here Kossuth received visitors. At these audiences he spoke but little, but listened attentively, occasionally taking notes of anything that seemed of importance. His secretaries were continually coming to him to receive directions, to present a report, or some document to receive his signature. These he never omitted to examine carefully before affixing his signature, even amidst the greatest pressure of business; at the same time listening to the speaker. "Be brief," he used to say, "but for that very reason forget nothing." These hours of audience were also his hours of work, and here it was that he wrote those stirring appeals which aroused and kept alive the spirit of his countrymen. It was only when he had some document of extraordinary importance to prepare, that he retired to his closet. These audiences usually continued until far into the night, the anteroom being often as full at midnight as in the morning. Although of a delicate constitution, broken also by his imprisonment, the excitement bore him up under the immense mental and bodily exertion, and while there was work to do, he was never ill.

He usually allowed himself an hour for rest or relaxation, from two till three o'clock, when he was accustomed to take a drive with his wife and children to a little wood at a short distance, where he would seek out some retired spot, and play upon the grass with his children, and for a moment forget the preasing cares af state.

At three o'clock he dined, and at the conclusion of his simple meal was again at his post. This round of audiences was frequently interrupted by a council of war, a conference of ministers, or the review of a regiment just on the point of setting out for the seat of hostilities. New battalions seemed to spring from the earth at his command, and he made a point of reviewing each, and delivering to them a brief address, which was always received with a burst of *"eljens"*.

At Debreczin, the sittings of the House of Assembly were held in what had been the chapel of the Protestant College. Kossuth attended these sittings only when he had some important communications to make. Then he always walked over from the Town Hall. Entering the Assembly, he ascended the rostrum if it was not occupied, if it was he took his place in any vacant seat, none being specially set apart for the Governor.

The defeat of Bem at Temesvar, on the 9th of August, gave the death blow to the cause. Two days afterwards, Kossuth and Görgey stood alone in the bow-window of a small chamber in the fortress of Arad. What passed between them no man knows; but from that room Görgey went forth Dictator of Hungary, and Kossuth followed him to set out on his journey of exile. On the same day the new Dictator announced to the Russians his intention to surrender the forces under his command. The following day he marched to the place designated, where the Russian general, Rudiger, arrived on the 13th, and Görgey's army numbering 24,000 men, with 144 pieces of artillery, laid down their arms.

Kossuth and his companions fled to the Turkish frontier, and threw themselves on the hospitality of the Sultan, who promised them a safe asylum. Russia and Austria demanded that the fugitives should be given up, and for some months it was uncertain whether the Turkish Government would dare to refuse. At first a decided negative was returned; then the Porte wavered; and it was officially announced to Kossuth and his companions that the only means for them to avoid surrendry would be to abjure the faith of their fathers; and thus take advantage of the fundamental Moslem law, that any fugitive embracing the Mohammedan faith can claim the protection of the Government. Kossuth refused to purchase his life at such a price; and finally Austria and Russia were induced to modify their demand and merely to insist upon the detention of the fugitives. On the other hand, the Turkish Government was urged to allow them to depart. Early in the present year, Mr. Webster, as Secretary of state, directed our Minister at Constantinople to urge the Porte to suffer the exiles to come to the United States. A similar course was pursued by the British Government. It was promised that these representations should be complied with; but so late as in March of the present year, Kossuth addressed a letter to our charge at Constantinople, dispairing of his release being granted. But happily his fears were groundless, and our Government was notified that on the 1st of September, the day on which terminated the period of detention agreed upon by the Sultan, Kossuth and his companions would be free to depart to any part of the world. The United States steam-frigate Mississippi was at once placed at his disposal. The offer was accepted. On the 12th of September the steamer reached Smyrna, with the illustrious exile and his family and suit on board, bound to our shores, after a short visit in England. The Government of France, in the meanwhile, denied him the privilege of passing through the territory.

Kossuth's endeavors have been attended neither by success nor martyrdom. He is the living leader of a lost cause. His country is ruined, its nationality destroyed; yet no Hungarian lays this ruin to his charge; and the first lesson taught the infant Magyar is a blessing upon his name. Whatever the future may have in store, his efforts have not been lost. The tree which he planted in blood, and agony, and tears, though its tender shoots have been trampled down by the Russian bear, will yet spring up again to gladden, if not his heart, yet those of his children or his children's children.

Battles of Hungary

We have already, in speaking of Kossuth's achievements, referred to the origin of the revolution in favor of Hungarian freedom, and it is only necessary now to briefly describe the several battles and their success.

Insurrection in Hungary, led on by Rajacsics

This prelate roused his religious brethren so speedily against Hungary, that symptoms of the greatest excitement were apparent among them as early as April, 1848. The insurrection broke out in July, and was conducted with cruelty such as rarely has disgraced barbarians. The misguided people attacked and burned German and Hungarian villages, murdering the inhabitants, from the child at the breast to the white-haired man of ninety. They bored out the eyes of their victims, cut off their flesh in strips, roasted them alive on spits, buried them up to their necks and so left them to be eaten by crows and swine. The wretches ripped open women big with child, and trampled the fruit of the womb before the eyes of the dying mother. All of these barbarities were the work of an unnatural woman and of a priest, who weekly exhorted his hearers to love each other as brethren.

Battle of Pakozd

The notorious Joseph, Baron Jellachich, Ban of Croatia; who held in readiness a rabble of fifty or sixty thousand men which he had assembled by force, entered Hungary near Letenye and marched in two columns directly upon Pesth, wasting and robbing as he went. The Hungarian forces were posted in the neighborhood of Stuhlueissenburg under Archduke Stephen, who left them on the approach of the enemy, in accordance with previous instructions. After this treacherous withdrawal of the Archduke, the command of the Hungarians, who had retired to Pakozd, was undertaken by Gen. Moga, an Austrian Lieutenant Field-Marshal, who gave battle to Jellachich at that place on the 29th of September, 1848. In this battle nearly all the inhabitants of Pesth took part. Jellachich was defeated, and the larger part of his cuirassiers driven into Lake Velencze. He applied for an armistice of three days, which was granted by Moga; after its ratification, he and his whole army decamped – and probably with the knowledge of the Hungarian commander. Although Jellachich's retreat was known next morning, immediate pursuit was delayed, and so this army, which could have been so easily taken, was suffered to escape.

Battles of Ozora, Dombo, Letenye, and Friedau

The Hungarian Diet determined that the main army should follow Jellachich. Perczel, with a small body under him, was to attack the other Croatian army under Generals Rott and Philippovics, who were approaching from Fanfkirchen. He only had three battalions of Honveds and a few sections of national guards. He pressed the enemy, who had already advanced as far as Ozora, so closely, that on the 10th of October they yielded unconditionally 9,000 strong, as prisoners of war. This able general then took his appointed station on the frontier. Besides the victories of Dombo and Letenye, he fought a brilliant battle at Friedau on the 25th of November, 1848, where the Pesth volunteers won immortal glory, driving General Buric's force of 10,000 men, with a great loss in dead and prisoners, far into Styria.

Battles of Fischamend and Albern and the Storming of Mannsworth

A large number of imperial troops had gathered about Vienna. The chief command was intrusted to Prince Windischgratz, a miserable aristocrat. This army was gradually increased by the obstinacy of the Viennese Diet, on the 28th, including the forces of Jellachich and Auersberg, to 85,000. They took Landstrasse, Leopoldstadt, and finally Vienna itself, and set the city on fire. Bem, general of the Garde Mobile, was wounded at this time while defending a barricade in the Jaeger Zeile.

Kossuth, seeing the flames from the capital on fire ordered the Hungarian army to march towards Vienna.

On the 30th of October the Hungarians, 21,000 strong, came up with the imperialists, and attacked them fiercely, drove them out of Fischamend and Albern, carried Mannsworth by storm, and pressed on towards Vienna, where thousands of their brethren panting for liberty, awaited their coming to rescue them from the hands of their destroyers.

Battles of Babolna and Teth

The barbarous Windischgratz having sufficiently gratified himself with executions by the score, and guarded the bastions of Vienna with cannon, marched his disposable force, amounting to 72,000 men, against the Hungarians. It was found impossible to resist such a power in extended cantonments, and after several unimportant actions, Görgey, who was then commander of the Hungarian forces, ordered a general retreat to Raab in the middle of December. Here intrenchments were thrown up, on which the noblest ladies worked with their delicate hands.

The early part of the winter of 1848–49 was very mild, and from this cause Görgey hoped to be able to maintain his ground behind the three rivers and his strong intrenchments, and check the further progress of the enemy. On the 20th of December, however, the weather suddenly became intensely cold, and by the 25th, the ice was so thick that a body of Austrians crossed the little Danube, and took a position with their artillery below Raab. Görgey found it necessary to retreat, but did so slowly, that he might join Perczel's army, which had been meanwhile ordered up from the frontier, before reaching Pesth, and give a decisive battle. While retreating, he fought the glorious battle of Babolna, where he engaged with three times his own number. Perczel had an unfortunate encounter, at first with Ottinger's brigade, and then with the main body of the Austrians at Moor on the 28th of December. Owing to his bad management, he lost nine cannon and about three thousand dead, wounded, and missing, and would perhaps have been totally defeated if a division of Görgey's had not come to his succor just before the close of the engagement.

Görgey received the broken remnants of Perczel's corps, and slowly retired beyond the Danube. On the 5th of January, 1849, his rear-guard fought with and again vanquished the enemy's cavalry at Teth. Under the constant pursuit of the enemy, in the depth of winter, and through the most inhospitable districts of the country, he afterwards conducted that series of retreats to Waitzen, Schemnicz, Neusohl, Leutshau, Eperjes, and Kachau, that distinguished him in Hungary, and in the course of which he gained decided advantages over his pursuers at Schemnicz, Iglo, and Braniczko.

Battles of Torczal, Bodrogkeresztur, Rakamaz, Hidas-Nemethi, and Kompolth

Encouraged by his success, Schlick, an Austrian general, began to act on the offensive and advanced with five thousand men against our position. The battles of the 22nd at Torczal, and of the 23rd at Bodrogkeresztur, were in extremely cold weather. Schlick, in spite of all his military stratagems; was defeated in both with a great loss in dead and wounded, and was forced back to Szanto. Klapka, a Hungarian leader whose main business was to prevent a passage of the Theiss, retired behind that river to Rakamaz on Schluczig's approach. He then took such admirable measures, that when the hostile generals, with their combined forces, attempted a passage on the 31st, they were not only vigorously repulsed but obliged to withdraw from that region altogether.

The rear-guard of Schlick was overtaken on the 8th of February at Hidas-Nemethi, where he had thrown up barricades behind the Hernat. The cold was so intense that our boots were frozen in the stirrups, but General Klapka ordered an assault at four in the afternoon upon the enemy's very strong position. At six the burning bridge over the Hernat, and in half an hour the barricades of the enemy were carried with triumph. They fled towards Szepsi, and General Klapka, having learned that the enemy had halted, and that their advanced guard of several divisions of cuirassiers were taking their ease in the castle of Count Karoy at Kompolt, planned a suprise. Our cavalry came suddenly upon them in the night of the 18th, killed a portion of them, and took the rest prisoners.

Battles of Kapolna and Szemere

The Austrian army was gradually drawing near our forces and Dembinsky resolved to hazard a decisive engagement with the Austrians.

The enemy attacked Kapolna at noon of the 26th, with a superior force. Mariassy maintained his ground bravely, and the battle lasted till late in the night. The Austrians twice carried the village, and were as often expelled, finally leaving it in our possession. On the 27th Schlick forced his way through the pass of Sirok, drove back our forces, who were guarding it, and fell upon our right flank while others of the enemy were marching from Nanar and Vecs against our centre. Klapka's corps had to bear alone the force of the first assault, and was forced from its position before succor arrived. There was hard fighting on both sides during the day and a half that this battle lasted, but had our troops been better directed, the issue had assuredly been in our favor.

Windischgratz had about sixty thousand men, and we numbered not quite forty thousand. Besides the almost total destruction of a regiment of Uhlans, and the Italian battalion Zanini, the enemy spiked and left behind in Kapolna eight cannon on the first day, and lost nearly four thousand in dead and wounded. Our loss in dead, wounded, and missing was greater by some two hundred than theirs. The next day, the enemy renewed the attack with five large bodies of cavalry, but were met so warmly by our brave Wilhelm and Palatinal hussars that they were glad to go back leaving their guns to our care. After overcoming great obstacles, we reached Egerfarmas in the afternoon of the 3rd of March. The troops were literally packed together on an open field behind the town. When the necessary guards had been set, the members of the staff (to which I had the honor of belonging) who, as well as the men, had scarcely eaten for three days, repaired to the table of a noble proprietor of the district to enjoy a splendid banquet.

But we had hardly seated ourselves, when a twelve pound ball dropped into the courtyard. We hurried out, sprang to our horses, and found that the enemy at Szemere had planted six batteries in a half circle, and turned their concentrating fire upon our wayworn, famished troops. If the Austrians had only shown a little vigor, and sent a column towards Tarkany, with orders to attack immediately on gaining our rear, not one thousand of our eighteen thousand would have escaped, for there was no room for necessary evolutions. But they permitted us to march off comfortably.

Battles of Szolnok, Hatvan and Tapiobicske

The attack by surprise near Szolnok, was conducted by Damjanics and Vecsey, with Klapka as a reserve, in an able manner. The enemy were either dispersed, or driven into the river Zagyva. We took nearly five hundred prisoners, most of their cannon, as well as any military wagons, chests, etc. Damjanics' troops, made the first charge upon the Austrians with the greatest bravery, and soon the victory was complete. After this victory, Kossuth came to the head-quarters, thanked the soldiers with glowing eloquence in the name of their country, and summoned them to further deeds of like glory.

It was now determined to resume the offensive, Görgey was to move in the direction of Gyongyos, and the army of 30,000, concentrated at Czibakhaza, near Szolnok, under Gen. Vetter, were to pass Nagy-Koros, and operate upon Pesth. On the 22nd of March, the latter army crossed the Theiss, at Czibakhaza; but when they learned that the enemy were gathered between 70 and 80,000 strong at Koros, they relinquished their design, and returned behind the Theiss. It was then decided that the two armies should operate together towards a common centre. President Kossuth named Görgey provisional commander-in-chief. On the 27th of March, Gen. Gaspar fought with the Austrians for six hours, and drove them behind Hatvan.

The corps under Klapka as the advance, Damjanics in the centre, and Aulich in the rear, marched on the 4th towards Tapiobicske. Klapka unadvisedly ordered his whole army across the only bridge over the Tapio, a fenny, unfordable stream. Between the river and the village, situated at the foot of a mountain, are nothing but quicksands. When near enough to the place, he gave orders to storm it. But to our astonishment, numberless batteries from houses opened upon us. Jellachich's entire corps, to which was added Rastich's brigade, lay here in ambush.

The sudden appearance of the enemy on all sides had so injurious an effect on our men that after a short resistance they began to retreat and many battalions ran in confusion to the bridge. Finally, however, Damjanics' corps, especially the brave 3rd and 9th battalions, came up, broke their way through the fugitives and amid the cross-fire of the enemy on the causeway carried the bridge at one charge and restored the battle; and in half an hour they not only recovered all advantages from the enemy, but forced them to retire from the village. The loss in this action, which lasted nearly ten hours, was quite large amounting on both sides to more than 1,000 killed and wounded.

Battle of Isaszeg

On the 5th of April we learned that the entire Austrian army was concentrated near Isaszeg, under Windischgratz. A column was sent out under General Dessewffy to turn the left flank of the enemy, which, however, owing to the difficulties of the ground, did not reach its destination till after the enemy were beaten. Windischgratz's main body, with 120 cannon, occupied the heights behind the town. It might well be called the Gibraltar of the country. Klapka approached by the road from Sap, Damjanics from Koka, Aulich forming a reserve between the two towards the woods before Isaszeg. About noon a terrible firing commenced. Our troops fought nobly and carried the woods three times, but were as often expelled by the greatly superior force opposed to them. At last, reinforced by Aulich's corps and the cavalry of Gaspar who had come up from Tura, they bore down all resistance, clearing the woods at one charge, and entering the village, which was burning in at least ten different places. Along the whole line of battle, for an extent of at least five miles, there was an incessant firing of artillery and small arms, and constant charges and attacks. When our column came out from the woods, though exposed to a dreadful fire from the heights; they stormed the enemy's stronghold. Before night the tricolor was planted on the works of the enemy, and waved in the last beams of the setting sun. The Austrians fought better than on any other occasion during the war, but they were beaten on all sides. The loss on both sides was several thousand in dead and wounded, but that of the enemy by far the greatest.

Proclamation of Independence

The Hungarian army next proceeded towards Godollo, the last tenable position of the enemy between us and Pesth; but they had retreated early in the day to Pesth, where they threw up strong intrenchments, and prepared for defence.

Having reached Godollo; and made it our head-quarters, Kossuth, with some of his ministry and deputies from the Diet, was preparing to declare the Independence of Hungary and the banishment of the Austrian Dynasty. The army received the announcement with the greatest enthusiasm. Kossuth and his associates returned to Debreczin, and on the 14th of April, 1849, the representatives of the Hungarian nation met in the Protestant church of that place, where the brave President, in an eloquent address, reported the late victories, presented the rights and claims of Hungary, the abuses and perfidy of Austria, and called upon the Diet and the assemled people, in the name of their country and of God, to shake off the fetters that had bound them for three centuries, and take their place among independent nations. The following propositions were then unanimously adopted:

1. Hungary with all its legal provinces and counties should be proclaimed as a free, independent, and self-subsistent state, whose integrity and unity can never be attacked.

2. The dynasty of Habsburg-Lorrain, whose treachery and perfidiousness took up arms against the Hungarian nation, which tried to divide the country, to annihilate the holy constitution, to produce hatred between the different races, and which was even so shameless as to make use of a foreign power (Russia) to butcher a whole nation; which in this way has torn in pieces the Pragmatic sanction; which has violated every mutual treaty, this faithless dynasty of Habsburg-Lorrain, should be deposed forever as ruler in Hungary and all its legal provinces and countries, should be exiled and banished forever from all the territories of Hungary, and should never be allowed the privilege of Hungarian citizenship. This banishment should be proclaimed in the name of the whole Hungarian nation.

3. The Hungarian nation being, by a holy, inalienable right, self-subsistent, free, and independent, may proclaim its decided will to keep peace and friendship with all nations of the world, so long as its rights are not violated; to keep particularly peace and friendship with those people who were before united with Hungary, under the same ruler; also with the neighboring Turkish and Italian countries, and to make treaties and alliances with them, founded on mutual interests.

4. The future system of government with its particularities shall be deliberated and decided by the National Assembly. Until the new principles of government are deliberated upon and accepted, a president, with

responsible ministers, should be elected and invested with the executive power.

5. A committee of three members should be authorized to publish a manifest of this resolution and its principles.

Battle of Waitzen

Our forces were disposed as follows: The corps of Klapka, Damjanics, and Gaspar, under the lead of Görgey, were to move forward to Comorn, which was hardly pressed by the enemy. Aulich, with his own corps, and the division of Vimety and Asboth, was to keep watch of Pesth. Görgey departed for Comorn on the 8th of April, while Aulich remained behind; and, having defeated the Austrians in four different actions, obliged them to evacuate Pesth; but they left a garrison of between 5,000 and 6,000 men, under Gen. Henzy, in the fortress of Ofen.

On the 9th of April, Görgey proceeded against Waitzen; which was held by 12,000 Austrians, under Generals, Jablonovsky, Gocz, and Fidler, drawn up behind a row of sand hills. Damjanics attacked them as soon as he came in sight, without waiting for the others to come up, and pressed them so hotly, in spite of a violent rain, that when Klapka appeared, they were already wavering, and soon after began their retreat. They were closely followed into the town, which was taken by storm. They again turned upon us on the heights outside, but after a spirited battle of two hours, they were completly routed and driven to Verocze. The Hungarians took a number of cannon and military wagons, and about 500 prisoners. Gen. Gocz, and several hundred of less rank, lay dead on the field. Our loss, in killed and wounded, was not more than thirty.

Battle of Grosz-Sarlo

On the 10th, the Hungarians, continued their course towards Comorn. When about crossing the Gran, at Levencz, we observed the outposts of the enemy, on the opposite bank. They had partly carried and partly burned the bridges on this stream. We collected mills, house-roofs, barrels, and timber, and commenced building a bridge at Obars and Levencz, at which latter place we completed a structure at the end of three days.

The corps of Klapka and Damjanics consumed the whole of the 18th in crossing the tottering bridge, which threatened every moment to give way, and we did not reach Lok till late in the evening. The enemy had gone down to the city of Gran, to which place we proceeded, on the 19th, with Klapka in advance.

To our astonishment, a very large body of the enemy was drawn up in order of battle near Grosz-Sarlo. We hastened forward, and saw a strong army, with its right wing resting on the town, its left on the range at mountains, and its centre supported by a forest. Görgey was still behind at Levencz, and Gaspar's corps had not yet even crossed the Gran. But not stopping long to deliberate, we charged upon the much superior force thus suddenly opposed to us. At first the conflict was fierce and doubtful; now we had no left wing, and now no centre; but the bravery of our soldiers supplied all deficiencies, and 22,000 new recruits without preparation defeated 84,000 choice Austrian troops fully provided with artillery and commanded by the ablest generals. Damjanics went around the town, which was defended by four battalions, two rocket and four field batteries, while Kazincy carried it by a masterly assault. The garrison defended themselves with desperation. We were obliged to storm every room, cellar, and door-way separately, and either cut down the occupants, or take them prisoners. The enemy then threw themselves violently in strong columns upon our centre, endeavoring to break it through and disperse our troops. A large flanking column of our cavalry partly broke their left wing. Two of our batteries then came up at not more than three hundred paces distant from their main column, causing fearful destruction in its ranks, and they were forced to abandon their design and commence a retreat. They were hotly pursued; but the commander of our extreme right neglected to keep close by the vineyards on his side, from which error we were unexpectedly assaulted in flank and rear by 8,000 men. There was at first a little confusion in this wing; but it would yield in nothing of bravery to the rest, turned fiercely back on the assailants, and in less than an hour not only repulsed them but cleared the wood whither they had retired after the first onset. The retreat now became general; the pursuit was kept up till ten at night.

The enemy lost some thousands killed, 3,000 prisoners, and a number of cannon. Our loss, in killed and wounded, was not far from 800.

Great Battle of Comorn

The Hungarian army received no further opposition until reaching Comorn. As it approached the city which was besieged by the Imperialists, General Guyon sallied out into the Schutt, an island in the Danube, and drove the besiegers who were on the left bank of the river behind Aranyos. The main body of the Austrians were on the right bank, and were constantly throwing bombs into the city and fortress. A bridge of boats over the Danube was completed in three days, in spite of an uninterrupted shower of bombs and balls. On the evening of April 25th, eight picked battalions, led by Colonel Knezics, crossed the bridge, and at two hours after midnight, stormed the hostile works opposite the fortress, captured all their defenders, and seized all their guns. Then they stormed Old and New Szony, opposite the fortress, took more prisoners, and large supplies of war material. At four in the morning the army began to cross the bridge, and at eight the battle commenced in earnest. The Austrian main army under Lieutenant Field-Marshal Velden, successor of Windischgratz, engaged against Klapka, Damjanics, and the troops of the garrison. The action began on the high grounds before New Szony, and was immediately decided in our favor, against, a much superior force, but as the enemy were driven back, they fought more obstinately. Their left wing finally entered the woods before Acs, with their centre turning towards Puszta-Herkaly, and their right wing to Nagy and Kis-Igmand. It was two in the afternoon, when General Nagy Sandor, commander of the Cavalry, received orders to flank the enemy's right wing, and drive them over the Csonczo; which would have made a general retreat necessary. But this brave general, pushing forward with too much ardor, suddenly brought our cavalry into a formidable cross-fire. Its flank was at the same time turned by Schlick's corps. A retreat, in utter corifusion, was the result.

The infantry soon recovering the advantages lost, the fighting ceased on both sides. The Hungarians captured a number of cannon, took many prisoners, and gained possession of two camps, with more than 3,000 tents. The enemy's loss, in dead and wounded, was over 4,000; ours not quite 1,000. During the night the Austrians crossed the river, and passed the frontier.

Battle of Ofen

Our blockading army did not make their entrance into Pesth, until the Austrians had left of their own accord. Görgey took command of all the blockading troops, distributed them on the heights about Ofen; a strong fortress opposite Pesth on the Danube, and fixed his headquarters on the so-called Schwabenberg. He then summoned the commandant of Ofen to surrender within forty-eight hours, and bade him beware of bombarding Pesth, as no operations would proceed from that quarter, threatening if the old arrangement in this respect were broken, to put the entire garrison to the sword when the fortress was taken. Henczy, an Austrian general, bombarded Pesth without the least provocation, and changed the elegant row of buildings on the river, and the finest streets and squares into heaps of ruins. The battering cannon were set up and an attack made upon the fortified aqueduct, and upon the fortress itself, but it was not sucessful. But when the first breach was made, our men could no longer be restrained. They looked down on Pesth, which lay in ruins, then upon the rocky fortress, above them, and they were impatient for the combat. At two o'clock, on the morning of the 21st of May, the assault began upon the breach, and by means of scaling ladders, on all sides of this fortress, perched upon a rock rising a thousand feet above the Danube. Two hundred and forty-seven cannon, and from 5,000 to 6,000 small arms, poured out death and ruin upon the assailants; but they could not be stopped. They clung, and crept, and sprang from ladder to rock, from crag to ladder. Occasionally a ball would strike a ladder, with a man grasping all around, and hurl all into the abyss. Thus Colonel Mariassy was thrice cast down; and though severely wounded, climed again, for the fourth time, and happily succeeded in gaining the fortress. At seven in the morning the first tricolor was floating from the battlements; at eight the conquest was complete. We made 5,000 prisoners. Henczy received a fatal wound, of which he died the same day.

Battle of Pered, and Second Great Battle at Comorn

After the Hungarian government had learned that the Russian intervention was a settled matter, they ordered Dembinsky to protect Upper Hungary against the Russian invasion; the main army resting on Comorn.

The southern army, under Vetter, was to remain in Baksa on both sides of the Danube, until Bem, with a part of his forces from Transylvania, should be advanced on a line with the other armies, when he was to take the chief command and resume the offensive. An army of reserve, was to be established at Szolnok, and 22,000 troops under Klapka's command, were to occupy a fortified camp at Comorn.

General Klapka gained an important victory on the 13th of June near Comorn, when the enemy left some hundreds of dead upon the field, Gen. Wyss among the number.

All was now ready for action against the enemy. On the 24th of June, when the reconnoitering had given the enemy sufficient warning to concentrate all their forces between the Waag and the Newhausler-Danube, the second and third corps attacked them at Kiralyrev, while Klapka, with a part of the eighth corps, endeavored to take Nyarasd. But the enemy were in large numbers at Nyarasd and its neighbourhood and by several vigorous charges of their Uhlans and cuirassiers, proved themselves an overmatch for the hussars of Karolyi, Lehel, and Hunyadi, who retreated, leaving their cannon behind. Görgey had better success, for he drove more than three times his own numbers behind Pered, and gained advantages that made good more than fourfold what Klapka had lost. Next morning, the combat commenced again with increased violence, at Pered. The enemy had been joined, during the night, by a large reinforcement of Russian troops, still they were at first repulsed; but, by their enormous superiority in numbers, they turned our flank, assailed the rear, and forced us to retire. We were 22,000 against 95,000 Austrians and Russians, under the barbarous Haynau. The battle lasted till evening, and when our men began to cross the bridge, the corps at Nyarasd, with which Klapka engaged the preceding day, advanced to Aszod; for the purpose of destroying it, but was this time vigorously repulsed by him. The loss on both sides was nearly 5,000 in killed and wounded. On the 27th of the month, Raab was attacked by 40,000 Austrians. The garrison, only 6,000 strong, held their position bravely from eight in the morning till three in the afternoon, when, without any considerable loss, they retreated to Comorn.

The Austrian army, commanded now by the Emperor himself pursued us. On the 2nd of July, with a force of 40,000, we gained a victory over 70,000 Austrians and 25,000 Russians. Early in the morning the intrenched camp before Comorn was assaulted on all sides. The Austrians turned their main strength, against the heights of Monostor, and carried the first four lines at the first charge. They then took the village of Oszony, without difficulty. Görgey took command of the right wing of the Hungarian forces, committed that of the centre to Klapka, and of the left to Gen. Leiningen. The combat now commenced in earnest, and continued vigorously till long past noon, when Klapka in less than an hour, after two repulses, took Oszony. The flying enemy were pursued in the direction of Todis. Görgey now came to the centre, took all the cavalry and six batteries, and charged upon the enemy's centre, which he immediately broke and pursued till evening.

The grand Austrian army, under the eyes of their Emperor, was obliged to yield before our troops, and he was compelled to take to his heels. Besides the many prisoners in our hands, the enemy left several thousand dead on the field. We had 2,000 dead and wounded – among the latter Gen. Görgey, who was grazed on the head by a grape-shot.

Battles in Transylvania under General Bem

Bem was appointed to the comand of the forces in Transylvania, and was soon ready to begin offensive operations. There were at that time opposed to him from thirty to forty thousand Wallachians, and fourteen thousand Austrian regulars. In spite of this great superiority of opposing numbers, he very soon took the chief city. With 20,000 men, Bem marched at first against General Gedeon, who stood, with six thousand Austrian and those Wallachians who were not yet pacified, about Besztercze.

Puchner, who was in the Saxon district with eight thousand men, and who had undoubtedly received powers from the Austro–Russian government to this end, now called for aid upon the Russian general, Luders, who was stationed in Wallachia. Luders immediately dispatched ten thousand men under General Scariatin to his assistance. But Bem pushed forward, and after having beaten the combined Austro–Russian forces five several times, carried Hermanstadt by storm, and soon after Kronstadt, the two main supports of the reaction. We drove the army itself through the Temeser pass into Wallachia. With a few exceptions, Transylvania was now entirely cleared of enemies, and held by an army 20,000 strong.

But this army was not able to contend successfully with the 40,000 Russians, the 14,000 Austrians, and the new insurrection of 30,000 well-armed Wallachians. Austrian and Russian gold corrupted the soldiers so that Bem lost four successive battles, together with his war material. The army which but a short time previous, had been the terror of Russians and Austrians, was utterly dispersed before the breaking up of that of Dembinsky.

Dembinsky, who had charge of the troops destined to guard against an invasion from Gallicia, though 70,000 men were at his disposal, declared himself unable to compete with the bloody Haynau and retreated. Some suppose that he was a traitor.

The Traitor Görgey's Shameful Surrender to the Russians

Görgey commanded the choicest troops of Hungary, who had fought many triumphant battles. The third corps had been victorious in 30 engagements, and could alone have successfully resisted the whole Austrian armies; but Görgey caused reports to be circulated among them, that they were not able to contend with their enemies. He received overtures from the enemy, and gave them all the advantages he could, in carrying out his traitorous purposes. He removed the chief of his general-staff, and substituted his own brother, Lieutenant-colonel Armin Görgey, that he might the better work in secret. He intentionally and rapidly weakened the physical and moral soundness of his forces by extraordinary marches, by frequent parleys with the enemy, by discouraging reports, and by all kinds of deprivations. All discipline was soon destroyed. Hundreds were left to die on the road; other hundreds were allowed to desert. The demoralization had gone so far, that at Putnok he ventured to speak openly and with impunity of a surrender to the Russians.

Görgey had on the 11th of August, at Vilagos, obtained a promise from all the commanders under him to act with him, on a pretence that they should unite with the Russians against Austria. The actual surrender took place at Boros Jeno, close by Vilagos:

An Austrian officer speaks of the vile surrender as follows:

"The hot sun of August 13th shone with its piercing rays on the parched and silent ranks of the insurgents, whose army was drawn up in two solid columns, on each side of the Szollos road. Groups of officers stood before their battalions, gloomily talking with each other. Staff officers, in their splendid uniforms, rode up and down, occasionally speaking a word of encouragement to the faint-hearted; for the usual noisy gayety so peculiar to the Magyars had given place to the most painful depression. 'Must it be carried so far with us?' was the despairing cry that arose on every side. Curses, such as no one can command but a Magyar in trouble, resounded from the closed ranks. Wherever the eye turned, there was lamentation and despair. It seemed like a vast field of death.

The hussars, leaning on their jaded; skeleton-looking horses, seemed to exchange with their comrades one last mute word, and to bid them a final farewell.

'I must leave you and go on foot like a dog', they murmured in the ear of their trusty companions. The greater part regarded this as a misfortune to break their hearts. They would prefer exposing themselves to the greatest dangers. They cast off their laced dolmans in which they took such pride, and bursting through the military shell, tore the saddles from their horses, and rushed off at full gallop, in order to become again what they were before, the wild Csikos (horse-tamer) of the boundless Puszta. Here was the brave regiment of the Ferdinand Hussars, with the old war-wolf, their Colonel, at their head. It was he who, at the council of war at Vilagos, most strenuously opposed the surrender. When he was out-voted, in his rage he threw his heavy sabre rattling at the feet of Görgey, so that the hall resounded with the noise.

After I had wound my way along, with a great deal of trouble, I reached a small straw-roofed building, the only inn in the place.

As soon as I entered I saw the Chief Commandant and Görgey, the Hungarian Dictator for the last 48 hours. He was dressed in his simple but romantic costume, which differed very much from that of the general-staff who stood round him. In a light-brown blouse, with a golden collar, riding-boots reaching far above the knee, a round black hat surmounted with a waving white feather, he was joking with a pretty young girl, into whose ear he whispered flattering nonsense. I was astonished. A few minutes before the catastrophe effected by him which decided the fate of Hungary, surrounded by men whose dark visages wore, the impression of the deepest despair, could this man, serenely smiling, be exchanging gallantries with a frivolous girl.

In the midst of this a general commotion took place. Görgey had thrown himself on his horse and after him his whole glittering suite. It was the last act which was to conclude the grand drama of the Magyar war. The splendid cavalcade had placed itself in motion; the bridge, unaccustomed to such a burden, groaned under the hoofs of the proudly-prancing horses, while the eye followed the historical procession with astonishment and dismay.

When Görgey, after the transactions were closed at Vilagos, went into the midst of the army and declared, 'that he no longer felt it in his power to defend the army, but if any was found willing to assume the command, he would gladly yield it to him,' there was but one man ready for the proposal. This was a grayhaired captain of the Hussars, who sprang forward, and, the tears which he never knew before falling on his grizzled beard, cried out it was his wish and that of his comrades to cut their way through, and this must be the feeling of the whole army.

Only a soldier's heart can comprehend the feeling with which a man is parted from his arms. Many seemed torn in pieces in helpless agony, others wept as they kissed the cold steel, while a great number shrieked out with rage to be led against the enemy, and not to be subjected to this disgrace. I saw how officers and men threw themselves into each other's arms, and sobbing, bid each other farewell. But in other places they raved against the officers and accused them of selfishness. No pen can describe the woe, the despair, which prevailed among the Hussars. He who felt so much at home on his horse, was now to be dismounted and creep along on foot like the meanest Baka. Many shot their horses and they who would have lost a limb without a groan, sobbed like children.

But their rest was not of long duration. The Russian escort came galloping up, and, accompanied by them, the Magyars were obliged the same day to start one stage towards Zarand. The march, under the Russian escort, from Szollos to Sarkad lasted no less than eight days. The sun poured down his hottest rays on the sandy plains, over which moved an endless throng of carriages, horsemen, and foot-travelers, in the wildest confusion. Every moment the procession stopped, when all began to quarrel, curse, scream, and for a change, to fisticuff each-other.

In a few days the Magyar army was transported from Sarkad to Gyula, with the immense number of those compromised in the political movement, and there delivered over to the Imperial Austrian troops.

Men and officers were robbed of whatever they possessed. Their physical wants were unattended to. On the slightest provocation they were beaten. Finally, without regard to their previous rank, they were forced to enter the Austrian service as privates. The wealthy, on the most shameless pretexts, were either hung or shot, that the sunken state of Austrian finances might receive a temporary revival from the confiscation of their estates."

Success of General Klapka and Capitulation of Comorn

General Klapka gained several victories before he heard of Görgey's outrageous conduct.

An expedition was undertaken early on the morning of the 30th of July, under the personal conduct of Klapka himself, to rally out from Comorn. The forces were divided into four columns of three battalions, one division of cavalry, and two batteries each. The first column operated in the Schutt towards Aranyos, the second attacked Kurta-keszi, the third Heteny, the fourth O-Gyalla at the same time. The enemy nowhere maintained their ground, and only offered a weak resistance for a quarter of an hour on the hights of St. Peter; but they were very soon driven from there, and pursued till three o'clock in the afternoon beyond Ersek-Ujvar. The enemy lost, on this occasion, two full ammunition-wagons, about 200 killed and wounded and 500 prisoners. Our loss was one officer wounded, and one horse shot. Gen. Klapka now determined to attack the besieging Austrian army with his whole force. Col. Asserman led a column of six battalions, three divisions of hussars, and three footbatteries, to flank the enemy, which broke up from the intrenched camp at midnight, and about four o'clock in the morning, Aug. 3rd, stormed Almas. The garrison were cut down, or put to flight. This column next marched against Todis and then against Komlod. At eight o'clock, another column of six battalions of infantry, one division of cavalry, and two batteries, advanced directly to Mocsa.

Asserman moved with his column towards Nagy-Igmand, then crossed the Csonczo and took possession, on his march thither, of forty loaded baggage-wagons, and 2,700 beef cattle, on their way to the Austro–Russian main army. Kosztolanyi advanced against the redoubt of the enemy between Csem and Herkaly, which was defended by nine eighteen-pounders. Meantime, the column at Schultz, consisting of three battalions of infantry one squadron of cavalry, and one battery, left our intrenched camp and approached the redoubt in front.

When the great redoubt was turned by the batallions of Kosztolanyi's column, Schultz began his attack; and although it was defended by twenty-one cannon, nine of which were eighteen-pounders, and six battalions of infantry, it was taken in less than half an our by two weak Honved battalions. The enemy, forced from their strong position, ran in the utmost disorder towards Acs, their last place of refuge.

Thousands of corpses strewed the field of battle; we had taken about 3,000 prisoners, and captured twenty-seven cannon; an enormous supply of provisions intended for the Austro–Russian main army, that formed the cargo of thirty-five large vessels on the right shore of the Danube, also fell into our possession.

Amid Klapka's brilliant success, he was astounded to hear of Görgey's treachery, and that probably all was lost. Soon a letter from the bloody Haynau was brought, in which he advised Klapka, with idle threats in case of refusal, to an unconditional surrender of the fortress of Comorn within forty-eight hours.

The following terms of surrender were proposed to the Austrian general:

1. A full amnesty for all political offences.
2. A general pardon for the surrendering army.
3. A sanctioning of the Hungarian paper-money.

In reply, he declared that he would lay our demands before the Emperor. No answer was ever returned. Soon news came that, the army in Transylvania, demoralized by the treason of Görgey, was dispersing, and that Bem, Kossuth, and some other generals, with a small remnant of the Hungarian forces, had taken refuge in Turkish territory. A few days after accounts reached us of the fall of Peterwardein. The fate of this fortress was also owing to Görgey, whose order to yield on the same conditions that had been extended to himself, caused a dissension in the garrison which resulted in its surrender.

At this time Haynau took command in person of the besieging corps, and invited Klapka, together with those officers who were most prominent in opposing a surrender to a meeting. In a council of war, it was determined to accept the invitation at ten o'clock on the following morning. Klapka, however, excused himself from attendance, under pretext of indisposition. On the 27th of September, those who afterwards signed the articles of capitulation, with an escort under the command of Colonel Asserman, proceeded to the place of meeting at the enemy's redoubt near Herkaly.

They finally agreed upon the following conditions:

1. The garrison are to be allowed freely to withdraw, without arms; the swords of the officers to remain in their possession.

Foreign passports shall be granted to those officers who have formerly served in the imperial army; to those who do not ask for passports to other countries, a free dismission to their homes – excepting such as voluntarily enter the imperial service.

A free residence at their homes shall be granted to the Honved officers not previously in the imperial service, without restriction as to their future conduct and occupation.

An amnesty is granted to the rank and file of the imperial regiments, and to those individuals who have been meantime promoted. They are to remain unmolested, and no legal prosecution shall hereafter be conducted against them.

2. Passports abroad shall be furnished to all who apply for them within thirty days.

3. One month's pay to the officers, and ten days wages to the rank and file, according to the rates of the Austrian service, shall be paid in Austrian national bank-notes.

4. For the settlement of the various obligations entered into by the garrison, as shown by their orders on the military chest, the sum of 500,000 guilders, *convention's munze*, (about $250,000,) shall be paid in Austrian bank-notes.

5. The sick and wounded in Komárom, and in the hospitals, shall be properly cared for.

6. Private property, both real and personal, shall be generally retained by the owners.

7. The place, time, and manner of giving up the arms, shall be hereafter determined.

8. All hostilities shall immediately cease on both sides.

9. The fortress shall be given up according to the usages of war, after a mutual ratification of the conditions.

{ Puszta-Herkaly, Sept. 27th, 1849.
Haynau, M. P.

Takats, captain.
Gasparetz, captain.
Mednyansky, colonel.
John Pragay, colonel.
Stefan Rutkay, colonel.
Count Otto Zichy, colonel.
Count Paul Esterhazy, colonel.

{ A true copy of the original,
Comorn, Sept. 29. 1849.

Szillanyi, lieut-colonel, chief of the general-staff.

John Janik, colonel.

Sigmund Szabo, colonel, commandant in the town.

Joseph von Kaszonyi, colonel.

Francis Asserman, colonel, commandant in the fortress.

George Klapka, commander-in-chief of fortress and troops.

The Austrians took possession of the intrenched camp on the right bank of the Danube on the 30th of September; of the *tête-du-pont* and the fortress on the 1st of October; of the *Palatinal lines* on the 2nd; and of Waag fort on the 3rd. The retiring divisions as they withdrew were furnished with a safe-conduct, and marched under the command of their officers to their homes, where they were disbanded. 260 of us, mostly officers, desired passports under the second article of the capitulation; some to Turkey, some to other European states, and a portion of us to America.

But there was great delay, and in many cases no passports could be obtained at all; and now, in spite of the 1st and 2nd articles, we must endure the oppressive yoke of Austria, or perhaps starve in our wretchedness. How carefully the remaining articles, which Haynau had declared to be sacred, were observed, is clearly enough shown in the execution of Major Repeczky, the imprisonment of Wiliam Csapo, the sequestration of Zichy's estates; and of others who were all in Comorn up to the end, and the first of whom was seized and executed while on his road home.

Public Speeches in Amercia

Arrival of Governor Kossuth at Quarantine

After a brilliant reception in England, the Governor arrived at the Quarantine, near New York, about one o'clock at night, December 4th, 1851, in the steamer Humboldt. As soon as her arrival was announced, the forts and various batteries fired a salute of thirty-one guns, one gun for each of the States of the Union. Their echoes awakened the island, and brought thousands of people to the shore. The noble steamer was stopped in the stream, when Dr. Doane, Col. Bercencey, and several of the Hungarians went off in the boarding boat, and asked for Kossuth. He was already on deck, and when the Hungarians and he met, their salutations were of the most joyful and enthusiastic kind. M. Pulsky was also warmly greeted, and others in the suite of the Governor.

After these demonstrations of friendship, Dr. Doane addressed Kossuth in brief but eloquent language of greeting.

The Doctor concluded his address by referring to the deep interest elicited in this country by the Hungarian struggle.

He then handed a letter to the great Magyar, of which the following is a copy:

CITY HALL, Nov. 24, 1851.

Dear Sir: – In order that our city may have notice to assemble and welcome you to our city and country as they desire, we would respectfully request you to leave the steamer at the Quarantine, and remain a few hours with Dr. Doane, who will, with great cheerfulness, tender to you the hospitality of his house, and where we are assured every attention will be paid to your comfort during the time it may be necessary for you to continue his guest.

We are with great-respect,
A. C. KINGSLAND, Mayor.
GEO. F. FRANKLIN, Alderman.

Kossuth was evidently much impressed by the sincerity and earnestness of Dr. Doane's address, and replied with much feeling:

"Thanks for your generous sentiments, expressed it such generous words! They are but the counterpart of the welcome I have met with in a great nation of the old world. But do not speak of your own nation as an infant – oh no! She is a giant, and in less than seventy years has grown to a stature which the elder nations have hot reached in a thousand. The genius of your Fulton has blotted out the distance across the Atlantic, and may the generous confidence of the young giant know no distance when I ask a fraternal hand for old Europe. (Kossuth here shook the Doctor warmly by the hand.) May your kind anticipations of me be not disappointed. I am a plain man. I have nothing in me but an honest fidelity to those principles which have made you great, and my most ardent wish is that my own country may be, if not great as yours, at least as free and as happy, which it will be in the establishment of the same great principles. The sounds I now hear seem to me the trumpet of resurrection for downtrodden humanity throughout the world."

This last allusion was to the cannon and shouts on shore, and at the close, Kossuth turned with great grace to the reporters and said that he had suffered all the voyage from sea-sickness and that his head was still dizzy. In a little while the whole party disembarked, Madame Kossuth apparently so ill that she had to be carried down the gangway. As they approached the shore the cheering was tremendous, and when they had landed, Major Hagadorn's command, who were awaiting the hero, escorted him to the house of Dr. Doane. A salute of guns from the steamship closed the ceremonies of the night.

Reception on Staten Island

A grand demonstration of the inhabitants of Staten Island took place at 12 o'clock on Friday Dec 5th. At sunrise the European revolutionary flags were hoisted in the Quarantine grounds, and a salute of twenty-one guns fired. Kossuth having accepted the guard of honor, tendered by the Major of the First Battalion, the officers entered on their honorable duty, wearing on their arms the Hungarian colors, with a portrait on satin of the great

Magyar. He stands about five feet 7 or 8 inches high; his figure is slight with full chest. He wears the large moustache flowing in with his bushy whiskers; which he wears under the chin. His forehead is well developed and expresses great mental power; his hair, once light brown, is beginning to be tinged with gray, "but not from years". He wore a handsome tight-fitting single breasted coat of black silk velvet, and the Hungarian hat and feather.

The procession was an imposing one. Kossuth finally ascended the platform, and was addressed by Mr. Locke. He replied as follows:

Kossuth's Speech to the Authorities on Staten Island

LADIES AND GENTLEMEN – The twelve hours during which I have had the honor and happiness of standing on your glorious shores gives me a happy augury of the circumstances that during my stay in the United States I will have the pleasant duty to answer many manifestations of the generous public spirit of the United States; and, therefore, you will be so kind, I hope, to take into consideration, these circumstances, that I have at the first moment a hard task – hard to me, because I will have to address your United States people in a tongue foreign to me; and therefore you will not desire from me a long or elaborate speech, but will be contented with a few warmly told, warmly felt words of thankfulness and gratitude to you. Citizens, be, therefore, fervently thanked for your generous welcome to me on my arrival to your happy shores. Be both thanked and blessed for the sanction of my hopes which you have expressed. You, sir, (turning to Mr. Locke,) have most truly expressed what are my hopes when you tell me that you consider the destiny of this glorious country to be, that from hence the spirit of Liberty is to go forth and achieve the freedom of the world. Yes, citizens, these are the hopes which induce me at the most important period, when every moment may be a turning point in Europe's destiny, to cross the Atlantic, with a risk that I shall be forced sooner to return back to my field of duty than I would expect or perhaps like.

I confidently hope, citizens, that as you have anticipated my wishes by the expression of the generous sentiments that you agree with me in the conviction that the spirit of liberty, not only the spirituality but the materiality, would go forth from your glorious country, in order that it might achieve freedom for the world. The spirit itself is but the inspiring power to deed, but yet in itself no deed; and you know that those who will be free must besides, be inspired to strike the blow. (Great applause.)

Despotism and oppression were never yet beaten but by heroic resolution and manly resistance. This is a sad necessity, but a necessity it is. I have so learned it out of the great book of life–history. I hope that the people of the United States will remember that in the hour of her glorious struggle, she received from Europe more than kind words and friendly sympathy. She also received material aid, and will readily, I hope, impart it, now that she has grown a mighty giant, in support of European liberty. (Applause, and cheers for Lafayette.) I have spoken but your own sentiments. You have given us assurance of this before I had even spoken a word to you of humble entreaty; and be sure, citizens, that the Independence of Hungary is not only a benefit to Hungary, but an indispensable condition to the freedom of the European Continent. (Great enthusiasm.)

Citizens, I thank you that you have addressed to me by your speaker not the language of party, but the language of liberty, and therefore I repeat to the *people* of the United States what I said in England, here and there, and on every opportunity, frankly and openly, that I desire to see respected the sovereign right of my nation to dispose of its own domestic concerns; and therefore, I myself must feel resolved in every place and in every country to respect the same principle, and therefore I came not here to the United States to mix with its interior affairs; that is your occasion, your concerns, you are the sovereign masters of your own fate; but I came here in the name of my down-trodden, but not broken people, humbly to entreat, in her name, the generous protection and aid of the people, but not of any party of the United States. (Here the speaker was interrupted with bursts of applause.)

I am sorry to mention, citizens, that having the consciousness before me, that I have never spoken in my life a single word which I have not felt in the bottom of my heart, I am sorry to say that that declaraton which I so often and solemnly professed in England, and to which declaration (as I was happy to hear from your address) you have paid your best and generous attention, was not sufficient to protect me, even before my arrival among you, from the charge of meddling with your domestic concerns, namely, with the question of your Presidential Election. (Here three groans were asked for the Courier and Enquirer, and given with great good will, and cheers for the Sun and other papers.) Because it so happened in one of my addresses in England; I mentoned one of your honorable fellow-Citizens, Mr. Walker; as one of the candidates for the

Presidency. Now, gentlemen, I feel quite at home in your midst and therefore speak familiarly, (Voices, "That's all right.") I confess, with the warmest feelings of gratitude that Mr. Walker has pronounced in England sentiments, such, that if it shall be my happy lot to see these sentiments to be the real feelings of the people of the United States, then I with fervent joy declare, "Hungary and Europe are free", and therefore I feel highly indebted to him and feel highly indebted to you, sir, (turning to Mr. Locke) for the enunciation of sentiments, quite and entirely like those which I heard from Mr. Walker in England.

But all this has nothing to do with the question of mixing myself up with the Presidential Election of the United States. The matter was simply that a gentlemen from America, in official capacity, had introduced to me Mr. Walker, whom I had not had the honor of knowing before, as one of the candidates proposed by one party in the United States, and that being the information I got, I mentioned the fact without having had the slightest meaning or idea in my mind to mix with any party question whatever in the United States. Yes, citizens, I declare that I consider no man to be honest who is not ready to respect those principles in other men which he would desire to see respected in himself. I desire to see respected by every person in the world the right of every state to dispose of its own domestic concerns, and therefore, he is no honest man who would not readily, and in every country, respect the same principles towards other men.

Allow me, citizens, to reflect upon the expression of your kind address, which is rather a delicate matter to me; but I confidently hope you will not misunderstand me. You have named me in the beginning of your address "Kossuth, Governor of Hungary". Now, citizens, my lot is a curious one. Never was there a man in this world more fond of tranquility and a retired life than myself, and I never in my life was able to enjoy that happiness for a single moment. I was not able to enjoy it, because I considered always the duty of patriotism to be the first duty of man, and after discharging that, then only to attend to his individual wishes and his individual inclinations. My nomination to the high station of Governor of Hungary was no satisfaction, as serving ambitious uses, because I know no other ambition than this one – not to be ambitious. I never in my life felt more sad than in the moment when I was named Governor, because I considered the feeble faculties of mind which I possessed, and the high duties laid upon my feeble shoulders. I was almost afraid of the high responsibility of this great station.

It is, therefore, not out of ambition that I thank you sir for your expressions where you designed and named me Governor of Hungary; but I thank you for it because this nomination on the part of the people of the United States, whom I now have the honor to address, is an acknowledgment of the righful existence of the Declaraton of Independence of Hungary, (cheers) and, Gentlemen, I frankly declare that I believe that the people of the United States are bound in honor and in duty to recognize this Declaration of Independence as a *righteously existing Fact*, because your very existence depends upon a similar declaration of Independence. This declaration of the Independence of Hungary is now the only existing public act of my nation, not the *Pronunciamento* of a single individual or a single party, but the solemn declaration of the whole nation lawfully assembled in Congress; as your forefathers were when they put forth the glorious Declaration of Independence and was sanctified by every village and municipality in the whole country. And to that Declaration of the Independence of Hungary there is no contrary act, no contrary protestation from my people that has yet come forth to the world; and therefore I have a right to say that the Declaration of the Independence of Hungary exists rightfully and now has the whole power of right and lawful existence. What is contrary to this existence? The only contrariety to it is that the Czar of Russia, a foreign power, who had no right to intermeddle with Hungarian affairs, had ambitious views, to impose upon us allegiance to him; and finding a Traitor in our ranks, to trample upon the liberties and national existence of Hungary.

Now, gentlemen from what time has violence power to annihilate right? Violence can establish a fact contrary to law and contrary to right, but violence never could destroy the source, the rightful source of that declaration of Independence. Take for instance; you have had, not long ago, a great struggle with Mexico – when General Scott had driven out the President of Mexico from his residence. Now suppose, on the contrary that General Santa Anna came to Washington with a victorious army, and drove from the capital President Taylor – would President Taylor, gentleman, by that fact cease to be the rightfully elected President of the United States because foreign powers came and forced him for a moment to leave his post? I believe there is not a single man in the United States would answer me, "he would". The violence of Santa Anna would not have taken away the sovereign right of the United States people to choose their own President; and if this is so, therefore it is right in me to say that it is the duty of consistency and the duty of logic for the people of the United

States to recognize the Declaration of Independence of Hungary as an existing law – the only existing public law of my poor downtrodden land.

This, gentlemen, is what I expect to find here, and whatever be the difference of sentiment of the Government in this respect, I know that I have the honor to be in a country where the sovereign is not the government but the people and where the government measures must be in that direction which the public spirit of the people commands; and it is therefore, that I thank you once more for the kindness of having named me Governor of Hungary, because by that you have paid the tribute of acknowledgment to the Declaration of the Independence of my native land.

My humble capacity, gentlemen, has not preserved me from calumnies. I can now almost tell what poor O'Connell once told: "I am the most calumniated man in the world" (Cries of no, no.) Gentlemen. I don't care much about it. So long as despotism will exist in the world, and so long as despots can *pay*, they will find calumniators – I mean men to calumniate those opposed to despotism and tyranny. But I don't care much about it because, suppose I was one of the most wicked creatures in the world; I put it to your judgment, in the name of what is most sacred and dear to you, what would this alter in respect to the cause of Hungary? Would the cause of Hungary by this become less just, less righteous, less worthy of your sympathy, because I, for instance, was a bad man? It is not the question of an individual, it is the question of the great cause of a country worthy to take a place in the great family of the free nations of the world – and therefore, gentlemen, I do not much care about these calumnies – but scarcely had I arrived here when I was told that I am attacked, even here in the United States, with the charge of being an irreligious man. Now gentlemen, this is a sacred ground. All these assertions do not affect either your judgment or your heart. (Cries of no, no.)

As to the praises which you were so kind as to bestow on me, it is no affectation of modesty in me when I declare that I am conscious of having no merit at all, but only that of being a plain, straight forward, honest man – a faithful friend of freedom and a good patriot – and I am somewhat susceptible on this matter; but notwithstanding, I will own at least that, as a good Christian, whose first moral principle to "Love thy neighbor as thyself" – I only wish that man who charged me with being irreligious, shall, in respect to this great principle of christianity, to love thy neighbor as thyself, stand with such open face before the Eternal Judge as I confidently hope I shall stand (M. Kossuth delivered this sentence with great devotional solemnity, and was loudly applauded), and therefore, even about these matters I don't care much.

But one thing I can scarcely comprehend, that the *Press*, the mighty vehicle of progress and of Justice, this champion of human rights, would have found one organ even in the whole of the United States, which, leaving aside its personal calumnies, would assert that it is not the people of Hungary, not myself and companions, that fought for liberty, but that it was the Emperor of Austria who was the champion of liberty. (Groans and execrations for the Courier and Enquirer.) Do not give him groans, gentlemen, but rather thank him, because I say that these could be no better service given to a cause than the proof of its justice, that its opponents have nothing to say but such *ridiculous* – I do not now find a word to convey my idea about it – it must be a sacred and just cause which by its opponents is attacked by the assertion that the Emperor of Austria is the champion of freedom throughout the European Continent! I thank you, citizens, that you have given me full proof that all these calumnies are qualities which are so natural to every right minded man that it is scarcely worthy to speak of them, because I cannot conceive how a man with common understanding and a good heart can be any thing else than a good patriot – a lover of freedom – and an honest man. (Loud and protracted cheers.)

I have heard with great pleasure the development of your views in your address, which prove that you have bestowed a kindly and investigating attention to the true nature of the cause of Hungary and those principles which we posess. I expected and desired nothing else. I desire only that the glaring eye of the people of the United States shall be pleased to read this open book in my heart – to read in this open book of the history of their struggle for Hungary. Hungary wants no advocate to recommend her cause to attention, that cause will sufficiently recommend itself. (Great applause.)

Now, gentlemen, it was not my intention to have spoken so much, and badly enough I have spoken it, I suppose. (Cries of no, no, go on.) I cannot go on, because I have got to speak tomorrow, and after tomorrow, and I don't know how many times today yet. I am the worst sailor in the world; I suffered very much in crossing the ocean, and have not slept for many nights. My bodily strength is broken, but, nevertheless, I give you my word that whenever the trumpet calls for a resurrection in the cause of freedom, I will not be sick, but will stand in my place on the battle field as an honest man, because the body must obey the spirit. (Great enthusiasm.)

Let me end, gentlemen, by once more repeating to you my most fervent thanks for this generous welcome, and these generous sentiments which I have had the honor here to listen to. And let me hope that before I leave the United States, as leave I must, because I have a suffering country in Europe which is only made dearer to my heart by its suffering. Let me hope, I say, that before I leave the United States, the generosity of the people of the United States will have given me *material* proof that these sentiments which I have had the honor to hear from you are the sentiments of the people – *of the whole people* of the United States and that the people of the United States are firmly decided to be as great in deeds and in acts as in words and sympathy. Excellent. In this hope I beg to be kindly remembered by you, and I take my leave of you, with the promise that as this place will be that from whence I start back to Europe, if you will give me the honor, I will once more have the joy and happiness to address you publicly, to say to you a public adieu, and give you, I trust, public thanks for facts, as I do now for *sentiments*.

Kossuth's Grand Reception in New York City

On Friday, December 5, extensive preparations were made throughout the city for extending a hearty welcome to the illustrious stranger. On all the hotels, and other public buildings, the National and Hungarian flags were displayed. At the eastern and western gates of the Park, two large triumphal arches were erected and decorated with evergreens and flags of the national colors of Hungary, red, white and green.

A committee of the Common Council, with a large number of guests in a steamer, accompanied Governor Kossuth to Castle Garden. Alderman Morgans addressed him at some length, to which he replied as follows:

[Kossuth commenced his address, but for many minutes the enthusiasm was so great that he could not make himself audible to the reporters, who were close beside him. At length, order having been partially restored, he re-commenced.]

Kossuth's Speech at Castle Garden
on the day of his Reception

Mr. Mayor and Gentlemen – If you are desirous to hear my humble thanks, for the generous respect with which you have honored me, then I humbly entreat you to keep silence, as it is not possible to speak in such confusion.

I am yet half sick, gentlemen – tossed and whirled about by a fortnight's gale on the Atlantic's restless waves, my giddy brain is still turning about as a whirlpool and this gigantic Continent seems yet to tremble beneath my quivering steps. Let me have, I beg of you, before I go to work, some hours of rest upon the soil of freedom, your happy home. (Enthusiastic cheers.) Freedom and home! What heavenly music is in those two words! Alas! I have no home, and the freedom of my people downtrodden. Young giant of free America – do not you tell me that your shores are an asylum for the oppressed, and a home for the homeles exile? An asylum it is, but all the blessings of your glorious country cannot drown to oblivion the fond desires and longings of this heart for my native land. (Great applause.)

My poor native land! The sufferings make thee but dearer to my heart; thy bleeding image dwells with me while I wake as it rests with me in the short hours of restless sleep; it has accompanied me over the waves, and will accompany me when I go back to fight over thy battles for liberty once more. (Cheers.) I have no ideas but thee – no sentiment but thee – even here, with this prodigious view of greatness, freedom and happiness before my eyes. My thoughts are wandering towards home, and when I look over thousands of thousands before me, the happy inheritors of yonder freedom, for which your forefathers fought and bled, and when I turn to you citizens, and bow before the majesty of the United States; and thank you for the generous share you have taken in our liberation, and return you thanks for the unparalleled honor of this reception, I see out of the very midst of this great assembly the bleeding image of Hungary rise before me; looking at you with anxiety, to see if there is in the lustre, of your eyes a ray of hope for her, if in the thunder of your hurras, she hears a trumpet-call of resurrection for her. If this were not so, if there were no ray of hope in your eyes, no such trumpet-call in your cheers, then woe to Europe's oppressed nations. They will stand alone in the hour of need. Less fortunate than you, they will meet no brother's hand to help them in the approaching giant fight against the leagued despots of the world, and woe to me also. I will feel no pleasure, even here. The days of my stay will turn out to be lost for my fatherland, at a time when every moment is teeming with the decisions of Europe's destiny.

Citizens, much as I have need of some rest, much as I want to be familiar with the ground on which I tread, I will have to stand before you in business matters publicly. I took it for my duty and honor not to let escape even this first moment of your generous reception without telling you plainly, openly, what kind of man I am, and what my hopes and expectations are, and what were the motives which brought me to your shores.

Here the clamor and confusion were so great that Kossuth was forced to desist from speaking.

After he had reached his hotel, his private secretary dictated the remainder of his speech from his manuscript to the reporters, who received at the same time the following from Mr. Pulszky:

"To the gentlemen of the press:

The enthusiasm of the people of New York, with which it espressed its noble sympathy for Hungary, was so great that its outburst made it impossible for the Governor to address the masses, but out of respect to the inhabitants of the Empire City, and to show his gratitude for the cordial welcome with which he was honored today, he wishes, by the mighty agency of the press, to give publicity to his feelings, and to have circulated what he would have said, if unfortunately for him, and for the cause of Hungary, the people assembled this morning, had had less sympathy, and had expressed it less warmly.

I am, gentlemen, your obedient servant,

Francis Pulszky"

Conclusion of Kossuth's Speech

Gentlemen: – I have to thank the people, Congress and Government of the United States for my liberation from captivity. Human tongue has no words to express the bliss which I felt when I, the down-trodden Hungarian, wandering chief, saw the glorious flag of the stripes and stars fluttering over my head when I first bowed before it with deep respect – when I saw around me the gallant officers and crew of the Mississippi frigate – the most of them the worthiest representatives of true American principles – American greatness – American generosity – and to think that it was not a mere chance which cast the star spangled banner around me, but that it was your protecting will – to know that the United States of America, conscious of their glorious calling, as well as of their power, declared, by this unparalleled act, to be resolved to become the protectors of human rights – to see a powerful vessel of America coming to far Asia to break the chains by which the mightiest despots of Europe fettered the captivity of an exiled Magyar, whose very name disturbed the proud security of their sleep, to feel restored by such a protection, and in such away to freedom – and by freedom to activity. You may be well aware of what I have felt and still feel at the remembrance of this proud moment of my life.

Others spoke; you acted; and I was free! You acted, and at this act of yours tyrants trembled. Humanity shouted out with joy; the down-trodden people of Magyar; the down-trodden, but not broken, raised his head with resolution and with hope, and the brilliancy of your stars was greeted by Europe's oppressed nations as the morning star of rising liberty. Now, gentlemen, you must be aware how boundless the gratitude must be which I feel for you. You have restored me to life, because restored to activity; and should my life, by the blessings of the Almighty, still prove useful to my fatherland and to humanity, it will be your merit – it will be your work. May you and your glorious country be blessed for it. Europe is on the very eve of such immense events; that however fervent my gratitude be to you, I would not have felt authorized to cross the Atlantic at this very time, only for the purpose to express to you my warm thanks. I would have thanked you by facts contributing to the freedom of the European Continent, and would have postponed my visit to your glorious shores, till the decisive battle for liberty was fought, if it were my destiny to outlive the day. Then, what is the motive of my being here at this very time? The motive, citizens, is, that your generous act of my liberation has raised that conviction throughout the world that this generous act is but the manifestatian of your resolution to throw your weight into the balance where the fate of the European Continent is to be weighed. You have raised the conviction throughout the world that, by my liberation, you were willing to say, "Ye oppressed nations of old Europe's Continent, be of good cheer; the young giant of America stretches his powerful arm over the waves, ready to give a brother's hand to your future." So is your act interpreted throughout the world. You, in your proud security, can scarcely imagine how beneficial the conviction has already proved to the suffering nations on the European Continent. You can scarcely imagine what self-confidence you have added to the resolution of the oppressed. You have knit the tie of solidarity in the destinies of nations. I cannot doubt that you know how I was received by the public opinion in every country which I touched since I am free, and what feelings my liberation has elicited in those countries which it was my lot to touch. You know how I, a plain, poor, penniless exile, have almost become a centre of hope and confidence to the most different nations, not united but by the tie of common sufferings. What is the source of this apparition, unparalleled in mankind's history? The source of it is, that your generous act of my liberation is taken by the world for the revelation of the fact that the United States are resolved not to allow the despots of the world to trample upon oppressed humanity. It is hence that my liberation was cheered from Sweden down to Portugal as a ray of hope. It is hence that even those nations which most desire my presence in Europe, now have unanimously told me, "Hasten on, hasten on to the great, free, rich and powerful people of the United States, and bring over its brotherly aid to the cause of your country, so intimately connected with European liberty." And here I stand to plead the cause of the solidarity of human rights before the great Republic of the United States. Humble as I am, God, the Almighty, has selected me to represent the cause of humanity before you. My warrant to this capacity is written in the sympaty and confidence of all who are oppressed, and of all who (as your elder brother, the people of Brittania,) sympathize with the op-pressed. My warrant to this capacity is written in hopes and expectations you have entitled the world to entertain by liberating me out of my prison, and by restoring me to activity. But it has pleased the Almighty to make out of my humble self yet another opportunity for a thing which may prove a happy turning point in the destiny of the world. I bring you a brotherly greating from the people of Great Britain. I speak not in an official character imparted by diplomacy whose secrecy is the curse of the world, but I am the harbinger of the public spirit of the people which has the right to impart a direction to its government, and which I witnessed pronouncing itself in the most decided manner – openly – that the people of England, united to you, with enlightened, brotherly love, as it is united in blood conscious of your strength, as it is conscious of its own, has for ever abandoned every sentiment of irritation and rivalry, and desires the brotherly alliance of the United States, to secure to every nation the sovereign right to dispose of itself, and to protect this sovereign right of nations against the encroaching arrogance of despots; and leagued to you against the league of despots, to stand together with you, godfather to the approaching baptism of European liberty. Now, gentlemen, I have stated my position. I am a straight forward man; I am a republican; I have avowed it openly in the monarchical but free England and I am happy to state that I have nothing lost by this avowal there. I hope I will nothing lose here in republican America by the frankness which most be one of the chief qualities of every Republican. So I beg leave frankly and openly to state the following points.

First, that I take it for a duty of honor, and of principle, not to meddle with whatever party question of your own domestic affairs. I claim for my country the right to dispose of itself so I am resolved and must be resolved to respect the same principle here and everywhere; may others delight in the part of Knights Errant for theories – that is not my case. I am the man of the great principle of the sovereignity of every people to dispose of its own domestic concerns, and I must solemnly deny to every foreigner, as to every foreign power, the right to oppose the sovereign faculty.

Secondly. I profess highly and openly my admiration for the glorious principles of union upon which stands the mighty pyramid of your greatness, and upon the basis of which you have grown in the short period of seventy-five years to a prodigious giant, the living wonder of the world. I have the most warm wish that the star-spangled banner of the United States may be for ever floating, united and one – the proud ensign of mankind's divine origin – and taking my ground upon this principle of union, which I find lawfully existing – an established constitutional fact, it is not to a party, but the united people of the United States, that I confidently will address my humble requests for aid and protection to oppressed humanity. I will conscientiously respect your laws, but within the limits of your laws I will use every honest exertion to gain your operative sympathy, and your financial, political and material aid for my country's freedom and independence and entreat the realization of those hopes which your generosity has raised in my and my peoples' breast, und also in the breast of Europe's oppressed nations; and therefore –

Thirdly, I beg leave frankly to state that my aim is to restore my Fatherland to the full enjoyment of that act of declaration of independence which, being the only rightful existing public law of my nation, can nothing have lost of its rightfulness by the violent invasions of foreign Russian arms, and which, therefore, is fully entitled to be recognized by the people of the United States, whose very existence is founded upon a quite similar declaration of independence.

What can be opposed to this recognition; which is a logical necessary consequence of the principle of your country's political existence? What can be opposed to it? The frown of Mr. Hulseman – the anger of that satellite of the Czar called Francis Joseph of Austria, and the immense danger with which some European and American papers threaten you, and by which, of course, you must feel extremely terrified, that your Minister at Vienna will have offered his passports, and that Mr. Hulseman leaves Washington, should I be received and treated in my official capacity.

Now as to your Minister at Vienna, how can you combine the letting him stay there with your opinion of the cause of Hungary, I really don't know – but so much I know, that the present absolutistical atmosphere of Vienna is not very propitious to American principles. I know a man who could tell some curious facts about this matter, but as to Mr. Hulseman; really, I don't believe that he will be so ready to leave Washington. He has extremely well digested the caustic pills which Mr. Webster has administered to him so gloriously, but, after all, I know enough of the sovereign people of the United States, that it would never admit, to whatever responsible depository of the Executive power should he even be willing to do so, which, to be sure, your highminded Government is not willing to do, to be regulated in its policy by the frowns of all the Hulsemans and all the Francis Josephs in the world. So I confidently hope that the sovereign of the country, *the people* will make the Declaration of the Independence of Hungary soon formally recognized, and that it will care not a bit about it, if Mr. Hulseman takes tomorrow his passports – *bon voyage* to him – but it is also my agreeable duty to profess that I am entirely convinced that the government of the United States shares warmly the sentiments of the people in that respect. It has proved it by the ready and dignified manner in executing the resolution of Congress in behalf of my liberation – it has proved it by calling on the Congress to consider how I shall be treated, and even this morning I was honored with an express order of the government, by an official salute from the batteries of the United States, in such a manner in which, according to the military rules, only a public high official capacity can be greeted.

Thus having expounded my aim, I beg leave to state that I came not to your glorious shores to enjoy a happy rest. I came not with the intention to gather triumphs of personal distinction, or to be the object of popular shows, but I came a humble petitioner in my country's name, as its freely chosen, constitutional chief, humbly to entreat you to give aid. To this aim I will devote every moment of my life with the utmost assiduity, with the utmost restlessness, as every moment may bring, a report of events which may call me to hasten to my place in the battle field, where the great, and I hope, the last battle will be fought between liberty and despotism – a moment marked by the finger of God to be so near, that every hour of delay of your generous aid may prove fatal to oppressed humanity. Thus, having stated my position to be an humble petitioner in the name of my oppressed country – let me respectfully ask you, do you not regret to have bestowed on me the high honor of the glorious reception unparalleled in history – I say unparalleled in history, though I know that your fathers have welcomed Lafayette in a similar manner – but Lafayette had a mighty claim to your country's gratitude – he had fought in your ranks for your freedom and independence, and what was still more, in the hour of your need, he was the link of your friendly connection with France – a connection, the result of which were two French fleets of more than 38 men-of-war, three thousand gallant men who fought side by side with you against Cornwallis before Yorktown, the precious gift of twenty-four thousand muskets, a loan of nineteen millions, and even the preliminary treaty of your glorious peace negotiated at Paris by your immortal Franklin. I hope the people of the United States, now itself in the happy condition to aid those who in need of aid as itself was once in need, will kindly remember these facts, and you, citizens of New York, you will yourselves become the Lafayettes of poor Hungary. Lafayette had great claims to your love and sympathy; but I – I have none. I come an humble petitioner, with no other claims than those which the oppressed has to the sympathy of free men who have the power to help – with the claim which the unfortunate has to the happy – and the down-trodden to the protection of Eternal Justice and human right. In a word, I have no other claims than those which the oppressed principles of freedom has to the aid of victorious liberty. Then I would humbly ask, are these claims sufficient to ensure your generous protection, not to myself, but to the cause of my native land – not to my native land only, but to the principle of freedom on Europe's Continent, of which the independence of Hungary is the indisputable keystone. If you consider these claims not sufficient to your action and operative sympathy, then let me know at once, that the hopes have failed with which Europe's oppressed nations have looked to your great mighty and glorious republic. Let me know at once the failure of our hopes, that I may hasten back and tell Europe's oppressed nations; "Let us fight forsaken, single handed, the battle of Leonidas. Let us trust to God, to our right, and to our good sword; there is no other help for the oppressed nations on earth" But if your generous republican hearts are animated by the high principle of freedom and the solidarity in the destinies of humanity – if you have the will, as to be sure you have the power, to support the cause of freedom against the sacrilegious league of despotism – then give me some days of calm reflection to become acquainted with the ground upon which I stand. Let me take the kind advice of some active friends, on the most practical course I have to adopt. Let me see if there be any preparatory steps taken in favor of that cause which I have the honor to represent, and then let me have a new opportunity to expound before you my humble requests in a practical way. I confidently hope, Mr. Mayor, the Corporation and citizens of the Empire City will grant me the second opportunity. If this be your generous will, then let me take this for a boon of happier days, and let me end with a sigh of thanksgiving to the Almighty God that it is your glorious country which Providence has selected to be the pillar of freedom, as it is already the asylum to oppressed humanity. I am told that I will have the high honor today to review your patriotic militia. Oh God! how my heart throbs at the idea to see this gallant army enlisted on the side of freedom against despotism. The world would be free, and you the saviours of humanity. *And why not?* These gallant men take part in the mighty demonstration of today, proving that I was right when I said that now-a-days even "the bayonets think."

Citizens of New York, it is under your protection that I place this sacred cause of the freedom and independence of Hungary.

Kossuth, on leaving the Garden, mounted a splended charger, and, accompanied by Maj. Gen. Sanford and suite, reviewed the troops; after which, on reaching the carriage provided for him, he dismounted and entered it amidst the loud shouts of the people.

The procession passed up Broadway, and such a cheering we never before heard. The display of flags and mottos were very imposing, and probably no mortal ever received a more enthusiastic reception.

57

Banquet given to Kossuth by the Corporation of New York

A Banquet to Kossuth, by the Corporation of New York, was given, Dec. 12, at the Irving House. Of its magnificence it is superfluous to speak. It was worthy of the occasion.

The company invited, consisted of not less than 350, embracing almost every man prominently connected with our city government; Judges on the Bench, members elect of the Common Council, members of the Bar, Proprietors and Editors of Newspapers, &c.; &c.

After a toast was given in honor of Kossuth, he addreased the company as follows:

Kossuth's Speech before the Corporation of New York

Sir, in returning you my most humble thanks for the honor you did me by your toast, and by the benefit of coupling my humble name with that cause which is the sacred aim of my life, I confess to be so overwhelmed with emotion by all it was my prodigious lot to experience since I am on your glorious shores, that unable to find words to express my feelings, and knowing that all the honor I meet with has the higher meaning of principles, I at once beg leave to fall back to my duties, which are the lasting topics of my reflections, my sorrows and my hopes. I take the present occasion for a highly important opportunily. I take it for such as will probably decide about the success or failure of my visiting the United States. I must therefore humbly embrace your indulgence for a pretty long, plain, in no case eloquent development of my humble views to the benefit of that cause which the citizens of New York, and you particularly, gentlemen, honor with, generous sympathy.

When I consider the sympathy af the people of the United States for the cause of Hungary, so generally diffused as to be almost universal and so resolutely pronounced as men pronounce these feelings which are intended to be followed by noble and great deeds, I would feel inclined to take your generous aid for the restoration of my native land to its sovereign independence, already as granted in principle, and for me nothing left to do but to enter into a negotiation about the arrangement of the details, were my confident hopes not checked by that idea, of noninterference in foreign, chiefly European affairs, which, according to the numerous testimonials of your most distinguished politicians, we are told to be one of the ruling and lasting principles of the policy of the United States.

I highly respect the source of this conviction, gentlemen. This source is your religious attachment to the doctrines of those great men, who highly proved to all posterity their wisdom, by bequeathing to you the immortal work of that Constitution which, sided by the unparalleled benefits of nature, has raised you, in the short period of seventy-five years, from the precarious position of an infant people to the prodigious strength of a giant nation. The beneficial results of the wisdom of the founders of your great Republic you see in a happy reality. What would be the consequences of the departure from that wisdom, you are not sure of. It is therefore natural that you feel an instinctive fear to touch, even with improving hands, the dear legacy of those great men.

And as to your glorious Constitution, all humanity can only wish, in the common interest of mankind, that you and your posterity may yet long conserve this religions attachment to its fundamental principles, which by no means exclude development and progress; and that every citizen of your great Union, thankfully acknowledging the immense benefits of this Constitution, may, even in the moments of the most passionate irritation, never forget to love that Constitution more than the momentary passion of his heart, or the egotistical interest of the passing hour. May every citizen of your glorious country for ever remember that a partial discomfort of a corner in a large, sure and comfortable house, may be well amended without breaking the foundation of it, and that amongst all possible means of getting rid of that corner's partial discomfort, the worst would be to burn down the house with our own hands.

But while I thus acknowledge the wisdom of your attachment to the fundamental doctrines of the founders of your Republic, I beg leave with equal frankness to state, that in my opinion, there can be scarcely anything more dangerous to the progressive development of whatever nation, than to take for a basis that which is none – to take for a principle that which is but the convenience of the passing situation – to take for substantial that which is but accidental, or take for a constitutional doctrine that which was but the momentary exigency of administrative policy. Such a cause of action would be like to that, when a healthy man would refuse to take substantial food, because when he was once laboring under weakness of stomach, his physician ordered him a severe diet to keep. The consequence would be consumption–death.

Let me suppose, gentlemen, that yonder doctrine of non-interference was really bequeathed to you by your Washington – and that it is not, I will prove to you afterwards – and let me even suppose that your Washington imparted such a meaning to yonder supposed doctrine – which were equivalent to the words of Cain – "Am I my brother's keeper?" – which supposition would be of course a sacrilege. But suppose all this. And I believe that, even under such suppositions, I may be entitled to ask – is the dress which suited the child, still convenient to the full grown man – nay to a *giant*, which you are? Would it not be ridiculous to lay the giant in the child's cradle, and to sing him to sleep by a lullaby?

In those times of the foundation of the United States, you were an infant people; and the large dress of your then comparatively not large territory, hung loose on your puerile limbs. In those times you had of course no wiser thing to do, but to grow, to grow, and to grow!

But now you are so far grown that there is no foreign power on earth from which you have anything to fear for your own existence – for your own security. This being your present condition, you have entered into the second *stadium* of political existence, the destination of which is not only to exist for yourself exclusively, but to exist as a member of the great human family of nations, having the right to all claims which are due from that family towards every one of its full grown members, but also engaged to every duty which that great family has the right to claim from every one of its full grown members.

A nation may be in the situation, either by a comparative weakness, or by choice and policy, as Japan and China, or by those motives, as Paraguay, under Dr. Fancia to live a life secluded from the world, indifferent to the doctrines of mankind, in which it cannot, or will not, have any share; but then it must be prepared to become also excluded from the benefit of progress, civilization, and national intercourse. Such a nation may well say, "I don't care about the fate of whatever other nations in the world."

But I am sure no citizen of the United States had, has, or ever will have, the wish to see this country degraded to the rotting vegetation of Paraguay, or the mummy existence of Japan and China! The feeling of self dignity, and the expansive quality of that enterprising spirit, which is congenial to free men, would revolt against the very idea of such a degrading national captivity. But, if there were even a will to live such a mummy life, there were no possibility to do so!

The very existence of your great country, the principles upon which it is founded, its geographical position, its present state of civilization, and all its moral and material interests, would lead on your people not only to maintain, but incessantly more and more to develop your intercourse with the world.

Then, of course, being in so many, respects linked to the world – connected with the world, you can have neither the will, nor be in the possibility, to remain indifferent to the condition of that outward world you are in so many respects connected with. And if you cannot remain indifferent, so you must feel resolved to down your own self consistent weight into that balance in which the fate and condition of the world is weighed.

In a word, the glorious Republic of the United States must feel resolved to be a power on earth – a power among the nations; or else itself would be doomed to continual decay, and soon cease to be great, glorious, and free.

You are a power on earth. You must be a power on earth. So, of course, you must also unhesitatingly accept all the natural consequences of this situation. You cannot allow that any power whatever should dispose of the fate of that great family of mankind of which you are such a pre-eminent member, or else you would resign your proud position, and resign your still prouder future, and be a power on earth no more.

Thus, I hope, I have suffciently shown, that, should even that doctrine of non-interference have been established by the founders of your Republic, that which would have been very convenient to your infancy, would not be convenient to your manhood.

It is a beautiful word of Montesquieu, that republics are to be founded on virtue. And you know that virtue, as sanctioned by our Christian religion, is but the effective exercise of a principle – "Thou shalt do to others as thou desirest others to do to thee." So, I am confident, that it were suifficient for me to rely simply – for the decision of the question I have the honor to treat – upon the virtuous feelings of your generous republican hearts, and the consistency of principles. But still I beg leave to mention also in material respects, some essential differences between your present condition and that of yore.

Then your infant Republic, composed of thirteen States, was restricted to the borders of the Atlantic. Now your giant Republic spreads to the Gulf of Mexico, the Pacific, and your territory is a world. Your right hand reaches

Europe over the waves, while your left hand reaches over the Pacific, the East of Asia; and then, in the midst of two great continents, there you stand in proud immensity, a world yourself!

Then you were a small people of three and a half millions. Now you are a mighty nation of twenty-four millions. And more than nineteen millions out of these twenty-four are over yonder immense territory, the richest in the world, employed in the cultivation of the soil – that honorable occupation which in every age has proved to be the most inexhaustible, the most unfaltering source of public welfare, and of private happiness – as also the most unwavering ally of love of freedom, the most faithful preserver of all those straight, noble, and generous sentiments which the constant occupation with ever young, ever great, ever beneficial Nature imparts to man. Add to this consideration, that this immense agricultural interest, which, deriving large markets and affording at the same time a most solid basis also to your manufactural industry and to your commerce, has developed in such an immense proportion, makes such a boundless difference between the infant Republic of the time of Washington and your present giant Republic, that though you may very well be attached to your original constitutional principles, because the principles of liberty are everlastingly the same; but in respect to the exigencies of your policy, it is impossible not to feel that, if you are to be regulated in your policy by interest, then your country has other interests today than it had then; and if ever you are to be regulated in policy by the higher consideration of principles, then you are already strong enough to feel that the time has come to do so. And I, standing here before you, to plead the cause of humanity – I resolutely declare that there may perhaps never again come a time when the elevation of your policy to the high level of principles identified with liberty could prove either more glorious to you, or more beneficial to humanity; because we in Europe are apparently on the eve of that day, when either the hopes or the fears of oppressed nations will be crushed for a long time.

Having stated so far the difference of the situation, I beg leave now to state that it is entirely an unfounded supposition that the doctrine of non-interference in foreign matters had been, to the people of the United States, by your great Washington, bequeathed to be a constitutional principle to you.

No! that is not the case.

Firstly. Washington never even recomended non-interference, or indifference to the fate of other nations, to you. He has only recommended *neutrality*. And there is a mighty difference between these two ideas.

Neutrality is an idea which has reference to a state of war between two belligerent powers, and it is this case which Washington contemplated when he, in his Farewell Address, advised the People of the United States not to enter into entangling alliances. Let quarreling powers – let quarreling nations war; you consider your own concerns, and let foreign powers quarrel about ambitious topics, or scanty, particular interests. Neutrality is a matter of convenience – not of principle.

But even as neutrality has reference to a state of war between belligerent powers, the principle of non-interference has, on the contrary, reference to the sovereign right of nations to dispose of their own domestic concerns.

Therefore these two ideas of neutrality and non-interference are two entirely different ideas, having reference to two entirely different matters.

The sovereign right of whatever nation to dispose of itself to alter its institutions, to change the form of its own government, is a common public law of nations, common to all, and therefore put under the common guarantee of all.

This sovereign right of every nation to dispose of itself, you, the People of the United States, must recognize, because it is a common law of mankind in which, being a common law of mankind, every nation is equally interested. You must recognize it, secondly, because the very existence of your great republic, as also the independence of every nation, rests upon this ground. If that sovereign right of nations were no common public law of mankind, then your own independent existence would be no matter of right, but only a matter of fact, which might be subject to whatever time, to whatever chances of power and of violence.

And where is the citizen of the United States who would not feel revolted against the idea that the existence of this great republic is not a righteous, nor a lawful one, but only a mere accident, a mere matter of fact?

If it were so, you were not entitled to invoke the protection of God for your great country; because the protection of God cannot, without sacrilege, be invoked, but in behalf of justice and right. You had no right to look to the sympathy of mankind for yourself, because you would profess an abrogation of the laws of humanity, upon which is founded your own independence, your own existence.

Now, gentlemen, if these be principles of common law, of that law which God has given to all, and to every nation of humanity; if the faculty to dispose of itself is the common lawful right of every nation, then the interference with this common law of all humanity, the violent act of hindering, by armed forces, a nation from exercising that sovereign right, must be considered as a violation of that common public law upon which your very existence rests, and which, being a common law of all humanity, is by God himself placed under the safeguard of all humanity, because it is God himself who commands us to love our neighbor as we love ourselves, and to do toward others as we desire others to do toward ourselves.

Upon this point you cannot remain indifferent. You may well remain *neutral* to every war between two belligerent nations, but you cannot remain indifferent to the violation of the common law of humanity. That indifference Washington has never taught you. I defy every man to show me, out of the eleven volumes of Washington's writings, a single word to that effect. He recommended *neutrality* in the case of foreign wars; but he never recommended indifference to the violation of the common laws of humanity, by interference of foreign powers with the sovereign right of nations to dispose of themselves.

And he could not have recommended this indifference without ceasing to be wise, as he was; because there is, without justice, no wisdom on earth. He could not have recommended it without becoming inconsistent, because it was this common law of mankind which your forefathers invoked, before God and mankind, when they proclaimed your Independence. It was he himself, your great Washington, who not only accepted, but asked again and again foreign aid – foreign help for the support of the common law of mankind, in respect to your own Independence.

Knowledge and instruction are so universally spread amongst the enlightened people of the United States; the history of your country is such a household science at the most lonely hearth of your remotest settlements, that it may be sufficient for me to refer, in that respect, to the instructions and correspondence between Washington and the Minister at Paris – the equally immortal FRANKLIN – the modest man, with the proud epitaph which tells the world that he wrested the lightning from Heaven, and the sceptre from the tyrant's grasp.

This I have proved, I believe: that Washington never bequeathed to you the principle of non-interference against the violation of the sovereign right of nations to dispose of themselves, and to regulate their own institutions, but he taught you only neutrality in respect to the wars of foreign nations.

I will go further. And I state that even that doctrine of neutrality he taught and bequeathed to you, not as a constitutional principle – a lasting regulation for all future time – but only as a matter of temporary policy. I refer in that respect to the very words of his Farewell Address. There he states explicitly that *"it is your policy to steer clear of permanent alliances with any portion of the foreign world"*. These are his very words. *Policy* is the word, and you know policy is not the science of principles, but of exigencies; and that principles are of course, by a free and powerful nation never to be sacrificed to exigencies. The exigencies are passing away, like the bubbles of a rain; but the nation is immortal; it must consider the future also, and not only the egotistical comfort of the passing hour. It must be aware that to an immortal nation, nothing can be of higher importance than immortal principles.

I will go yet further; and state that even this policy of neutrality Washington taught you, not as a permanent rule, but as a temporary convenience.

I prove it again by referring to the very words of his Farewell Address, when he, in reference to his policy of neutrality, explicitly says, that *"with him (Washington) a predominant motive has been to endeavor to gain time to your country to settle and mature its institutions, and to progress, without interruption, to that degree of strength and consistency which is necessary to give it the command of its own fortunes."*

These are highly memorable words, gentlemen. Here I take my ground, and casting a glance of admiration over your glorious land, I confidently ask you, gentlemen are your institutions settled and matured, or are they not? Are you, or are you not, come to that degree of strength and consistency to be the masters of your own fortunes?

Oh, my God, how I thank thee for having given me the glorious view of this country's greatness, which answers this question for me!

Yes! you have attained that degree of strength and consistency, when your less fortunate brethren in mankind may well claim your brotherly, protecting hand.

And here I stand before you – to plead the cause of these, your less fortunate brethren – the cause of humanity. I may succeed, or I may fail. But I will go on, pleading with that faith of martyrs, by which mountains were moved; and I may displease you, perhaps still I will say with Luther, *"May God help me – I can do no otherwise!"*

One word more, to prove that Washington never attached to his doctrine of neutrality more than the sense of temporary policy. I refer to one of his letters, written to Lafayette, wherein he says: – "let us only have *twenty years* of peace, and our country will come to such a degree of power and wealth that we will be able in a *just cause* to defy whatever power on earth!"

"In a just cause!" Now in the name of eternal truth, and by all that is sacred and dear to man since the history of mankind is recorded, there has been no cause more just than the cause of Hungary! Never was there a people without the slightest reason more sacrilegiously, more treacherously, and by fouler means, attacked than Hungary. Never has crime, cursed ambition, despotism and violence, in a more wicked manner united to crush freedom and the very life, than against Hungary. Never was a country more mortally offended than Hungary is. All your sufferings, all your complaints, which with so much right drove your forefathers to take up arms – are but slight grievances in comparison with those immense, deep wounds out of which the heart of Hungary bleeds! If the cause of my people is not sufficiently just to insure the protection of God, and the support of good-willing men – then there is no just cause, and no justice on Earth – then the blood of no new Abel will move towards Heaven. The genius of charity, Christian love and justice will mourningly fly the Earth; a heavy curse will upon morality fall – oppressed men despair, and only the Cains of humanity walk proudly, with impious brow, about the ruins of Liberty on Earth!

I have shown, gentlemen, that Washington has never bequeathed to his country the doctrine of not caring about the violation of international law – has not bequeathed the doctrine of indifferentism to his countrymen, but only neutrality. I have shown that these two ideas are essentially different. I have shown that even the doctrine of neutrality he never intended to recommend to his country as a lasting constitutional principle; but only as a measure of temporary policy advisable until the United States should progress in strength and consistency, to which end he judged twenty years to be sufficient – after which he himself declared to be resolved to expose any just cause. Now allow me briefly to consider how your policy has been developed in the course of time, with respect to the principle of non-intervention in foreign concerns.

I will only recall to your memory the mesage of President Monroe, when he clearly stated that the United States would take up arms to protect the American Spanish Colonies now free Republics, should the so-called Holy (rather unholy) Alliance make an attempt either to aid Spain to reduce the new American Republics to their ancient colonial state, or to compel them to adopt political systems more comfortable to the policy and views of that Alliance. I entreat you to mark well, gentlemen, that not only the forced introduction of Monarchical Governments, but in general the interference of foreign powers in the contest for independence of the Spanish Colonies was declared sufficient motive for the United States to protect the natural right of these nations to dispose of themselves.

I beg leave to desire you to remember that this declaration of President Monroe was not only approved and confirmed by the people of the United States, but that *Great Britain itself joined the United States* in the declaration of this decision and this policy.

I further recall to your memory the instructions given in 1826 to our Envoys to the Congress of Panama, Richard Anderson and John Sergeant, where it is clearly stated that the United States would have opposed, with their whole force, the interference of Continental Powers with that struggle for independence.

It is true, that this declaration to go even to war, to protect the independence of foreign States against foreign interference, was not only restricted to the Continent of America; but President Monroe declares in his message that the United States can have no concern in European struggles, being distant and separated from Europe by the great Atlantic Ocean.

But I beg leave to remark that this indifference to European concerns is again a matter, not of *principle*, but of temporary exigency, the motives of which have, by the lapse of time, entirely disappeared – so much that the balance even turned to the opposite side.

President Monroe mentions *distance* as a motive of the above stated distinction. Well, since the prodigious development of your Fulton's glorious invention, distance is blotted out of the dictionary – or rather – replaced by the word *time.* Distance is no more calculated by miles, but by hours. And being so, Europe is of course less distant from you than the greater part of the American Continent. But, let even the word distance be taken in nominal sense – Europe is nearer to you than the greatest part of the American Continent, yea, even nearer than perhaps some parts of your own territory.

President Monroe's second motive is, that you are separated from Europe by the Atlantic. Now, at the present time, and in the present condition of navigation, the Atlantic is no separation, but rather a connecting benefit – the facilitating source of that commercial intercourse which brings the interests of Europe home to you, connecting you with it with every tie of moral as well as material interest.

It is chiefly in New York that I feel induced to speak so because New York is by innumerable ties connected with Europe, more connected than several parts of Europe itself.

It is the agricultural interest of this great country which chiefly wants, an outlet and a market. Now it is far more to Europe than the American Continent to which you have to look in that respect. This very circumstance cannot allow you to remain indifferent to the fate of freedom on the European Continent, because, be sure gentlemen – and let me have spoken this chiefly to the gentlemen of trade – should absolutism gain ground in Europe, it will, it must, make every possible obstacle to the commercial intercourse of Republican America, because commercial intercourse is the most powerful *locomotive of principles;* and be sure the victory of Absolutism on the European Continent will in no quarter have more injurious national consequences than it will in the vast extent of your agricultural and commercial interests.

Then why not prevent it – while yet there is a possibility to do so with none, or comparatively small sacrifices – rather than to abide that fatal catastrophe, and to mourn the immense sacrifices it would then cost?

Even in political considerations nowadays you have stronger motives to feel interested in the fate of Europe than even in the fate of the Central or Southern parts of America. Whatever may happen in the institutions of these parts, you are too powerful to see your own institutions affected by it. But let Europe become absolutistical – as without the restoration of Hungary to its independence, and the freedom of Italy so strongly connected with Hungary, to be sure it will – and your children will see those words which your National Government spoke in 1827 fulfilled on a larger scale than they were meant, that *"the absolutism of Europe will not be appeased until every vestige of human freedom has been obliterated even here"*. And oh! do not rely too fondly on your power. It is great to be sure. You have not to fear whatever single power on earth; but look to history. Ancient Rome has fallen, and mighty empires have vanished from earth. Let not the enemies of freedom grow too strong. Victorious over Europe, and then, united, they would be too strong even for you! And be sure that they hate you with an infernal hatred. They must hate you even more than me. They consider you as their most dangerous opponents. Absolutism cannot tranquilly sleep while the Republican principle has such a mighty representative as your country is.

Yes, gentlemen: it was the fear from the political reaction of the Absolutistic principles, which induced your great statesmen – that principle which they professed for Central and Southern America – not to extend to Europe also, and by no means the publicly avowed feeble motives. Every manifestation of your public life out of those times, shows that I am right to say so. Europe's nations were, about 1823, in such a degraded situation that indeed you must have felt anxious not to come into any political contact with that pestilential atmosphere of Europe, when, as Mr. Clay said in 1818, in his speech about the emancipation of South America, "Paris was transferred to St. Petersburg."

But scarcely has, within a year later, the Greek nation come in its contest to an important standing, which gave you hope that the spirit of freedom is waking again, and at once you abandoned your principle of political indifference for Europe. You know how your Clays and your Websters spoke, as if really they were speaking for my very case. You know how your citizens acted, in behalf of that struggle for liberty in that part of Europe which is more distant than Hungary; and again, when Poland fell, you know what spirit pervaded the United States.

So I have shown you how Washington's doctrine of perfect neutrality in your foreign relations has by-and-by changed into the declaration to oppose, with all your forces, absolutistical Europe, in interfering with the independence of republican institutions of Central and Southern America. I have shown you why this manly resolution was not extended then to Europe. I have shown you the further differences between your present convenience and that of the time of President Monroe – not less important than those between Monroe's and Washington's time. But one mighty difference I must still commemorate – that is, that your population has, since Monroe's time, nearly doubled, I believe – at least increased by millions. And what sort of men are these millions? Are they only native born Americans? No. European emigrants they are men who, though citizens of the United States, are by the most sacred ties of relationship attached to Europe's fate. That is a consideration worthy of the reflection of your calmest and wisest men, who, after calmest reflection, must agree with me, that in your present condition you are at least as much interested in the fate of Europe, as your fathers twenty-eight years ago declared themselves interested in the fate of Central and Southern America.

69

And really so it is. The unexampled, immense, prodigious sympathy for the cause of my Country which I meet with in the United States, proves that it is so. Your general interference with the Turkish captivity of the Governor of Hungary, proves that it is so. And this development, rather than change in your foreign policy, is not even more an instinctive ebullition of public opinion, which is called by-and-by to impart a direction to your National Governmental policy; the direction is already imparted, and the opinion of the people is already an avowed principle of the policy of the Government.

I have a good, I have a most decisive authority, to rely upon in saying so: it is the Message which the President of the U.S., His Excellency Millard Fillmore, communicated to the Congress a few days ago; there I read the paragraph – "The deep interest which we feel in the spread of liberal principles, and the establishment of free governments, and the sympathy with which we witness every struggle against oppression, *forbid that we should be indifferent to a case in which the strong arm of a foreign power as invoked to stifle public sentiment and repress the spirit of freedom in any country.*" Now, gentlemen, here is the ground which I take for my earnest endeavors to benefit the cause of Hungary. I have only respectfully to ask, is a principle which the public opinion of the people of the U.S. so resolutely professes and the Government of the U.S. with the full sentiment of its responsibility declares to your Congress to be a ruling principle of your national government; is that principle meant to be serious? Indeed I confess that it would be the most impertinent outrage towards your great people, and your National Government, to entertain the offending opinion, that what the people of the United States, and its National Government; in such a solemn diplomatic manner, profess to be a ruling principle of your policy, should not be meant to be but a joke about the most sacred interests of humanity. God forbid that I should feel the impertinent arrogance to think so! therefore I take the principle of your policy as I find it established, without any interference – and I come in the name of oppressed humanity, to claim the natural, logical, unavoidable, pratical consequences of your own freely chosen Government policy which you have avowed to the whole world – the right to claim the realization of those expressions which your Sovereign people of the United States have chosen out of your own accord, to raise in the bosom of my countrymen and of oppressed humanity. You will excuse me, gentlemen, for having dwelt so long about that principle of non-interference with European measures, but I have found this rock thrown in my way when I spoke of what I humbly request from the U.S. I have been charged to have the arrogance to change your existing policy; and as in one speech I of course cannot exhaust the whole mighty complex of my mission, I choose for the present opportunity, to develop my views about that fundamental principle of not caring about European concerns; and having shown not theoretically but practically, that it is a mistake to think that you had, at whatever time, such a policy, and having shown that should you ever have entertained such a policy, you had abandoned it, and were forced by circumstances to abandon it, so much, at least, I hope to have achieved. My humble requests to your operative sympathy may be still opposed by, I don't know what other motives; but that objection I will never more meet – not to interfere with European concerns – this objection is disposed of, and forever, I hope. It remains now to investigate, that having professed not to be indifferent to the cause of European freedom, is the cause of Hungary such as to have just claims to your active and operative assistance and support? It is, gentlemen – to prove this I do not now intend to enter into an explanation of the particulars of our struggle, which I had the honor to direct, as the chosen Chief Magistrate of my native land – it is highly gratifying to me to see the cause of Hungary is – excepting some ridiculous misrepresentations of ill-will – correctly understood here. I will only state one fact, and that is that our endeavorings for independence were crushed down by the armed interference of a foreign despotic power – the principle of all evil on earth – Russia. And stating this fact, I will not again intrude upon you with my own views, but recall to your memory the doctrines established by your own statesmen. Firstly. Again I return to your great Washington. He says, in one of his letters to Lafayette, "My policies are plain and simple: I think every nation has a right to establish that form of government under which it conceives it can live most happy, and that no governments ought to interfere with the internal concerns of another." Here I take my ground – I take my ground upon a principle of Washington – a *principle*, and no doctrine of temporary policy, calculated for the first twenty years of your infancy. Russia has interfered with the internal concerns of Hungary, and by doing so has violated the policies of the United States, established as a lasting principle by Washington himself. It *is* a lasting principle – I would invoke in my support the opinion of every statesman of the United States; of every party; of every time – but to save time I come from the first President of the United States at once to the last, and recall to your memory this word of the present Annual Message of His Excellency President Fillmore, "Let every people choose for itself, and make and alter its political institutions to suit its own condition and convenience." Here again I take my ground upon this principle established by Washington – making the basis of your own existence, and professed and acknowledged by your very present Government, only to show that I am aware of the policy and political opinion of your present Government also. I beg leave to quote your present Secretary of State, Mr. Webster's statement, who, in his speech on the Greek question, speaks so – "The law of nations maintains that in extreme cases resistance is lawful, and that one nation has no right to interfere in the affairs of another." Well, that precisely is the ground upon which we Hungarians stand. But I may perhaps meet the objections – I am sorry to say I have met it already – "Well, we own that it has been violated by Russia in the case of Hungary, but after all what is Hungary to us? Let every people take care of itself; what is that to us?" So some speak – it is the old doctrine of private egotism, "every one for himself and God for all." I will answer the objection, not by my own humble views, but again by the words of Mr. Webster, who, in his alluded-to speech on the Greek question, having professed the sovereign right of every nation to dispose of its own concerns, to be a law of nations – thus is going on: "But it may be asked what is all that to us?" The question is easily answered. We are one of the nations, and we as a nation have precisely the same interest in international law as a private individual has in the laws of his country.

You see, gentlemen, I had again a good authority to quote. The principle which your honorable Secretary of War professes, is a principle of eternal truth. No man can disavow it, no political party can disavow it. Thus I am in the happy condition to address my humble prayers in that respect, not to a party, but to the whole people of the United States, which I will go on to do so long as I have no reason to contemplate our party opposite or indifferent to my country's cause, because else of course I would have to address those who are either indifferent or antagonistic. But it may be from some quarters avowed, "will we acknowledge the justice of that principle of every nation's sovereign right to acknowledge it to be a law of nations that no foreign power has a right to interfere in the affairs of another, and we are determined to respect this common law of mankind, but if others do not respect that law, it is not our business to meddle with them." Let me answer by an analysis:

"Every nation has some interest in the international career, as a private individual has in the laws of his country." That is an acknowledged principle of the United States. Consequently every nation is, in respect to international law, precisely in the same condition as a private individual is in respect to the laws of his Country. Well, where is the condition of a private individual in respect to the laws of his country? Is it only that he has himself not to violate the law? or is it that so far as is in his power he should also prevent others to violate the law? Suppose you see that a wicked man is about to rob – to murder your neighbor, or to burn his house, will you wrap yourself in your own virtuous lawfulness, and say, "I don't rob – don't murder – don't burn, but what others do is not my business – I am not my brother's keeper – I sympathize with him; but I am not obliged to help him that he may not be robbed, murdered or burnt?" What honest man of the world would answer so? None of you. None of the people of the United States, I am sure. That would be the damned maxim of the Pharisees of old who thanked God that they were not as others were. Our Saviour was not content to go himself treading in the hall of the temple, but he had driven out those who were treading there. Now, what the duty of an individual is in respect to the laws of his country, the same duty has a nation in respect to international law.

The duty has no other limit, but only the power to fulfil it. Of course, it cannot be expected that the republic of St. Marino, or the Prince of Morocco should stop the Czar of Russia in this ambitious annoyances. It was ridiculous when the Prince of Modena refused to recognize the government of Louis Philippe – but "to whom much is given, will much be expected from him," says the Lord. And every condition has not only its rights, but also its own desires, and any which is in the condition to be a power on earth, has the duty to consider himself as a part of the executive power of mankind called to maintain the law of nations.

Woe, a thousandfold woe to humanity should there nobody on earth be to maintain the laws of humanity. Woe to humanity, should even those who are as mighty as they are free, not feel interested in the maintenance of the laws of mankind, because they are laws, but only in so far as some scanty money interests would desire it. Woe to humanity if every despot of the world may dare to trample down the laws of humanity, and no free nation arises to make respected these laws. People of the United States, humanity expects that your glorious republic will prove to the world, that republics are formed on virtue – it expects to see you the guardians of the laws of humanity.

Well, I will come to the last possible objection. I may be told, "You are right in your principles, your cause is just, and you have our sympathy; but after all we cannot go to war for your country; we cannot furnish your armies and fleets we cannot fight your battles for you." There is the rub. Who can exactly tell what would have been the issue of your own struggle for Independence, though your own country was in a far happier geographical position than we, poor Hungarians – should France have given such an answer to your forefathers in 1778 and 1781, instead of sending to your aid, a fleet of 38 vessels of war, and auxiliary troops, and 24,000 muskets; and a loan of nineteen millions? And when I take far more than all this, does it not show that France resolved with all its power to espouse the cause of your Independence? But, perhaps, I will be told that France did this not out of love for freedom, but out of hatred against England. Well, let it be: but let me ask, shall the cause of olden times – hatred – be more efficient in the destinies of mankind, than love of freedom, principles of justice, and the laws of humanity? Perhaps I will be told that Europe is so far from America. But let me ask, is America in the days of steam navigation more distant to Europe today than France was to America 73 years ago? However, I most solemnly declare that it is not my intention to rely literally upon this example. It is not my wish to entangle the United States in war, or to engage your great people to send out armies and fleets to restore Hungary to its sovereign Independence. Not at all, gentlemen. I most solemnly declare that I have never entertained such expectations, such hopes, and here I come to the practical point.

The principle of evil in Europe is the enervating spirit of Russian absolutism. It is upon this rests the daring boldness of every petty tyrant to trample upon oppressed nations, and to crush down liberty. To this Moloch of ambition has fallen a victim my poor native land. It is this with which Montalambert threatens the French republicans. It is Russian intervention in Hungary which governed French intervention in Rome, and gave the temerity to German tyrants to crush down all the endeavors for freedom and unity in Germany. The despots of the European continent are leagued against the freedom of the world. That is a matter of fact. The second matter of fact is that the European continent is on the eve of a new revolution. It is not necessary to be initiated in the secret preparations of the European democracy to be aware of that approaching contingency. It is pointed out by the French constitution itself prescribing a new Presidential election for the next spring. Now, suppose that the ambition of Louis Napoleon, encouraged by Russian secret aid, awaits this time, (which I scarcely believe,) and suppose that there will be a peaceful solution, such as would make contented the friends of Republic in France – of course the first act of the new French President must be, at least, to recall the French troops from Rome. Nobody can doubt that a revolution will follow, if not precede this recall in Italy. Or if there is no peaceful solution in France, but a revolution, then every man knows that whenever the heart of France boils up, the pulsation is felt throughout Europe, and oppressed nations once more rise, and Russia again interferes. Now I humbly ask, with the view of these circumstances before my eyes, can it be convenient to such a great power as this glorious Republic, to await the very outbreak, and then only to discuss and decide what direction you will be willing to take in your foreign policy? It may come again, so as under the late President, at a late hour, agents to see low matters stood in Hungary.

Russian interference and treason achieved what the sacrilegious Habsburg dynasty failed to achieve. You know the old words, "while Rome debated Saguntum fell." So I respectfully entreat the people of the United States, in time, to express its will as to what course it wishes to be pursued by its national government in the case of the approaching events I have mentioned. And I most confidently hope that there is only one course possible, consistent with the above recorded principles. If you acknowledge the right of every nation to alter institutions and governments to be a law of nations – if you acknowledge the interference of foreign powers in that sovereign right, to be a violation of the law of nations, as you really do – if you are forbidden to remain indifferent to this violation of international law, as your President openly professes that you are, then there is no other course possible than not to interfere in that sovereign right of nations, but also not to admit whatever other powers to interfere.

But you will, perhaps, object me, that is so much as to go to war. I answer, *no* – that is so much as to prevent war. What is wanted to that effect? It is wanted, that being aware of the precarious condition of Europe, your national government should so soon as possible send instructions to your Minister at London, to declare to the English government that the United States, acknowledging the sovereign right of every nation to dispose of its own domestic concerns, have resolved not to interfere, but also not to let interfere whatever foreign power with this sovereign right, in order to repress the spirit of freedom in any country. Consequently to invite the

Cabinet of St. James to unite with the United States in this policy, and to declare that the United States are resolved to act conjointly with England in that decision in the case of that approaching crisis on the European continent; which is impossible not to foresee. If the citizens of the United States, instead of honoring me with the offers of their hospitality, would be pleased to express this their will, by passing convenient resolutions, and ratifying them to their national government – if the people by all constitutional means – if the Independent press would hasten to express the public opinion in a similar sense – if in consequence of this, the national Government would instruct its Minister in England accordingly, and by a convenient communication to the Congress, give, so as it is wont to do, publicity to this his step, I am entirely sure that you would find the people of Great Britain heartily joining this direction of policy – nobody in the world could feel especially offended by it, and no existing relation would be broken or injured, and still the interference of Russia in the restoration of Hungary to its independence (formally declared in 1849) prevented – Russian arrogance and preponderance checked, and the oppressed nations of Europe soon become free. There may be some over anxious men who perhaps would say, "but if such a declaration of your Government will not be respected and Russia still does interfere, then you would be obliged by this previous declaration to go to war, and you don't desire to have a war." That objection seems to me like as if somebody would say: "If the vault of Heaven breaks down, what will we do?" My answer is, "But it will not break down" even so I answer – but your declaration will be respected – Russia will not interfere – you will have no occasion for war, you will have prevented war. Be sure Russia would twice, thrice consider, to provoke against itself, besides the roused jury of nations – besides the legions of Republican France, also the English Leopard and the star-surrounded Eagle of America. Please to consuler the fact that you, united to England, have made already such a declaration, not to admit any interference of the European Absolutistical powers into the affairs of the formerly Spanish Colonies of America; and has this declaration brought you to a war? Quite the contrary; it has prevented war – so it would be in our case also. Let me therefore most humbly entreat you, gentlemen – let me entreat you on this occasion by the means of publicity – the people of the United States, to be pleased to give such practical direction to its generous sympathy for Hungary, as to arrange meetings and pass such resolutions here and there, and in every possible place of this great Union, as I took the liberty to mention above. Why not do so? I beg leave to reiterate what I had the honor to say yesterday to a Committee of Baltimore. Suppose there should in Cuba a revolution occur, a revolution from the inhabitants of Cuba themselves, and whatever European power would send down a fleet to support Spain against this revolution, would you admit this foreign intervention in a foreign country? I am confident there is not one in the United States who would not oppose this intervention. Then what is the difference between this supposed case and the case of Hungary? Is there a difference in principle? No. Then what? The difference is that Cuba is at six days distance from New York, and the port of Hungary, Fiume, at eighteen days distance. That is all; and who would affirm that the policy of such a great free and glorious nation as the U.S. shall be regulated by hours and not by principles? Allow me to remark that there is an immense truth in that which the French Legation in the U.S. expressed to your Government, in an able note of 27th October past, which I beg leave to quote: – "America is closely connected with Europe, being only separated from the latter by a distance scarcely exceeding eight days' journey, by one of the most important of general interests – the interest of commerce. The nations of America and Europe are at this day so dependent upon one another, that the effects of any event, prosperous or otherwise, happening on one side of the Atlantic, are immediately felt on the other side. The result of this community of interests, commercial, political, and moral, between Europe and America of this frequency and rapidity of intercourse between them, is that it becomes as difficult to point out the geographical degree, where American policy shall terminate, and European policy begin; as it is to trace out the line where American commerce begins and European commerce terminates. Where may be said to begin or terminate the ideas which are in the ascendant in Europe and in America?" The second measure which I beg leave to mention has reference to commercial interests. There has in latter times a doctrine stolen into the code of international law which is even as contrary to the commercial interests of nations as to their independence. The pettiest despot of the world has the faculty to exclude your commerce from whatever port it pleases to do so. He has only to arrange a blockade, and your commerce is shut out; or if down-trodden Venice, bleeding Lombardy, or my down-oppressed but resolute Hungry, rises to shake off the Austrian tyrant's yoke, as surely they will, that tyrant believes to have the right from the very moment to exclude your commerce with the risen nations.

Now, this is an adsurdity – a tyrannical invention of tyrants, violating your interest – your own sovereign independence. The United States have not always regarded things from this point of view. I find, in a note of Mr. Everett, Minister of the United States in Spain, dated "Madrid, Jan. 20, 1826," these words – in the war between Spain and the Spanish American colonies, the U. States have freely granted to both parties the hospitality of their ports and territory, and have allowed the agents of both to procure within their jurisdiction, in the way of lawful trade, any supplies which suited their convenience. Now, gentlemen, this is the principle which humanity expects, for your own, and for mankind's benefit, to see maintained by you, and not yonder fatal course, which admits to tyrants to draw from your country whatever supply of oppression against their nations, but forbids to nations to buy the means of defence.

That was not the principle of your Washington; when he speaks of harmony, of friendly intercourse and of peace, he always takes care to speak of nations, and not of governments – still less of tyrants who subdue nations by foreign arms. The sacred word of nation, with all its natural rights, should, at least of your political dictionary, not be blotted out; and yet I am sorry to see that the word nation is replaced by the word government. Gentlemen, I humbly wish that public opinion of the United States, conscious of its own rights, should highly and resolutely declare that the people of the United States will carry on trade and continue its commercial intercourse with whatever nation, be that nation in revolution against its oppressors or not; and that the people of the United States express confidence from its government, to provide for the protection of your trade.

I am confident that your national government, seeing public opinion so pronounced, will judge it convenient to augment your naval forces in the Mediterranean; and to look for some such station for it as would not force the navy of republican America to such abrogations towards tyrants, which cannot be consistent with republican principles or republican dignity, only because the king so-so, be he even the cursed King of Naples, grants you the favor of an anchoring place for the naval forces of your republic. I believe your glorious country should everywhere freely unfurl the star-spangled banner of liberty with all its congenial principles, and not make itself dependent on whatever respect of the glorious smiles of the Kings Bombaste Compagne. The third object of my humble wishes, gentlemen, is the recognition of the independence of Hungary.

Your glorious Declaration of Independence proclaims the right of every nation to assume among the powers of the earth the separate and equal stations to which the laws of nature and nature's God entitle them. The political assistance of your glorious Republic is founded upon this principle, upon this right. "My nation stands upon the same ground, and there is a striking resemblance between your cause and that of my country. On the 4th of July, 1776, John Adams spoke such in your Congress; "Sink or swim, live or die, survive or perish, I am for this declaration." It is in the beginning we arrived not at independence, but "there is a divinity which shapes our ends." These noble words were present to my mind on the 14th of April 1849, when I moved the Declaration of Independence in the National Assembly of Hungary.

Our condition was the same, and if there be any difference, I dare say it is in favor of ourselves. Your country was before this declaration not a self consisting, independent State. Hungary was. Through the lapse of a thousand years, through every vicissitude of this long period, while nations vanished and empires fell, the self-consisting independence of Hungary was never overthrown, but recognized by all powers of the earth, sanctioned by solemn treaties with the Hapsburg dynasty, when this dynasty by the free will of my nation, and by a bilateral part was invested with the kingly crown of Hungary. Even more, this independence of king was acknowledge to make a part of the international law of Europe, and was guaranteed not only by the foreign European governments, such as Great Britain, but also by several of those when yet constitutional nations, which belonged formerly to the German, and after its dissolution, to the Austrian empire.

This independent condition of Hungary is clearly defined in one of our fundamental laws of 1791, in these words: "Hungary is a free and independent kingdom, having its own self consistent existence and constitution, and not subject to any other nation or country in the world." This therefore was our ancient right. We were not dependent upon, nor a part of the Austrian Empire as your country was dependent upon England. It was clearly defined that we were to Austria nothing but good neighbors and the only tie between us and Austria was, that we elected to be our kings the same dynasty which were also the sovereigns of Austria and enjoyed the same line of hereditary succession of our Kings; but by accepting this, our forefathers, with the consent of the King, again declared that though she accepts the dynasty to be our hereditary Kings, all the other franchises, rights and laws of the nation shall remain in full power and intact;

and our country shall not be governed like the other dominions of that dynasty, but according to our constitutionally established authorities. We would not belong to the Austrian empire, because that empire did not exist, while Hungary did already nearly a thousand years exist, and existed some 280 years under the government of that Hapsburgian dynasty. The Austrian empire, as you know, was only established in 1806 when the Rhenish confederation of Napoleon struck the death blow to the German empire, of which Francis II. of Austria, was not hereditary, but elected Emperor.

That Hungary had belonged to the German empire, that is a thing which no man in the world ever imagined yet. It is only now when the Hapsburgian tyrant professes the intention to melt Hungary into the German Confederation; but you know this intention to be in so striking opposition to the European public law, that England and France solemnly protested against this intention, which is not carried out even today. The German empire having died, its late Emperor Francis, also, King of Hungary, established the Austrian empire in 1806; but even in that fundamental charter of the new established Austrian empire, he solemnly declared that Hungary and its annexed provinces are not intended, and will not make a part of the Austrian empire. Subsequently he entered with this empire into the German Confederation of 1805, but Hungary, as well as Lombardy and Venice, not making part of the Austrian empire, remained again separated, and were not entered into the confederacy. The laws which I succeeded to carry in 1848 did of course nothing alter in that old chartered condition of Hungary. We transformed the peasantry into freeholders, free proprietors, abolished feudal incumbrances. We replaced the political privileges of aristocracy by the common liberty of the whole people; gave political representation to the people for the legislature; transformed our municipal corporations into democratic corporations; introduced equality in rights and duties, and before the law, for the whole people, abolished the immunity of taxation of the nobility, secured equal and religious liberty to all, secured liberty of the press and of association, provided for public gratuitous instruction for the whole people of every confession and of whatever tongue; but not injuring, in any way, the rights of the King. We replaced our own aristocratical constitution by a democratic constitution founded upon nearly universal suffrage of the whole people – of whatever religion, of whatever tongue. All these were, as you see, internal reforms which did in no way interfere with our allegiance to the King, and were carried lawfully in peaceful legislation, with the sanction of the King. Besides this there was one other thing which was carried. We were formerly governed by a Board of Council, which had the express duty to govern according to sure laws, and be responsible for doing so; but we saw by long experience that this responsibility is an empty sound, because a corporation cannot really be responsible; and here was the reason why the absolutistical tendency of the dynasty succeeded to encroach upon our liberty. So we replaced the Board of Council by Ministers: the empty responsibility of a board by the individual responsibility of men – and the King consented to it. I myself was named by him Minister of the Treasury. That is all. But precisely here was the rub. The tyrant could not bear the idea that I would not give to his ambitionary disposal the life-sweat of my people; he was not contented with the one million five hundred thousand dollars which we generously appropriated to him yearly. He would have his hands in our pockets, and he could not bear the idea that he should never more be at liberty to dispose, without any control, of our brave army, and to crush down the spirit of freedom in the world. Therefore he resorted to the most outrageous conspiracy, and attacked us by arms, and by a false report of a victory which never was won, issued a proclamation declaring that Hungary shall not more exist – that its independence, its constitution, its very existence is abolished, and it shall be melted, like a farm or fold, into the Austrian Empire. To this we answered, "Thou shalt not exist, tyrant, but we will;" and we banished him, and issued the declaration of our independence. So you see gentlemen, that there is a very great difference between yours and ours – it is in our favor. There is another similar difference; you declared your independence when it was yet very doubtful if you would be successful. We declared ours, when we, in legitimate defence, were already victorious; when we had beaten our enemies, and so proved, before our declaration, that we had strength and power enough to become one of the independent powers on earth. One thing more, our declaration of independence was not only voted unanimously in our Congress, but every county, every municipality, has solemnly declared its consent and adherence to it; so it became not the supposed, but by the whole nation positively, and explicitly sanctioned by the fundamental laws of Hungary. And so it is even now. There happened since nothing contrary to this declaration on the part of the nation. No contrary law nor declaration issued. On thing only happened – a foreign power, Russia, came with his armed bondsmen, and, aided by treason, overthrew us for a while.

Now I put the question before God and humanity to you, free sovereign, people of America, can this violation of international law abolish the legitimate character of our declaration of independence? If not, then here I take my ground, because I am in this very declaration of independence entrusted with the charge of Governor of my fatherland. I have sworn before God and my nation to endeavor to maintain and secure this act of independence. And so, may God the Almighty help me as I will – I will; until my nation is again in the condition to dispose of its government, which I confidently trust, yea more, I know; will be a republican. And then I retire to the humble condition of my former private life, equalling, in one thing at least, your Washington, not in merits, but in honesty – that is the only ambition of my life – Amen. So my third humble wish is, that the people of the U.S. would be pleased, by all constitutional means of its wonted public life, to declare that, acknowledging the legitimate character of the declaration of independence of Hungary, it is anxious to greet Hungary amongst the independent powers of the earth; and invite, the government of the United States to recognize this independence at the earliest convenient time. That is all. Let me see the principle announced; the rest may well be left to the wisdom of your government, with some confidence in my own respectful discretion also. And so, gentlemen, I have respectfully stated what are my humble requests to the sovereign people of this country, in its public and political capacitiy. It is that the people of the United States may be pleased, by all constitutional means, to declare – First, that feeling interested in the maintenance of the laws of nations, acknowledging the sovereign right of every people to dispose of its own domestic concerns to be one of these laws, and the interference with this sovereign right to be a violation of these laws of nations, the people of the United States – resolved to respect and to make respected these public laws – declare the Russian past intervention in Hungary to be a violation of these laws, which, if reiterated, would be a new violation, and would not be regarded indifferently by the people of the United States – that you, therefore, invite your government to act accordingly, and so invite Great Britain to unite with the United States in this policy. Second, that the people of the United States is resolved to maintain its right of commercial intercourse with the nations of Europe, whether they be in a state of revolution or not – and that, with the view of approaching scenes on the continent of Europe, the people invite the government to take appropiate measures for the protection of the trade of the people on the

Mediterranean; and 3rd, that the people of the United States pronounces its opinion in respect to the question of independence of Hungary, so as I had the honor to state. I hope nobody can reproach me to have done by this anything inconsistent with the high regards which I owe to the United States, or not appropiate to my capacity. I would regard it as a very judicious and beneficial thing, if those generous men who sympathize with the cause of Hungary would form committees through the different part of the United States, with the purpose to occassion appropiate meetings, to pass such resolutions as I had the honor humbly to suggest. So much for the generous people of the United States, in its public and political capacity. And if that sympathy which I have the honor to meet with in the United States is really intended to become beneficial to the cause of my poor native land, then there is one humble wish more which I anxiously entertain; but that is a private business, it is a respectful appeal to the generous feelings of individuals. Gentlemen, I would rather starve than rely for myself and family, on foreign aid; but for my country's freedom, I would not be abashed to go a begging from door to door. (Great cheering.) Gentlemen, I mean financial aid; money to assist the cause of freedom, and independence of Hungary. I took the advice of some kind friends, if it be lawful to express such an humble request, because I feel the honorable duty neither to offend nor to evade your laws. I am told it is lawful. There are two means to see this, my humble wish, accomplished. The first is from spontaneous subscriptions, to put the offerings of kind friends at my disposal, for the benefit of my country's cause. The second is a loan. As to this loan, that is a business of a more private nature, which, to be carried on in an appropriate way, requires private consultation in a more close circle. So here I only mention that if there are such generous men, who are willing to enter into the idea, provided it will be arranged in an acceptable way, I would most humbly entreat them to enter into a private communication about the subject with me; and secondly, I express my conviction that even this matter of loan could be efficiently promoted by the other measure of free, gratuitous subscriptions, which would afford me the means necessary for the practical initiation of the loan business itself. Now, as to these subscriptions, the idea was brought home to my mind by a plain but very generous letter, which I had the honor to receive, and which I beg leave to read. It is as follows:

Cincinnati, O., Nov. 14. 1851.

M. Louis Kossuth, Governor of Hungary: – Sir – I have authorized the office of the Ohio Life Insurance and Trust Company, in New York, to honor your draft on me for one thousand dollars.

Respectfully yours,

W. SMEAD.

I beg leave here publicly to return my most humble thanks to the gentleman, for his ample aid, and the delicate manner in which he offered it; and it came to my mind, that where one single individual is ready to make such sacrifices to my country's cause, there may perhaps be many who would give their small share to it, if they were only apprised that it will be thankfully accepted, however small it may be. And it came to my mind then, that drops of millions make an ocean, and the United States number many millions of inhabitants, all attached with warm feelings to the principles of liberty. A million of dollars agglomerated by single dollars is equally as good as if it were one single draft, but to me yet more precious, because it would practically show the sympathy of the people at large. I will consider it highly beneficial, should I be so happy to see that generous men would form committees throughout the United States, to raise out of the free offerings of the people, some material aid to assist the second cause of freedom and independence of Hungary. It is a delicate matter, gentlemen, for me to speak so. It is, perhaps, one of the greatest sacrifices to my country that I do so, (Great applause.) But I love my country. (Renewed cheering.) And I will undergo even this torturing humiliation for her sake. Would I were so happy as your Washington was, when for your glorious country's sake in the hours of your need, he also called for money in France. Sir, I have done. Conscious of no personal merit, I came to your shores as a poor persecuted exile, but you poured upon me the triumph of a welcome, such as the world has never yet seen; and why? Because you took me for the representative of that principle of liberty which God has designed to become the common principle of all humanity; and it is a glorious sight to see a mighty, free, powerful people, come forth to greet with such a welcome the principle of freedom, even in a poor, persecuted, penniless exile. Be blessed for it? Your generous deed will be recorded to all posterity; and, as even now millions of Europe's oppressed nations will raise their thanksgiving to God for the ray of hope which you by this, your act, have thrown on the dark night of their fate; even so, through all posterity, oppressed men look to your memory as to a token of God that there is a hope for freedom on earth, because there is a people like you to feel its worth and to support its cause.

Governor Kossuth resumed his seat amid the most enthusiastic manifestations of applause, which were kept up for several minutes. His speech occupied two hours and a half in delivery.

Banquet given by the Press of New York to Governor Kossuth

This imposing affair occurred Dec. 15, 1851, at the Astor House. After several toasts had been offered and speeches made by distinguished members of the press, Kossuth arose, and spoke as follows:

Kossuth's Speech before the New York Press

GENTLEMEN: – Rising, respectfully to return my most warm thanks for the honor of the toast, and the high benefit of the sympathy manifested by this solemn demonstration it is with a mingled feeling of joy and fear, that I address you, gentlemen!

I address you with joy, because, conscious of the immensity of the power which you wield, it is natural to feel some awe in addressing those in whose hands the success or the failure of our hopes is placed; still I equally know that in your hands, gentleman, the independent Republican Press is a weapon, but a weapon to defend truth and justice, and not to offend it is no screen to hide, no snuffers to extinguish the light, but a torch lit at the fire of immortality, a spark of which is glistening in every man's soul, to prove its divine origin; a torch which you wield loftily and high to spread light with it to the most lonely regions of humanity.

And as the cause of my country is the cause of justice and truth; as it has in no respect to fear light, but rather wants nothing but light to see secured to it the support and protection of every friend of freedom, of every noble-minded man, these are the reasons why I address you with joy, gentlemen.

The more with joy, because, though it is sorrowful to see that ill-willed misrepresentations or secret Austrian intrigues, distorting plain open history to a tissue of falsehood and lies, know how to find their way even to a small insignificant part of the American press, still I am proud and happy to see that the immense majority of the American press not only proved inaccessible to these venomous intrigues, but conscious of the noble vocation of an independent press, and yielding to the generous inclination of Freemen, of protecting truth and justice against the dark plots of tyranny, has, without any interference from my part, come forth to protect the sacred cause of Hungary.

The Independent Press of this great Republic has in this very case also proved to the world that even against the mischievous power of calumnies the most efficient protection is the Freedom of the Press, and not preventive measures, condemning human intellect to eternal minority.

I address you, gentlemen, the more with joy, because through you I have the valuable benefit to address the whole university of the great, glorious and free people of the United States.

That is a great word; gentlemen, and yet is literally true.

While eighty years ago immortal Franklin's own press was almost the only one in the Colonies, now there are over three thousand newspapers in the United States, having a circulation of five millions of copies, and amounting in their yearly circulation to the prodigious number of nearly four and a half hundred millions; every grown man in the Union reads on the average two newspapers a week, and one hundred and five copies a year; nearly eighteen copies fall, in the proportion to the population, to every human being in the Union, man, woman, and child.

I am told that the journals of New York State alone; exceed in number those of all the rest of the world beyond your great Union, and the circulation of the newspapers of this city alone nearly exceeds those of the whole Empire of Great Britain.

But there is yet one particularly remarkable fact which I cannot forbear to mention, gentlemen.

I boldly declare, that beyond the United States there exists scarcely a practical Freedom of the Press; at least in Europe, not except perhaps, Norway, of whose condition in that respect I am not quite aware. You know, gentlemen, how the press is fettered throughout the European Continent, even for the present in France itself whose great nation, by a strange fate, sees under a nominally Republican, but centralized Government, all the glorious fruits of their great and victorious Revolutions wasting between the blasting finances, centralized administrative and legislative omnipotence. You know how the Independent Press of France is murdered by imprisonment of their editors and by fines; you know how the present government of France feels, unable to bear the force of public opinion – so much, that in the French Republic the very legitimate shout of "Vive la Republique" has almost become a crime.

This very circumstance is sufficient to prove that in that glorious land where the warm and noble heart of the French nation throbs with self-confidence and noble pride, a new Revolution is an unavoidable necessity. It is a mournful view which the great French nation now presents, but it is also an efficient warning against the propensities of centralization, inconsistent with freedom, become inconsistent with self-government, and it is also a source of hope for the European continent, because we know that things in France cannot endure thus as they are; we know that to become a true Republic is a necessity for France, and thus we know also, that whoever be the man who, in the approaching crisis, will be honored by the confidence of the French nation; he will, he must be, faithful to that great principle of Fraternity towards the other nations, which, being announced by the French Constitution to the world, raised such encouraging, but bitterly disappointed espectations through Europe's oppressed continent.

But it is chiefly, almost only Great Britain in Europe which boasts to have a Free Press, and to be sure during my brief stay in England, I joyfully saw that really there is a freedom to print, almost an unlimited one, so far that I saw printed advertisements, spread at every corner, and signed by the publishers, stating that that Queen Victoria is no lawful Queen – that she ought to be sent to the Tower, and all those who rule ought to be hanged. Men laughed, and nobody cared about the foolish extravagancy.

And yet I dare say and I hope the generous people of Great Britain will not feel offended at my stating the fact, that there is no practical freedom of the press.

The freedom of the Press, to be a practical one, must be a common benefit to all – else it is no freedom, but a privilege. It is wanting two ingredients – freedom of printing and freedom of reading. Now there is no freedom of reading there, because there is no possibility for the people at large to do so. Because the circulation of newspapers, the indispensable moral food of human intellect, is by a heavy taxation, checked. The Press is a source of public revenue, and by the encumbrance of stamp and paper duties made almost inaccessible to the poor. Hence it is that the newspapers in the United States are only one-tenth, and in some cases one-twentieth the price of English or French papers, and hence, again, is the immense difference in their circulation. In the United States several of the daily papers every morning reach from thirty to forty thousand readers, whereas the *London Times* is considered to be a monster power, because it has a circulation of from twenty-five to thirty thousand copies, of which, I was told during my stay in England, that the good generous sense of the people has abated some six thousand copies in consequence of its foul hostility to the just and sacred cause of Hungary.

Such being the condition of your Press, gentlemen, it must, of course, be a high source of joyful gratification to me, to have the honor to address you, gentlemen; because in addressing you I really address the whole people of the United States – not only a whole people, but a whole intelligent people, gentlemen.

That is the highest praise which can upon a people be bestowed, and yet is no praise – it is the acknowledgment of a real fact. The very immensity of the circulation of your journals proves it to be so – because this immense circulation is not only due to that constitutional right of yours to speak and print freely your opinions; it is not only due to the cheap price which makes your press a common benefit to all, and not a privilege to the rich but it is chiefly due to the universality of public instruction which enables every citizen to read. It is a glorious thing to know that in this flourishing young city alone, where streets of splendid buildings proudly stand, where a few years ago the river spread its waves, or the plough tilled, nearly one hundred thousand children receive public education annually.

Do you know, gentlemen, where I consider the most glorious monuments of your country? If it be so as I have read it once – it is that fact, that when in the steps of your wandering squatters, your engineers go on to draw geometrical lines, even in the territories where the sound of a human step never yet has mixed with the murmurs by which virginal nature is adoring the Lord; in every place marked to become a township, on every sixteenth square you place a modest wooden pole, with the glorious mark – "POPULAR EDUCATION STOCK." This is your proudest monument.

However, be this really the case or not, in every case, in my opinion, it is not your geographical situation; not your material power, not the bold enterprising spirit of your people which I consider to be the chief guarantee of your country's future, but the universality of education; because an intelligent people never can consent not to be free. You will be always willing to be free, and you are great and powerful enough to be so good as your will.

My humble prayers to benefit my country's cause; I must so address to the public opinion of the whole intelligent people of the United States. You are the mighty engineers of this sovereign power upon which rests my country's hope – it must be, therefore, highly gratifying to me, to see not isolated men but the powerful complete of the great word "PRESS" granting me this important manifestation of generous sentiments and of sympathy. Still I address you with fear, gentlemen, because you are aware that since my arrival here, I had the great honor and valuable benefit to see my whole time agreeably occupied by the reception of the most noble manifestations of public sympathy, so much so that it became entirely impossible for me to be thus prepared to address you gentlemen, in language which I but very imperfectly speak – as the great importance of this occasion would have required, and my high regards for yourselves, had pointed out as a duty to me.

However, I hope you will take this very circumstance for a motive of excuse. You will generously consider that whenever and wherever I publicly speak, it is always chiefly spoken to the Press, and, lowering your expectations to the humility of my abilities, and to the level of the principal difficulties of my situation, you will feel inclined to some kind indulgence for me, were it only out of brotherly generosity for one of your professional colleagues, as I profess to be one.

Yes, gentlemen, it is a proud recollection of my life that I commenced my public career in the humble capacity of a journalist. And in that respect I may perhaps be somewhat entitled to your brotherly indulgence, as you; in the happy conditions which the institutions of your country insure to you cannot have even an idea of the tortures of a journalist who has to write with fettered hands and who is more than fattered by an Austrian arbitrary preventive Censorship. You have no idea what a torture it is to sit down to your writing desk, the breast full of the necessity of the moment, the heart full of righteous feelings, the mind full of Convictions and of principles – and all this warmed by the lively fire of a patriot's heart – and to see before your eyes the scissors of the Censor ready to fall upon your head, like the sword of Damocles, lopping your ideas, maiming your arguments, murdering your thoughts; and his pencil before your eyes, ready to blot out, with a single draught, the work of your laborious days, and of your sleepless nights; and to know that the people will judge you, not by what you have felt, thought and written, but by what the Censor wills; to know that the ground upon which you stand is not a ground known to you, because limited by rules, but an unknown slippery ground, the limits of which lie but within the arbitrary pleasure of your Censor – doomed by profession to be stupid, and a coward, and a fool; to know all this, and yet not to curse your destiny – not to deny that you know how to read and to write, but to go on, day by day, in the torturing work of Sysiphus. Oh! it is the greatest sacrifice which an intelligent man can make to his fatherland and humanity!

And this is the present condition of the Press, not in Hungary only, but in all countries cursed by Austrian rule. Our past revolution gave freedom to the Press, not only to my fatherland, but by indirect influence also to Vienna, Prague, Lemberg; in a word to the whole empire of Austria. This very circumstance must be sufficient to insure your sympathy to my country's cause; as, on the contrary, the very circumstance that the victory of the Hapsburgian dynasty, achieved by treason and Russian arms, was a watchword to oppress the Press in Hungary, in Austria, in Italy, in Germany – nay throughout the European continent. The contemplation that the freedom of the Press on the European continent is inconsistent with the preponderance of Russia, and the very existence of the Austrian dynasty, the sworn enemy of freedom and of every liberal thought – this very circumstance must be sufficient to insure your generous support, to sweep away these tyrants and to raise liberty where now foul oppression proudly rules.

Gentlemen, a considerable time ago there appeared in certain New York papers a systematic compound of the most foul calumnies, falsehood and misrepresentations about the Hungarian cause, going so far as, with the most unexampled effrontery, to state that we struggled for oppression, while it was the cursed Austrian dynasty that stood forth for liberty. Now *there* is a degree of effrontery, the temerity of which becomes astonishing even to me, who, having seen the unexampled treachery of the House of Austria, became familiar with the old Roman maxim, *"nil admirari"*, through my tempest-tossed life. We may be misrepresented, scorned, jeered, charged with faults; our martyrs, the blood of whom cries for vengeance, may be laughed at as fools; and even heroes, commanding the veneration of history, may be represented as Don Quixottes of tragi-comedy, – all this I could, if not bear, at least conceive. I have seen strange specimens of the aberrations of the human mind; but that, in the midst of the most mournful sufferings, not even the honor of an unfortunate nation should be sacred to some men, who enjoy the benefit of free institutions and profess to be Republicans – that is too much! It is a sorrowful page in mankind's history.

You cannot of course, expect to see me, on this occasion, entering into a special refutation of this astonishing compound of calumnies. I will reserve it for my pen, as soon as I can have a free day for it. It will be very easy work, because all artificial compounds of misrepresentations must fall into dust before the dispassionate plain statement of facts, the greatest part of which I thankfully have to acknowledge are already not unknown to you. But one curious incident I may perhaps be permitted to state, which must be entirely new to you.

I was at Kutahia, a prisoner, when, several weeks before the alluded to article appeared printed here, I got, by the kindness of some brave friends from Vienna via Constantinople (mark well, gentlemen – from Vienna,) a manuscript with the intimation that it was a copy of the article which would soon appear in an American newspaper, the copy taken for my use by an honest man in the very bureaus of the Austrian Ministry. I have shown the manuscript to my associates, several of whom being here can remember and testify to the curious fact; and indeed some weeks later the very article appeared in an American newspaper, and it is that very compound of misrepresentations and calumny, to which I was alluding. Now it is not mine to investigate this strange affinity between an "independent" American journal and the secret Cabinet of Austria; it may be quite an innocent accident. I only mention it as a contribution to the Cabinet of curiosities of the world. Let it be; it is not worth while to dwell upon it.

Permit me rather to make some humble remarks upon the question of "nationalities" which play such an important, and, I dare say, such a mischievous part in the destinies of Europe. I say mischievous, because no word ever was so much misrepresented or mistaken as the word "nationality;" so that it would be indeed a great benefit to humanity, could I succeed to contribute something to the rectification of this idea, the misrepresentation of which became the most mischievous instrument in the hands of absolutism against the spirit of liberty.

Let me ask you, gentlemen, are you the people of the United States, a nation or not? Have you a National Government or not?

Have you? You answer yes; and yet you the people of the United States are not all of one blood and speak not one language. Millions of you speak

English, others French, others German, others Italian, others Spanish, others Danish, and even several Indian dialects – and yet you are a nation!

And your Government, even the Governments of your single States, nay, the Municipal Governments of your different cities, are not legislating, and governing and administering in all and every language spoken in your Union; in the respective States and in the respective cities themselves – and yet you have a National Government!

Now, suppose that one part of the people of the United States, struck by a curse like that with which the builders of Babel were once struck, should at once rise and say – "the Union in which we live is an oppression to us. Our laws, our institutions, our State and City Governments; our very freedom, is an oppression to us! What is union to us? what rights? what laws? what freedom? what history? what geography? what community of interests? They are all nothing. Language – that is all. Let us divide the Union; divide the States; divide the very cities. Let us divide the whole territory by, and according to languages, and then let the people of every language live distinct, and form each a separate State. Because every nation has a right to a national life, and to us the language is the nation – nothing else; and your Union, your rights, your laws and your freedom itself, though common to us, is an oppression to us, because language is the only basis upon which States must be founded. Everything else is tyranny."

What would you say of such reasoning? What would become of your great Union? What of your Constitution – this glorious legacy of your greatest man, those immortal stars on mankind's moral canopy? What would become of your country itself, whence the spirit of freedom spreads its mighty wings and rising hope clears up the future of humanity? What would become of this grand, mighty complex of your Republic, should it ever be attacked in its consistency, by the furious hands of the fanaticism of language? Where now she wanders and walks among the rising temples of human happiness; she soon would tread upon the ruins of liberty, mourning over the fragility of human hopes.

Happy art thou, free nation of America, that thou hast founded the house upon the only solid basis of a nation's liberty! Liberty! A principle steady like the world, eternal like the truth, and universal like every climate, for every time, like Providence! Thou hast no tyrants among thee to throw the apple of Eros into thy Union. Thou hast no tyrants among thee to raise the fury of hatred in thy national family – hatred of nations, that curse of humanity, that venomous instrument of Despotism.

What a glorious sight it is to see the oppressed of so many countries, different in language, history and habits, wandering to thy shores, and becoming members of thy great nation, regenerated by the principle of common liberty!

Would I could do the same! but I can't because I love my native land, inexpressibly, boundless, fervently. I love it more than life, more than happiness; I love it more in its gloomy sufferings than I would in its proudest, happiest days.

What makes a nation? Is it the language only? Then there is no great, no powerful nation on earth, because there is no moderately large country in the world, whose population is counted by millions, where you would not find several languages spoken.

No! It is not language only which makes a nation. Community of interests, community of history; community of rights and duties, but chiefly community of institutions of a population, which, though perhaps differing in tongue, and belonging to different races, is bound together by its daily intercourse in their towns, the centres of their homely commerce and homely industry, the very mountain ranges, and system of rivers and streams, the soil, the dust of which is mingled with the ashes of those ancestors who bled on the same field, for the same interest – the common inheritance of glory and of woe, the community of laws, tie of institutions, tie of common freedom or common oppression – all this enters into the definition of a nation.

That this is true – that this is instinctively felt by the common sense of the people, nowhere is more apparently shown than at this very moment in my native land. Hungary was declared by Francis Joseph of Austria no more to exist as a Nation, no more as a State. It was and is put under martial law; strangers rule, in a foreign tongue, where our fathers lived and our brothers bled. To be a Hungarian became almost a crime in our own native land. Now, to justify before the world the extinction of Hungary, the partition of its territory, and again the centralization of the dissected limbs into the common body of servitude, the treacherous dynasty was anxious to show that the Hungarians are in a minority in their own native land.

They hoped that intimidation and terrorism would induce even the very Hungarians – Magyars, as we are in our own language termed – to abnegate their language and birth; they ordered a census of nationalities to be made; they performed it with the iron rule of martial law; they employed terrorism in the highest degree, so much that thousands of women and men, who protessed to be Magyars, preferred not to know, nay, not to perhaps have heard any other language than the Magyar, notwithstanding all their protestations, were put down to be Slavs, Serbs, Germans, or Wallachians, because their names had not quite a Hungarian sound. And still what was the issue of this malignant plot? Out of the twelve millions of inhabitants of Hungary proper, the Magyars turned out to be more than eight millions, some two millions less than we know the case really is.

The people instinctively felt that the tyrant had the design to destroy with the pretext of language the very existence of the nation formed by the compound of all those ingredients which I have mentioned above, and with that common good sense which every nation possesses, met the tyrannic plot as if it answered, "We want to be a nation, and if the tyrant takes language only for the mark of our nationality, then we are all Hungarians." And mark well, gentlemen! this happened not under my governorship, but even under the rule of Austrian martial law. The Cabinet of Vienna became furious; it thought of a new census, but prudent men told them that the new census would give the whole twelve millions as Magyars, and thus no new census was taken. (So true is my assertion that it is not language alone which makes a nation – an assertion which of course your own great republic proves to the world.)

But on the European continent there unhappily grew up a school which bound the idea of language only to the idea of language, and joined political pretensions to it. There are some who advocate the theory that existing countries must cease, and the territories of the world be anew divided by languages and nations, separated by tongues.

You are aware that this idea, if it were not impracticable, would be but a curse to humanity – a death blow to civilization and progress, and throw back mankind by centuries – it were an eternal source of strife and war, because there is a holy almost religious tie by which man's heart to his home is bound, and no man ever would consent to abandon his native land only because his neighbors speak another language than he himself; and, by this reason, claims for him that sacred spot where the ashes of his fathers – where his own cradle stood – where he dreamed the happy dreams of youth, and where nature itself bears a mark of his manhood's laborious toil. The idea were worse than the old migration of nations was – despotism only would rise out of the strife of mankind's fanaticism.

And really it is very curious. Nobody of the advocates of this mischievous theory is willing to yield to it for himself – but others he desires to yield to it. Every Frenchman becomes furious when his Alsace is claimed to Germany by the right of language, or the borders of his Pyrenees to Spain – but there are some amongst the very men who feel revolted at this idea, who claim for Germany that it should yield up large territory because one part of the inhabitants speak a different tongue and would claim from Hungary to divide its territory (which God himself has limited by its range of mountains and the system of streams, as also by all the links of a community of more than a thousand years), to cut off our right hand, Transylvania, and to give it up to the neighboring Wallachia – to cut out like Shylock one pound of our very breast – the Banat – and the rich country between the Danube and Theiss – to augment by it Turkish Servia, and so forth. It is the new ambition of conquest, but an easy conquest, not by arms but by language.

So much I know, at least, that this absurd idea cannot, and will not be advocated by any man here in the United States, which did open its hospitable shores to humanity, and greet the flocking millions of emigrants with the right of a citizen, in order that the Union may be cut to pieces, and even your single States divided into new-formed independent countries by and according to language.

And do you know, gentlemen, whence this absurd theory sprung up on the European Continent? It was the idea of Panslavismus – that is the idea that the mighty stock of Sclavonic races is called to rule the world, as once the Roman did. It was a Russian plot – it was the infernal idea to make out of national feelings a tool to Russian preponderance over the world.

Perhaps you are not aware of the historical origin of this plot. It was after the third division of Poland, this most immoral act of tyranny, that the chance of fate brought the Prince Czartorisky to the Court of Catharine of Russia. He subsequently became minister of Alexander the Czar. It was in this quality that, with the noble aim to benefit his down-trodden fatherland, he claimed from the young Czar the restoration of Poland, suggesting for equivalent the idea of Russian preponderance over all nations of the old Sclavonic race. I believe his intention was sincere. I believe he thought not to misconsider those natural borders, which, besides the affinity of language, God himself has between the nations drawn. But he forgot that the spirits which he raises, he will not be able to master more, and that uncalled fanaticism will sundry fantastical shapes force into his frame, by which the frame itself must burst in pieces soon. He forgot that Russian preponderance cannot be propitious to liberty; he forgot that it can even not be favorable to the development of the Sclav nationality, because Sclavonic nations would, by this idea, be degraded into individuals of Russianism – all absorbed by Russia, that is, absorbed by depotism.

Russia got hold of the sensible idea very readily. May be that the young Alexander had in the first moment noble inclinations; he was young, and the warm heart of youth is susceptible to noble instincts. It is not common in history; such Francis Josephs of Austria – so young and yet such a Nero as he is! But a few years of power were sufficient to extinguish every spark of noble sentiment – if there is one in Alexander's young heart – upon the throne of the Romanows is the man soon absorbed by the Autocrat. The air of the traditional policies of St. Petersburgh is not that air where the plant of regeneration can grow, and the sensible idea became soon a weapon of honor, oppression and Russian preponderance – Russia availed herself of the idea of Panslavism to break Turkey down, and to make an obedient satelite out of Austria. Turkey withstands yet, but Austria has fallen in the snare.

Russia sent out its agents, its moneys, its venomous secret diplomacy through the world; it spoke to the Sclav nations of the hatred against foreign dominion – of independence of religion connected with nationality under its own supremacy; but chiefly it spoke to them of Panslavism under the protectorate of the Czar. The millions of its own large empire also, all oppressed – all in servitude – all a tool to his ambition; he flattered them with the idea to become the rulers of the world, in order that they might not think of liberty; he knew that man's breast cannot harbor two passions at once. He gave them ambition and excluded the spirit of liberty. This ambition got hold of all the Sclav nations through Europe; so became Panslavism the source of a movement, not a nationality, but of the dominion of languages. That word "language" replaced every other sentiment, and so it became the curse to the development of liberty.

Only one part of the Sclavonic races saw the matter clear, and withstood the current of this infernal Russian plot. They were the Polish Democrats – the only ones who understand that to fight for liberty is to fight for nationality. Therefore they fought in our ranks, and were willing to flock thousands of thousands to aid us in our struggle; but I could not arm them, so I could not accept them. We ourselves, we had a hundred fold more hands ready to fight, than arms – and nobody was in the world to help us with arms.

There is the same origin and real nature of the question of nationalities in Europe.

Now let me see what was the condition of Hungary under these circumstances.

Eight hundred and fifty years ago, when the first King of Hungary, St. Stephen, became Christian himself, converted the Hungarian nation to Christianity, it was the Roman Catholic clergy of Germany whom he invited to assist him in his pious work. They did, but it was natural that the pious assistance happened also to be accompanied by some worldly designs. Hungary offered a wide field to the ambition of foreigners; and they persuaded the King to adopt a curious principle, which he laid down in his political testament. That is, that it is not good, when the people of a country is but of one extraction and speakes but one tongue. There was yet adopted another rule, that is, to advise the language of the Church – Latin – for the diplomatic language of the Government, Legislature, law and all public proceedings. So it became, of course, that the real manners of the country, that spoke Latin. The Hungarian, scarcely yet believing Christian, spoke not – the Latin of course. This is the origin of that fatality that Democracy did not develop for centuries in Hungary.

The public proceedings having been carried on in Latin, the laws given in Latin, the people were excluded from the public life. Public instruction being carried on in Latin, the great mass of the people, being agriculturers, did not partake in it, and the few who, out of the ranks of the people, partook in it, became by the very instructions, severed and alienated from the people's interests. This dead Latin language, introduced into the public life of a living nation, was the most mischievous barrier against liberty. The first blow to it was stricken by the Reformation. The Protestant Church, introducing the national language into the Divine services, became a medium to the development of the spirit of liberty. So were our ancient struggles for religious liberty always connected with the maintenance of political rights. But still, Latin public life went on so far as to 1780. At that time, Joseph of Hapsburg, aiming at centralization, re-placed the Latin by the German tongue. This raised the national spirit of Hungary; and our forefathers seeing that the dead Latin language excluded the people from the public concerns, cannot be propitious to liberty, and anxious to oppose the design of the Viennese Cabinet of

Germanizing Hungary, and so melting it into the common absolutism of the Austrian dynasty – I say – anxious to oppose this design by a cheerful public life of the people, itself begun in the year 1790, passed laws in the direction that by-and-by, step by step the Latin language should be replaced in the public proceedings of the Legislature and of the Government by a living language, familiar to the people itself. And Hungary being Hungary, what was more natural than that, being in the necessity to choose one language, they chose the Hungarian language in and for Hungary, the more because that was the language spoken in Hungary; not only by a comparative majority of the people, but almost by an absolute majority that is, those who spoke Hungariatian were not only more than those who spoke whatever one of the other languages, but if not more at least equal to, all those who spoke several other languages together.

Be so kind to mark well, gentlemen, no other language was oppressed – the Hungarian language was upon nobody enforced – wherever another language was in use even in public life; for instance, of whatever church – whatever public school – whatever community – it was not replaced by the Hungarian language. It was only the dead Latin which by-and-by became eliminated from the diplomatic public life, and replaced by the living Hungarian in Hungary.

In Hungary, gentlemen, be pleased to mark it, never was this measure extended into the municipal public life of Croatia and Sclavonia which, though belonging for 800 years to Hungary, still were not Hungary, but a distinct nation, with distinct municipal public life.

They themselves Croatians and Sclavonians repeatedly urged it in the common parliament to afford them opportunity to learn the Hungarian language, that having the right they might also enjoy the benefit of being ewployed to common governmental offices of Hungary. This opportunity was afforded to them, but nobody was forced to make use of it if he desired not to do so; but with their own municipal and public life, as also with the domestic, social, religious life, of whatever other people in Hungary itself, the Hungarian language did never interfere, but replaced only the Latin Language, which no people spoke, which to no living people belonged, and which therefore was contrary to liberty, because it excluded the people from any share in the public life. Willing to give freedom to the people we eliminated that Latin tongue, which was an obstacle to its future. We did what every other nation in the world did, clearing by it the way to the people's common universal liberty.

Your country is a happy one even in that respect being a young nation, you did not find in your way the Latin tongue when you established this Republic; so you did not want a law to estimate it from your public life. You have a living diplomatic life, which is spoken in your Congress, in your State Legislatures, and by which your Government rules. That language is not the native language of your whole people – scarcely of that of a majority; and yet no man in the Union takes it for an oppression that Legislature and Government is not carried on in every possible language that is spoken in the United States; and yet are found in your common law, inherited from England, some Latin expressions, the affidavits, &c.; and having found it in law, you felt the necessity to stimulate it by law; as you really did.

And one thing I have to mention yet. This replacing of the Latin language by the Hungarian was not a work of our revolution, it was done before, step by step, by-and-by from 1791. When we carried in 1848 our democratic reforms, and gave political, social, civil and full religious freedom to the whole people without distinction of religion or tongue, considering that unhappy excitement of the question of languages prevailing through Europe in consequence of the Russian plot, which I developed, we extended our cares to the equal protection of every tongue and nationality, affording to all equal right, to all aid out of the public funds for the moral, religious, and scientific development in churches and in schools. Nay, our revolution extended this regard even to the political development of every tongue, sanctioning the free use of every tongue, in the municipalities and communal corporations, as well as in the administration of justice itself. The promulgation of the laws in every tongue, the right to petition and to claim justice in whatever tongue, the duty of the government to answer accordingly, all this was granted, and thus far more done in that respect also, than whatever other nation ever accorded to the claims of tongues; by far more than the United States ever did, though there is no country in the world where there are so many different languages spoken as here.

It is, therefore, the most calumnions misrepresentation, to say that the Hungarians struggled for the dominion of their own race. No; we struggled for civil and religious freedom, common to all against Austrian despotism. We struggled for the great principle of self-government, and not for centralization – because centralization is absolutism. Yes, centralization is absolutism; it is inconsistent with constitutional rights. Austria has given the very proof of it. The House of Austria had never the slightest intention to grant constitutional life to the nations of Europe. I will prove it on another occasion. It hates constitutions as hell hates the salvation of human souls. But the friends of the Hapsburghs say it has granted a constitution – in March, 1849. Well, where is that constitution now? It was not only never executed, but it was three months ago formally withdrawn.

Even the word Ministry is blotted out from the dictionary of the Austrian Government.

Swarzenburg is again House, Court, and State Chancellor, as Metternich was; only Metternich ruled not with the iron rule of martial law over the whole empire of Austria: Swarzenburg does. Metternich encroached upon the constitutional rights of Hungary, Transylvania, Croatia and Sclavonia. Swarzenburg has abolished them, and the young Nero, Francis Joseph, melted all nations together in a common bondage, where the promised equality of nationalities is carried out most literally, to be sure, because they are all equally oppressed, and all are equally ruled by absolutistical principles in the German language. And why was that illusory constitution withdrawn? Because it was a lie from the beginning; because it was an impossibility. And why so? Because it was founded upon the principle of centralization, and thirteen different nations, which now groan under Austrian rule; and yet, to have a constitutional life, is more than an impossibility. It is an absurdity, it is an oppression augmented by deceit.

I cannot exhaust this vast topic in one speech, so I go to the end. I only state clearly my own and my nation's ruling principle, even my respect to the claims of the nationalities of languages; and that is, we will have Republican institutions, founded on universal suffrage, and so the majority of the sovereign people shall rule, in every respect, in the village, in the city in the country, in the Congress and Government – in all and everything. What to the public concerns of the village, of the city, of the country, of the Congress belongs – self-government everywhere – the people sovereign everywhere – and universal suffrages and the rule of the majority everywhere. That is our principle, for which we live and are ready to die. This is the cause for which I humbly request the protecting aid of the people of the United States, and chiefly your aid and protection, gentlemen – you, the mighty engineers of the public opinion of your glorious land!

Let me entreat you, gentlemen, to accord this protection to my downtrodden land; it is the curse of oppressed humanity on the European continent. It is the curse of Germany, bleeding under the scourge of some thirty petty tyrants, all leaning upon that league of despots, the basis of which is St. Petersburgh. It is the curse of fair but unfortunate Italy, which in so many respects is dear to my heart. We have a common enemy; so we are brothers in arms for freedom and independence. I know how Italy stands, and I dare confidently declare there is no hope for Italy but in that great Republican party, at the head of which Mazzini stands. It has nothing to do with the communistical schemes or the French doctrines of Socialism. But it wills Italy independent, free, and republican. Whither could Italy look for freedom and independence, if not to that party which Mazzini leads? To the King of Naples, perhaps? Let me be silent about that execrated man. Or to the dynasty of Sardinia and Piedmont? It professes to be constitutional; and it captures those poor Hungarian soldiers who seek an asylum in Piedmont; it captures and delivers them to Austria to be shot – and they are shot, increasing the number of those 3,742 martyrs whom Radetzsky murdered on the scaffold during 3 short years. The house of Savoy became the blood-hound of Austria to spill Hungarian blood.

Gentlemen, the generous sympathy of the public opinion of the United States – God be blessed for it – is strongly aroused to the wrongs and sufferings of Hungary. My humble task in that respect is done. Now I look for your generous aid to keep that generous sympathy alive, that it may not subside like the passing emotion of the heart.

I look for your generous aid to urge the formation of societies to collect funds and create a loan.

I look for your generous aid to urge the public opinion of the sovereign people of the United States to pronounce in favor of the humble propositions which I had the honor to express at the Corporation Banquet of the City of New York, until the resolutions of the people succeed to impress the favorable decision to the policy of the United States.

In that respect, I beg leave one single remark to make. In speaking of the principle of non-admission of any interference in any country's domestic concerns, I took the liberty to express my humble wish to see Great Britain invited to unite in this protective policy. The reason is, because I take the present French Government for one of the oppressors – it has interfered, and continues to interfere in Rome. But the French nation I take for one of the oppressed. The French nation will do the same as Hungary, Italy, and Germany. The alliance of the French nation is insured by its necessary principles, if the Republic becomes a reality. The decisive question is, what the neutral powers will do – and those are Great Britain and the United States.

Let me hope, gentlemen, that however low I may have fallen in your expectations by this my humble address, which, though sketched down, was still without eloquence, nor by want of time elaborate. Still, following the generous impulse of your Republican hearts, and considering not the immerit of my humble self, but merit of the cause which I plead, you will accord me that protective aid of the free, independent Press upon which rest, for the greater part, the hopes of my nation and those of opprossed humanity. And if you generously accord me that protective aid, I will yet also see fulfilled, in my own country's cause, those noble words which you, Sir, (to the chairman) from that height where the genius of poetry soars, have told your people, who so like to listen to the noble inspiratious of its Bryant,

"Truth crushed to earth shall rise again;
The eternal years of God are here
But error, wounded, writhes in pain
And dies among –

Let me add, Sir, *with*

– his worshippers."

While Kossuth was delivering this speech, he was again and again interrupted by outbursts of applause.

Kossuth's Speech at Castle Garden,
before the First Division New York State Militia

Gov. Kossuth entered the room about 8 o'clock and was introduced and addressed by Gen. Sandford. He came forward, and was hailed with uprorious applause.

Kossuth's Response

He accepted, with gratification, the honor of meeting the First Division of New York State Militia, which participated, on his arrival, in the demonstration of public welcome, which must prove beneficial to the cause of freedom and independence on the European continent. The honor they showed him was an important circumstance, which cannot fail to produce a deep impression in Europe. Being amongst brethren-in-arms, he would feel gratified if he were able to address them in such an elaborate manner, as he felt it his duty to do. But he was sick, very sick indeed, so much so, that last night he was obliged to leave the banquet, with which he was honored by the mighty engineers of public opinion, THE PRESS. (Applause.) It very often happens, that searching to find true words, he forgot the ideas. It is only the lark and nightingale who can give forth their harmonions eloquence without thinking, but he was now growing old; hardships and toil had worn away his brain, and he was now more soldier than orator; and so he begged excuse for his plain, frank, soldierly speech. (Applause.)

What is the finest speech I ever heard or read? It was at the address of Garibaldi in the last war, when he said to his soldiers: "Soldiers! what I have to offer you is fatigue, danger – death – a continued struggle of the bayonet against batteries – those who love their country may follow me." (Cheers.)

That was the most glorious speech he ever heard, and would be the speech which he would address to his own soldiers, when they met again to fight the battles of liberty and independence. He recollected another great speech, that of an old covenanter to his soldiers, before the battle: "Soldiers put your trust in God, and keep your powder dry!" (Loud Cheers.) That will be my motto. We will put our trust in God, but I do not know about preserving my powder – (his health.)

Gov. Kossuth then turned to Major General Sandford and pronounced a high eulogy on the appearance of the men under him, and the obedience paid by the people to his command. He took it for a new truth of the vitality of free institutions. Your republic proves that order is founded upon the freedom of the People. Here is a regiment which had not long ago to fulfil the difficult duty of enforcing public order. The fact was as glorious to the regiment as honorable to the people. Today was the Anniversary of the great fire of 1835; but the city had become greatly enlarged since. Its present magnitude and social order is attributable to the discipline and order of the State Militia, as much almost as to the good practical sense of the people. You give many lessons to Europe, but the greatest of them is the organization of a great National Militia. Standing armies must cease, but cannot till the nations are free, for they are not

National institutions, but the tools of despotism. Where Nations become free, they will not be wanted, for Nations will no longer war with each other. Thirty-seven years ago was a battle fought in New Orleans, which proved the power of a defensive militia. They also proved this power in offensive war, if necessary. The war in Mexico was carried on by Volunteers, and it must be acknowledged they have high claims to the praise of their brilliant brethren. He knew what a distinguished part the Volunteers of New York took in the various battles, and how they partook in the glory of entering the metropolis of Mexico; and who were those Volunteers? They were out of your Militia, where they learned the military spirit which is the true bulwark of freedom. (Applause.) It was his determination to carry out this organization in Hungary. One of our common duties to our native land is to take up arms for its freedom and independence. He would lay down such a system in the public schools that every boy in the land would be trained up to military duties, and those who in their more advanced views feel inclined to take higher parts in the profession, should be trained in the universities. To defend the country is a common duty, and every man should know it and be prepared to perform it. That the militia of Hungary, so developed, would be the most solid guarantee of her freedom and independence, is proved by the heroic defence of their native land. They achieved brilliant ambition of glory, greater deeds than are recorded of the heroes of Mythology. To the sustenance of the country's independence they had established a National Guard. It was like a porcupine going quietly and inofficiously looking for food, but which when menaced would use its bristling points against the enemy.

Russia is the scourge of liberty; Austria is its satellite. Now, the question is; can Hungary be a barrier to secure Europe against the encroachments of Russia? I answer, yes. She can have a million of organized citizen soldiery, which can and will form a barrier to Russia. Russia is not such a mighty power. Its whole power does not exceed 750,000 men, and in Russia itself the contentment of the grave is the false tranquility which it presents. It wants at least 100,000 men to guard its frontiers, and 100,000 men is necessary to keep down the noble aspirations of Poland. In no case could she spare more than 300,000 men for a foreign war, and the million of Hungarian soldiers would not want to be so brave as they are, to be more than a match for Russia. We would find for allies in Russia the oppression of the nation, and the Polish nationalities which are spread through the broad provinces of the Russian empire; so that the might of Russia is not so strong as to intimidate a nation in a just cause. But Russia is to Hungary very near – within thirty hours distance stands one of its great armies, ready to crush down Hungary before she could organize; but Hungary once organized, she fears not the whole power of the Russian empire. This is the motive of his application to the U.S. to become the defender of the Executive power of every nation to dispose of its own domestic affairs. That is the only lustre wanting to the glory of their mighty stars, and he hoped the militia would not deny him their support in preventing Russian interference in the coming struggle of Hungary. (Great applause.) His second wish was the secured commerce of the citizens of the United States with every country in the world; and he hoped the militia of N. York would be ever found ready to protect those ships whose glorious flag waved over him. (Loud cheers) His third request was the legitimate acknowledgment of the Independence of Hungary. (Cheers.) As to the financial aid, it was a delicate matter, which he would entirely leave for their generosity. It was not, however, his design to ask for money to carry on war in Hungary, but only to prepare for that contingency. Hungary would be ready to fight her own battles at her own expense; but now the slightest manifestation of patriotism was a crime, the penalty of which would be enforced by the hangman. Whatever financial aid he would get would be employed by him within the observance of the laws of the United States; but when the battle of freedom would be fought again, he hoped to see in the ranks of the patriots individuals of the New York Militia (cheers) – provided, of course, that such would not be a transgression of the laws.

He thanked the Militia for the manifestation which they had shown him of their love for the cause of freedom, and for the honor which they had conferred upon his gallant and brave companions, who had fought so nobly by his side; and he would assign to them in the coming struggle the post of greatest danger, to give them an opportunity of testifying that the honors conferred on them were not undeserved.

As to myself (here Gov. Kossuth took in his hand the handsome sword which he wore), I have a sword by my side, given to me by an American citizen. This being a gift from a citizen of the United States, I take it as a token of encouragement for me to go on in this work, which, with the blessing of Almighty God, will perhaps lead us to see our fatherland independent and free, (great applause); and I swear here, before you, gentlemen, that this American sword in my hand will be always faithful to the cause of freedom; that it will be the foremost in the battle-field, and that it never will be polluted either by ambition or cowardice. (Enthusiastic cheers.)

First Division of the New York State Militia, I engage you to become the controlling power of this my solemn oath, and I thank you once more for your generous sympathy.

Kossuth's Address at the Plymouth Church, Brooklyn, L.I.

Governor Kossuth stepped forward, and remarked that he felt a little embarrassed. Expectations might have been formed of him, but his time had been so much occupied that he could deliver no eloquent speech. His honorable friend had remarked that he (Beecher) was but the shadow of good things to come. But it was not now morning, but the evening time, when the shadow does not precede the object, but follows it. (Applause.) If it might be anticipated that ladies and gentlemen might have come here to listen to an eloquent speech from him, he would have begged to be excused. Every moment of his time was engaged since he came here, and he did not, therefore, intend to make an eloquent speech, but to meet those whose sympathies were extended to the oppressed nations of Europe. He was unprepared to speak, but must depend on inspiration, and did not know whether he would have that inspiration, or not. Two considerations present themselves to my mind. The first was that he was in the power of God. The second that he met those who were ready to assist him in the cause of his Fatherland when he was a captive in far Asia, and did not dream that the heart of humanity bled for him. You, under the guidance of that noble man whom you have elected to preside over your spiritual wants, did not neglect to pray for me. He believed the Christian religion was the everlasting source of freedom on earth; he said Christ's kingdom was not of this world, but He taught his followers to be free on earth, as they would be equally free in heaven. The next change will be a reformation in Christianity; not in principle, but in the performance of that commandment to love our neighbors as ourselves:

The cause of Hungary is strongly connected with the principle of religious liberty on earth. When in the first war of the 16th century, a battle was fought by the Moslems in Hungary, by which the power of his nation was almost overthrown – at that time the monarchy was elective – a Hungarian, who was Governor of Transylvania, was chosen King, but another party elected Ferdinand of Austria to be King of Hungary. A long struggle ensued in which the Princes of Transylvania invoked Turkish aid against the House of Austria.

In the hour of need the House of Austria complied with the wishes of his nation, when his country had taken up arms; but no sooner was the sword laid down, than Austria neglected to perform its promises. In the midst of the last century, under Maria Theresa, those who did not belong to the Catholic faith were almost excluded from offices; and when Joseph succeeded, who was a tolerant man, scarcely was he in his grave when the Emperor Francis, who succeeded him, renewed persecution against religious liberty, and it was only in '48 that religious liberty was established to every creed; and when the House of Austria took arms against these laws, they took arms against religious liberty. He belonged to the Lutheran church – it was quite a democratic institution, as the congregations had shared in the elections of ministers. It was a true democratic institution. Now it is the House of Austria which disposes of religion and public religion – therefore he had reason to state that Hungary was the cause of Religion.

In our Parliament also, it was Roman Catholics who stood in the van of battle for religious liberty, but when I say this, I must state it without drawing any commentary from it. It was reserved to our revolution to show the development of the glorious cause of freedom. When my nation imposed on me the duty to govern the land, I was ready to show the confidence I had in religious freedom, and I chose a Catholic Minister to be Minister of Education in Hungary, and he fully justified the confidence I reposed in him. He has shown that to him the Constitution of a country is founded upon equality; that Constitution regards all men citizens, and makes no distinction of profession. It is only under free institutions that a clergyman can remain a clergyman with burning heart to those his duties, but when he is called to perform the duties of a citizen, he is no longer a clergyman but a citizen. You never would have found a Catholic King appoint a Protestant Minister to be Minister of Education, nor a Protestant King appoint a Catholic Priest. It was only possible Protestant King appoint a Catholic Priest. It was only possible for a Republic. Could the Church of Rome have appreciated this principle, and have acted upon it, my friend Mazzini was not now necessary for the freedom of Italy. But the

Church of Rome did not appreciate the value of this principle, and Mazzini becomes necessary. The power of the Pope is about to fall down for ever. This is rny conviction. The temporal power of the Pope will probably fall down at the next revolution. It was already felt on the air, and pointed out by the finger of God. I say it prophetically. I have read it in the book of history, which is made to be a revelation to mankind.

My principles are, that the Church shall not meddle with politics, and government will not meddle with religion. In every society there are political and civil concerns on one side, and on the other side social concerns; for the first civil authority must be established – in political and civil respects has to acknowledge the power of this jurisdiction. But, in respect to social interestst it is quite the contrary. Religion is not an institution – it is a matter of conscience – it is connected with the soul of man; but the church is the institution, for the church can only be founded on social interests. Now, if this principle be true, therefore the consequence of it must be, that no state in the world can be founded upon any other basis than on the basis of civil and political authority.

It was for the support of these principles he asked their generous aid, because the freedom and independence of Hungary was the question of civil and religious liberty throughout Europe. The House of Austria, they knew, was never propitious to the principles of religious liberty; for whenever it attained to any strength, its first step was to break down religious liberty. And Austria is helped by Russia, which is even still less propitious to these principles; they remembered the great cruelty to which in Russia are subject those people who do not belong to the Greek Church, and at the present time the poor Jews are subjected to great indignities, and compelled, if not to shave of their hair, to cut it in a particular manner, so as to distinguish them from members of the Greek Church. This is the power which now preponderates and rules over Europe, and what is the power which can be opposed to this terroristical power? It is only Hungary, which, by the Providence of God, is destined to become once more the vanguard of civilization, the vanguard of religious liberty for the whole of the European Continent against the encroachments of Russian despotism, as it has already been the barrier of Christianity against Islamism; so it will now be the barrier of civilization and liberty against Russia, and this he believed was a mighty claim to the generous aid of every freeman in the world. He was told that the ladies and gentlemen present were willing to bestow to this cause something, to speak plainly, that they were willing to give money to the cause of Hungary. It was not his intention to employ this aid to carry on war, but it was his intention to employ it in such a manner as not to be unprepared for the exigences of approaching circumstances (laughter), to have it prepared for that opportunity which God will soon give to restore their fatherland to freedom and independence. It was no joke he meant when he said so. He knew what the expense of war was. The year of the revolutionary struggle in Hungary cost them thirty-five millions of dollars (and he thought that it was unprecedented in history to carry on so great a war at such slight cost); but he had no expectation of raising that sum here – he did not dream of it, and therefore it was true what he said, that he did not want their aid to carry on the war, but he believed that it was possible for Hungary to attain freedom and independence without entering into a long, bloody war, if they would only carry out this principle of international law which he suggested, and become the executive power enforcing it; and then, besides, give him some aid, not thirty-five, nor twenty, nor ten, but even five millions of dollars; and then what would be the consequence? probably that they would scarcely have to fight more than one battle? On what did the Austrian power repose? on the love of the nation? It cannot be expected that a nation should love tyranny. On the contentment of its people? no nation can be content without freedom. On what then did the power of Austria repose? On three props – its loans, its army, and Russia. These were its three supports; are these bases so strong as to give security for the future? he believed it was quite the contrary. The loans are consumed so fast, that it is necessary, every three or four months, to make a new loan. Loans cannot give security to the House of Austria, but rather bankruptcy, and bankruptcy is not the surest prop of the existence of power. Its second prop was the army. But of what was the army composed? It was composed of the sons of those nations who are oppressed by the house of Austria and they must hate it as a man would hate one who had spilt the blood of his mother. There is no country, except perhaps the Tyrolese, under the Austrian government, which has not been bombarded, where the scaffolds do not rise – where the prisons are not filled with patriots. Will the armies raised by force and violence, not by voluntary choice out of the midst of those nations; give security to the existence of the despot? He believed not. And in that array are some hundred thousand Hungarians, enrolled by force – such Hungarians who have fought two years ago against the House of Austria for the freedom and independence of their country, and fought so as that the fame of their exploits had come over the ocean to the American people. Now what had happened since, that this hundred thousands men, who fought their father's country against Austria, should now become the friends of Austria? If the blood of their best martyrs, or the sufferings of their country, or the down-trodden existence of Hungary, or the numerous persecutions and material oppression which now Hungary endures, be motives by which this hundred thousand men fought against Austria – then they might be supposed to be loyal towards that prefidious house. In former times there never was any higher tax imposed upon Hungary than 9 or 10 millions of florins (some five millions of dollar), now the tax which is imposed is sixty millions; was that a motive that three hundred thousand men would fight for Austria? It would be a motive why they would fight not for Austria, but for the liberty of their country – therefore the army will not give any security to the house of Hapsburgs, but will give somewhat less than security – it will be a practical school for that hundred thousand men to become good drilled soldiers. But then the third prop was that Austria leaned upon Russia. This is the only possible prop for its vegetation for some days yet in the future. He therefore claimed that the people of the U.S. would move their government to establish the principles of international law in the way he has laid down, and thereby prevent whatever nation from interfering in the domestic concerns of any other nation; and, it was his firm conviction that should this be done, and some material aid given to his cause, the freedom of Hungary would be secured; for although Austria would not, of course, quietly resign her claim – for tyrants never resign out of their own free will – yet Austria would not have the means of making a long war against them for their independence, and with one or two battles, success would ensue. But he was told there were men of peace, who say after all (very fine if you please) we cannot have war, we must have peace at every price. Now many things in this world depend on their true definition, and this term applied to them is not true; they are not men of peace who speak so; they are only men who would conserve at every price the present condition. Is that present condition peace? Is the scaffold peace? the scaffold on which in Lombardy the blood of 3,742 patriots was spilled during three short years of this peace? "peace" or the prisons of Austria filled with patriots? or is the murmur of discontent of all the nations peace? He believed the Lord did not create the world to be in such a peaceful condition. He did not create it to be the prison to humans. No! the present condition is not

110

peace. The present condition is one of oppression on the European continent, and because it is a condition of oppression, there cannot be peace for so long as men and nations are oppressed. So long as men and nations are discontented, there cannot be peace – there cannot be tranquility. But it is a volcano, boiling up and ready at the first opportunity to break out and to sweep away all the artificial obstacles. This is the condition which these "men of peace" wish to conserve; but the tranquility of affairs is merely the prison of nations. His principles were really those of peace, because he was always a faithful servant of the principles of liberty, and on them only can nations be content, and only with the contentment of natious can there be peace on the earth. With him and his principles there was peace – lasting peace – consistent peace; with the tyrants of the world, there was oppression, and, consequently, the breaking forth of war. Gov. Kossuth then explained his views in respect to the right of the people of the U.S. to carry on commerce with whatever other nation who were willing to negotiate with them without the hindrance of any foreign government, or having their commerce interrupted by internal quarrels between the people and its government with which they (the people of the U.S.) had both to do, and to protect these, their commercial interests: they should have ships of war in the Mediterranean.

In conclusion, he asked that they should also go on to express their will in respect to the recognition of the legitimate character of the declaration of Independence of Hungary. Carry out, said he, this great principle of international law in the case of my poor suffering country, and give me some substantial aid also to that cause – by this aid, your great nation will be not only the saviour of mankind, in respect to their political, social and religious liberty, but you yourselves, gentlemen, in that circumstance, will have relieved your own country from the necessity of being forced to take up arms and fight for our principles of liberty; because if you now permit them to be overthrown, you will have to redeem this lost opportunity by bloody wars of long duration; whereas, now by a firm manly attitude in pronouncing these eternal principles, and some little substantial aid, you can avert this great necessity from the nation.

Kossuth's Address before the New York Bar

Several thousand persons having assembled in this splendid Hall, Mr. Edward Sandford read an address from the Bar.

Kossuth's Reply

Gov. Kossuth said in reply, he would have felt most embarrassed in addressing this large assembly, but for the confidence which he received from the announcement of those principles of truth which he had heard. Let him as an ancient member of the profession explain his views as to qualification and admission; he was no friend of the system of qualification, but of free unarrested progress, and the code hinders progress and fetters development. Nations are yet festering under the iron grasp of Justinian. Law must be developed in proportion as other social institutions, and whenever prejudice or custom succeeds to establish what is contrary to Justice, it was one of their noblest powers to show that it should not be continued. If this is the case in reference to private law, let them extend it to international law. In this field there is no code but that of nature and nature's God. When artificial cunning succeeds in introducing those principles which are contrary to justice, it is the duty of free nations to restore the true principles, and place high the torch of truth over the barriers of prejudice. This country would do so. He knew how to read their people's heart, because it was open like nature; and unpolluted as a virgin's heart. (Tremendous applause.) Therefore it is conscious of its power to restore to the law of nations the principles of justice and right, and is willing to exercise this power. Let his country, let Hungary be the opportunity for this restoration. Now is the hour, and if allowed to pass, the fate of humanity might be sealed. He had before stated three of his humble wishes. The first was – that the United States should declare the right of nations to dispose each of its own domestic concerns, and not permit the interference of foreign powers. This intervention had been described yesterday by a gentleman from Cincinnati as an act of piracy. He felt the truth of it. There is a striking power in a single word of truth, and that word had relieved him of many speeches. There can be no doubt about the law – the duty against pirates. He had however, to contend against two principles which had gained ground here: first, that the

United States could not interfere in European concerns. Every independent power had a right to form alliances, but might or not do so. Alliances were not matters of duty, but merely of policy. By forming alliances or abstaining from them, they might give offence to the wishes of some other nation, but this could not offend their duty. There is an essential difference between neutrality and non-interference, alliance and its opposite: neutrality may hurt interests, but not violate law. Interference is quite the opposite. It is a violation of nature, and the law of nature's God. He who violates that law is like a pirate, and every nation on earth must chase it down. Your naval forces are and must be instructed to chase down pirates without being limited as to latitude or longitude, or whether on American or European waters. How, in the name of all that is sacred, if all men are ready to cry out against a freebooter is there no hope to hear a universal cry against those pirates who spill blood; not by drops, but by torrents, and murder and destroy the very existence of a whole nation? (Applause.) These execrated criminals trample on humanity, and degenerate humanity bows before them. But blessed be God, there is a free nation here, ready to defend Justice against crowned pirates and their satellites. (Cheers.) The U.S. sympathize deeply, I am told, with the principles of international law, but have not the interest to make it respected by others. He answered with the words of a member of their own profession, and now Secretary of State, that nations have the same interest in defending international law, as every citizen has in protecting the law of his State. He is now in the position to carry out this principle, and he (Kossuth) hoped he would be as good as his word. M. Kossuth then adverted to this suggestion of a coalition between England and the U. S. for the enforcement of this international law. It was not his own original idea; it had been before acted on. The next struggle for independence would be the last war, because it would make nations contented – contented because free. America had nothing to fear for her own security from that war; if he thought so, he would not have appeared before them. It is time to establish that rule, that policy must be subservient to justice. There is an axiom in jurisprudence which they would not contradict – laws are mere empty words if there is nobody to enforce them. From the people of the United States he claimed that they would raise their gigantic arm, and be the executive power of the laws of nature; and of God – that they would protect and defend these laws, even if they had to go to war for them – it would be a holier war than ever yet was carried on, and they would have the blessing of God with them.

The Muscovite Government was not a very foolish one; though it was cruel, and they would not dare to enter into a war with the United States; therefore there was little fear of war by insisting on the observance of this principle. The Czar would show that he was prudently afraid. He did not even interfere with the Hungarian struggle, without considering what would England think "what would Turkey think"? So to try their pulse he sent first a small army into Hungary, pretending it was not only on the invitation of Austria, but on the invitation of a portion of the people. But he would not look back – the past is past, and "forward" is now his word; and he would go on with unabated energy, because he knew there was a God in Heaven, and such a people as they on earth, and the resolution and courage of his own mind. His motto still would be, "there is no difficulty to him who wills."

He wished also to see established the true principles of commercial and international intercourse; and his third wish was to see recognized the declaration of Hungarian Independence; but he was now too unwell to develop his ideas. He could not now go on, but he would make use of the mighty engine of public opinion, the Press, to lay his views before them and the whole people of the United States. He then concluded as follows:

Gentlemen of the Bar: – You have devoted your lives to maintain Justice, right and law, against all who would violate them. I put these principles under your protective care, and trust they will find mighty advocates in you. Gov. Kossuth resumed his seat amid loud applause.

At the conclusion of the Address, the members of the Bar entertained Gov. Kossuth and suite at a magnificent banquet.

Kossuth's Farewell Address to the Ladies of New York

Rev. S.H. Tyng said he was deputed to convey to Gov. Kossuth an expression of the sentiments of the Ladies of New York, and read a paper embodying them.

Governor Kossuth's Reply

Ladies: – I would I were able to answer that call. I would I were able conveniently to fill the place which your kindness has assigned me, but really I am in despair of being able to do so, for I do not know how many times I have spoken during the fourteen days I have been in New York. Permit me, however, to make some few remarks suggested to my mind by what I have heard. You have been pleased to say that Austria was blind to let me escape. Be assured, ladies, it was not the merit of Austria. Austria would have been very glad to burry me, if not in the cold grave of death, at least in the equally cold grave of moral idleness, in an Eastern exile. But the generosity of the Emperor of Turkey took courage at the interference of America, and not withstanding all the proclamations of Austria, I have been restored to life because I have been restored to duty and activity. It is a curious fate which I have had. Perhaps never was there a man in the world so fond of the idea of tranquility. Never, perhaps, was there a man in the world so fond of the idea to do as much good as possible, without wishing to be even noticed or known of whomever in the world; and this longing for tranquility, it was my destiny that I had never a single moment in my life to see fulfilled. But my guiding star was, is, and will be forever the word "duty" (Applause.) And the pleasure and delight of my heart must wait even forever, if necessary, when duty calls.

Ladies, outworn as I am, still I am glad, very glad indeed, that it is the Ladies of New York who have condescended to listen to my farewell. It cannot and will not be eloquent, this my farewell. While in the moments of the busy day, the watchful care of our guardian Angel throws some flowers of joy in the thorny way of man; he gathers them up with thanks, and a cheerful thrill strikes through his heart like the melody of an Eolian harp, but the earnest duties of life soon claim his attention, and on he must go, and on he goes, joyless, cheerless, cold, every fibre of his mind bent to the earnest duties of the day; but when the hard work of the day is done, and the stress of mind for a moment subsides; then the heart claims again its right, and the tender fingers of memory gather again the violets of joy which our guardian Angel threw in our way, and we look at them with as much joy, and cherish them as the fairest gifts of life, and we are so glad, so glad as a child on Christmas eve. (Applause.) These are the happiest moments of our life, but then we are not noisy, not eloquent, we are silent, almost mute like nature on a midsummer night, reposing after the burning

115

heat of the day. (Renewed Applause) Ladies this is my condition; it was indeed a hard day's work which I had to do here – now the work is done, and I am at my farewell; and every compassionate smile, every warm grasp of the hand, every token of kindness which I met, (and I met much, very much,) every flower of consolation which the Ladies of New York have poured on me and thrown in my way, rushes with deep force into my memory, and I feel so happy at the memory! I feel so much solemn tranquility about my mind, that at such a moment I had rather be silent than speak – scarcely can I do it. You know it, Ladies; they are not the deepest feelings, those which are loud – and, besides, I have to say "farewell" to New York, and that is a sorrowful word indeed. What immense hopes are linked in my memory at that word, "New York"! Hopes of resurrection for my downtrodden fatherland: hopes of liberation for oppressed nations on the European continent. Will the expectations which the mighty outburst of New York's young generous heart raised in my mind – will they be realized? (Shouts of "yes") Will these hopes be fulfilled, or will the joys of consolation which New York has cast on the dark night of my native land, pass away like an electric flash? Oh, that I could cast one single glance into futurity's book! But no. God forgive me this impious thought – it is He who hath hid the future before man's eye, and what He does is well done. It is not good for man to know his destiny. The energy and the sense of duty would falter or subside, could we know either the failure of our aim, or its assured success. It is better not to know the future, and to retain the whole energy of duty. So I will go on in my work, with the full energy of my humble abilities, without despair, as without precedent, but with hope. It is Eastern blood that runs in my veins. I came from the East, and I have somewhat of its fatalism; but the fatalism which I have, is that of Christianity, which trusts with unwavering faith in the boundless goodness of Divine Providence. (Great applause.) But among all these different feelings and thought, coming upon me in the hours of my farewell, one thing is indispensable almost to me, and that is, the knowledge that the sympathy which I met here will not pass away like the cheers which the warbling girl meets on the stage – that it will be fostered like principles, and when emotion subsides, clearness of reflection will but strengthen it, because it is a principle. This is the consolation I want, and this is the consolation I have; because I leave to you, mothers, sisters, the cares and the hopes of Europe's oppressed nations – the hopes of my bleeding fatherland – the hopes of social, political, civil and religious liberty. Oh, let me entreat you with the brief stammering words of a warm heart overwhelmed with emotion and with sorrowful cares, let me entreat you, ladies, be watchful over the sympathy of your people like the mother over the cradle of her beloved child. (Enthusiastic cheers.) It is worthy of your watchful cares, because it is the cradle of regenerated humanity, and especially as to my poor fatherland.

We Hungarians have three particular claims to the sympathy of the fairer and better half of humanity, which you are – the first is that there is, perhaps, no nation on earth which, even in its institutions, has shown more chivalric regard for woman than Hungary did; this is a precious, worthy part of the Oriental character which we inherit. M. Kossuth then adverted to the peculiar treatment of ladies in Eastern countries; the women of the East were not he said to be pitied, because they were happy, and it were ridiculous to pity those who feel happy. He also refered to the laws of Hungary, which made the widow entitled to the property of her deceased husband, so long as she remained a widow – gave her authority to vote at elections, and, if the widow of a noble, to send a representative to Parliament. He continued: Perhaps this chivalric character of my nation, so full of regard towards the fairer sex, somewhat entitles my nation to the particular sympathy of the ladies of America.

Our second particular claim is, that the source of all the misfortunes which now so heavily weigh upon our bleeding fatherland, is in two ladies – Catharine of Russia and Sophia of Hapsburgh – the ambitious, cruel mother of the young Nero, Francis Joseph. He illustrated his meaning as to the first by reference to the historical fact, that when Charles the 12th of Sweden, foreseeing and dreading the growing power of Russia, ventured, with a handful of soldiers, to overthrow that rising power, and though he had performed almost incredible feats, yet, having been defeated in the battle of Pultowa, and obliged to take refuge with the Sultan of Turkey, he persuaded the latter to oppose Russia also; and having driven the Emperor into such a pass that the distruction was inevitable, Catharine of Russia had gone into the camp of the Sultan, and, by her beauty and the value of her jewels, had procured the cessation of hostilities, and thereby Russia was saved. And, continued he, from that untoward day dates the downfall of Turkey and Russia's growth; and out of that source flowed the stream of Russian preponderance over Europe. Down-trodden liberty there, and the sufferings of Poland and my poor native land are the dreadful fruits of Catherine's success on yonder day, cursed in the records of humanity. The second lady who will be cursed through all posterity, is Sophia, the mother of the Usurper of Hungary, who had the ambitious dream to raise the limited power of a child over the ruins of liberty, and on the neck of downtrodden nations. (It is unnecessary to follow the speaker in his recital of the deeds of that ambitious and cruel woman, they are too well known to need recapitulation.)

Our third particular claim (continued M. Kossuth) is the behavior of the ladies of Hungary during the past war. It is no wanton praise – it is the fact which I say, that in my hard task to lead on that struggle and govern Hungary in those difficult days, I had no more powerful auxiliaries – no more faithful executors of the will of the nation than the women of Hungary. (Applause.) You know ladies the history of ancient Rome; after the battle of Cannae, won by Hannibal, the victor was afraid to come down to the very walls of Rome. The Senate had called upon the people spontaneously to sacrifice all their wealth upon the altar of their fatherland, and the ladies first brought every jewel and ornament they possessed; so that it was afterwards judged necessary to pass a law which prohibited the ladies of Rome to wear any jewels or any silk, in order that the simplicity of the Roman ladies might appear, not as chance only, but rather a command and order of law. In Hungary we wanted no such law. The women of Hungary brought all that they had, everything to the altar of their country's liberty.

I saw many, many brides, who, with smiling faces, wiped off one single tear, and urged on their bridegroom to delay the day of happiness, till he might return victorious out of the battle for the cause. That country deserves to live; that country deserves to have a future yet, when even the women of that country so much love, so much cherish it. But I have a stronger motive yet than these to claim your protecting sympathy for my country's cause; it is her nameless woes – her nameless suffering. In the name of that ocean of bloody deeds which flowed from the sacrilegious hand of the tyrant – in the name of the sufferings of the mothers rendered childless – of the brides who beheld the executioner's sword flash between them and their wedding day – in the name of all those mothers, wives, daughters, and sisters, who have wept over the graves of martyrs so dear to their hearts – in the name of all those torturing stripes, in which the flogging hand of the Austrian tyrant dared to outrage humanity on the womankind of my native land – in the name of the daily curse against Austria, with which even the prayers of our women are mixed – in the name of the nameless sufferings of my own dear wife – (Here the feelings of the audience were raised to such a pitch that they could no longer restrain them, and they burst forth in a shout of enthusiasm as the noble Magyar pointed to his lady, who rose and bowed in acknowledgment to the plaudity of the assembly) – the faithful companion of my sorrows, and the consolation of life – in the name of her who for months and months was hunted by my country's tyrants, like a noble deer, not having for months a moment's rest, nor a place to rest her wearied head, and no hope, and no support, and no protection, but at the humble abodes of the hard-working people, ever so noble, ever so generous as poor – in the name of my poor little children, who so young that they are scarcely conscious of their life, had already to learn what an Austrian prison is – in the name of all these, and what is still more, in the name of downtrodden liberty, I claim, Ladies of New York, your protecting sympathy for my country's cause. The heart of man is as soft as wax in your tender hands; mould it, Ladies, mould it into the form of generous compassion; inspire it with the noble feelings of your own heart – inspire it with the consciousness of your country's power, dignity and might. (Applause.) You are framers of man's character. Whatever be the fate of man, one stamp he always bears upon his brow – that with the mother's hand impressed upon the soul of the child. The smile of your lips can make a hero out of the coward, a generous man out of the egotist. One word of yours inspires the youth to noble resolution; the lustre of your eye is the fairest reward for the toils of life. You can even blow up the feeble spark of energy in the breast of barren age, that it may once more blaze up a noble, generous deed before it dies. All this power you have. *Use it, Ladies* – use it in behalf of your country's glory, and in behalf of oppressed humanity; and when you meet with a cold calculator, who thinks by arithmetic, who is too cold to feel for the wrongs of oppressed nations – convert him, Ladies. Your smiles are commands, and the truth but pours forth instinctively from your hearts. The *Peri* excluded from paradise, brought many precious gifts to heaven, to get in again. She brought the dying sigh of a patriot; she brought the kiss of a faithful girl, imprinted on the lips of her bridegroom, destroyed by the venom of plague. She brought many other fair gifts, but the doors of paradise opened before her only when she brought with her the prayer of a man converted to charity and brotherly love for his oppressed brethren of humanity. (Great applause.)

Now, Ladies, I am worn out very much, so I have done. Only one word now remains to be said – a word of deep sorrow to me the word – "FAREWELL, NEW YORK" New York! – that word will forever make thrill every string of my heart. I am like the wandering bird; I am worse than the wandering bird; he may return to his summer home; I have no home, alas! Here at New York I felt almost at home; but "forward" is my call, (applause,) and I part with the hopes that the sympathy which I met here has been the trumpet-sound of rescue to my native land. I part, with the hope that my having found here a short transitory, will bring me back to my own beloved home, that my ashes may yet mix with the dust of my native soil. Ladies, remember poor Hungary, and farewell!

Kossuth's Corporation Speech in Independence Hall, Phil'a, Pa.

After a splendid reception, Gov. Kossuth was conducted into Independence Hall, and addressed by Mayor Gilpin.

Kossuth replied: – Sir, this is perhaps the proudest welcome which you could give me. The very fact of knowing that I am standing here amongst the happy inheritors of that freedom and independence for which your forefathers fought and bled – the welcome by the happy inheritors of the great deeds here in the very cradle of your glorious liberties – this circumstance is enough to impress upon my mind a religious awe, which includes my heart silently to raise itself to God, wondering at the ways of his Providence, rather than to find expressions in words. I will only tell you, sir, that this Independence Hall – the words spoken here, and the act declared here – represent to my mind, when I, in my native land – not in the ambition to copy your glory, but from a sentiment of duty, and from a conscientiousness that my country was atso entitled to freedom, did even that which your forefathers did here. Your history inspired my people and myself with resolution, with inspiration, with encouragement, and with hope. You succeeded, and we failed; not because we were not as resolved and as decided to sacrifice life and all that to man on earth is dear, for our fatherland; but because we were not in so happy a situation as you. Foreign armed interference came, and wrested out of our hands the fruits of already achieved victories. I can tell you that much of the spirit of your freedom and independence, and of your republican institutions, came over the waves of the ocean to Hungary. Let me hope that my very standing here, welcome by your nation, may be a pledge for the future, that the spirit which came over to us from this place, may yet be attended by that ultimate success which was your happiness, your glory, and your merit also; because upon that basis you here founded a building of human freedom, and of the development, of human intellect, and of civilization, prouder, loftier, than that which humanity before you has beheld through five thousand years.

To your welcome I return my most hearty thanks – your welcome of the poor exile; but in the proud position of your nation's guest. Be thanked for your hospitality – be thanked for your welcome. Be thanked, because I know that the welcome of a free, mighty and powerful people like you, is the assurance that that mighty, free and powerful people feels inclined to become the executive power of the laws of nature and of nature's God; which were proclaimed out of the very ark of your hopes to be not your right alone, but the right of all humanity.

Kossuth's Corporation Speech in Independence Square, Phil'a, Pa.

Kossuth was introduced to the Corporation authorities, and other public men, after which he was conducted through the building to a covered platform erected in Independence Square, where he spoke as follows:

I would like to address you, gentlemen – (order, order, order,) – but when we will have order, we must call order very often. The despots of the world cry order, and you see by such words the liberty of the old world is murdered. Permit me, gentlemen, to cover my head – (putting on his hat.) Your hearts are warm, like Christian brethren, but the air is a little chilly. It is indeed, with deep emotion, that I thank you for the honor of this reception and for the manifestations of your generous sympathy. It has been my lot, during a tempest-tossed life, very often to experience that the people are everywhere highly honorable, generous, noble, and good – that they are imbued with instinctive sentiments of true principles, with a sympathy for every just cause, and filled with that manly resolution to support right and truth, which manly resolution is the inheritance of the most noble deeds.

I have very often, in my life, where the wisest men were at a loss as to what was the best course to pursue, noticed that the people's uncorrupted sentiment pointed out at once the true way. I have often seen the strongest man falter under the weight of an event, while the people stood firm; never wavering in their confidence in the justice of God – never wavering in their sympathies for a just cause, and never wavering in their resolution to carry it to a happy issue. And perhaps this experience has never brought more hope and consolation than in this very place. I feel now that I am upon sacred ground. In this very place was read to your forefathers seventy-five years ago, the Declaration of your Independence. It is here your forefathers achieved that declaration – (Applause) – although that declaration, then proclaimed, was no more than a call to the people to be ready to sacrifice life and all they held dear, for their Fatherland; it was a path full of danger which was pointed out to your forefathers.

But still they, upon that appeal, vowed to be ready to sacriflce life and everything to maintain their independence.

Now you, gentlemen, the happy inheritors of that independence for which your forefathers fought and bled, are in the proud condition that you have nothing more to fear, no further risk to run for your own security, when you resolve to put the whole weight of your mighty country into that balance in which the destinies of mankind are weighed.

Gentlemen – I hope that this demonstration of your sympathy is a token of this, your resolution, which is as glorious to you as it is beneficial to humanity. I thank you, with the warmest sentiments of an honest heart, for your kindness and sympathy, and beg you to be assured, that the remembrance of your sympathy will always be cherished in the heart of my people, as an object of your everlasting thanks and gratitude. (Immense cheering.)

Kossuth's Banquet Speech at Philadelphia, Pa., on the French Usurpation by L. Napoleon

This Speech was delivered on the occasion of a Grand Banquet to Gov. Kossuth by the citizens of Philadelphia, in the Musical Fund Hall.

In the opening of Governor Kossuth's speech, he noticed some annoyances to which he has been exposed in the U.S., which he had not expected to meet in this land of freedom. I have received, said he, four checks of considerable amount, from different places, during my sojourn in New York, as substantial aid for Hungary, and kind letters accompanying them, signed by well known, honorable names. It turned out the letters and checks were forgeries. Now, how base a trick! I can scarcely imagine its intention, if it be not to hurt my fealings and excite disappointment.

It was reported, in one organ of the daily press; that the news of L. Napoleon's stroke fell like a bomb-shell upon me, and that my movements will be arrested by them. Now I confidently state that this news, instead of arresting my movements, can only have the effect to hasten them, to forward their aim, and bring them in a much shorter time to a happy, at least to a speedier definitive decision than the case would have been without this intelligence.

I fear, indeed, no harm from that bomb-shell, and not only I feel neither scathed nor stunned by Monsieur Napoleon Bonaparte's sacrilegious blow aimed at the very life of republicanism in France, but rather I take it for one of those providential facts by which the very crime turns out only to promote that just cause which it was intended to suppress. I could not become scathed or stunned by it, because it was not unexpected by me. I have in New York very often publicly and privately foretold that every steamer may bring us tidings of the outbreak, of the unavoidable crisis of the European continent. The ambition of Louis Napoleon Bonaparte, pushed on by Russian and Austrian craft, will not await the day, but calls forth the struggle at the earliest time.

You know how he exhausted every possible plan to secure his reelection; but every device broke to pieces on the rock of the Constitution, which explicitly forbade a re-election of the actual President. So every man might have forseen, that, having failed in these attemps, he would resort to violence to shatter down that Constitution which excluded him from power, and by this exclusion, from the treacherous realization of his ambitious dreams. The Emperor of Russia and his satellites were well aware that a new peaceful presidential election would consolidate republicanism in France and make it dangerous to their absolutism. They wished to overthrow it; and there was but one alternative for that purpose, either a war or a *Coup d'etat* by their tool, Napoleon. A war would have been dangerous; because against foreign invasion the French nation would unite, and the French Republic attacked by Continental despotism would undoubtedly rouse all the nations of that Continent to take sides with France. They well remember those portentous words of Martin de Thiouville: "If they send us war, we will send them back liberty". There was, therefore, no mistake possible about the fact, that the Czar and his satellites would resort to the other more easy, and to them more agreable alternative, to make the hated French nation bleed by its own hands – in fratricidal combat – and so murder the republic by the very man who was appointed its chief guardian. This was an easier part for the despots to play than a war. A little money and a little diplomacy, that was all they had to play.

But only imagine, gentlemen, because a public officer fears to be accused of having violated the Constitution, he takes that for a motive to annihilate the Constitution. I am entirely sure that to such a motive for an inglorious usurpation, the great French nation will never submit.

But if there is neither the fascination of glory, nor the delusive pretext of liberty, which could induce the French nation to submit to this usurpation of Louis Napoleon, it is perhaps the word "Peace at any price" which might promise any duration to it? There can be no mistake about the matter. Where is the political party in France which would support him for tranquility's sake – support him only to have peace, when every man knows that to support him, would be only so much as to plunge France into the horrors of a long civil war, instead of plunging it into a dishonorable peace?

The Legitimist party must of course be violent against him; the Orleanist party equally so – their leaders, the Joinvilles and Aumales, are already threatening him from Belgium. The Republicans, of course, must hate him – the murderer of the Constitution, so nobly won and so dearly prized. The party of glory must look with contempt upon him, he has no glory to offer them, there is no glory to be earned on the side of the despots of the European continent.

Indeed many a thing may be possible in France, even the restoration of the Bourbons, if you please, but Louis Napoleon's ludicrous and yet bloody ambition triumphant over France – that is impossible! The French nation may bear delusion, it way bear deceit for awhile – alas, too often it has – but insult, never! An insult to the French nation is an earthquake in Europe – history proves it, and Louis Napoleon's act is an insult and this, at least, the French nation never will bear. It is mournful enough that humanity submits to the ambition of happy soldiers, or the vain prestige of a false principle, such as the pretended legitimacy of dynastical rights, often did submit to. Caesars, Cromwells, *General* Napoleons, may succeed, and Romans trample for awhile upon oppressed nations; but ambition without glory – ambition without a principle to lean upon, never yet was borne by manhood, even when "mankind" was yet a child – it will not be borne now when it is grown up a man. To use a characteristic word of your own, *humbug* never yet ruled the destinies of a nation, and the ambition of Louis Napoleon is a *humbug*, and criminal and ridiculous too.

It would be a great mistake to believe that the momentary success of the first days was of any importance at all. No it has none. I will explain this success, and the real nature of it. Existing governments have always a power in a great standing army; that is a logical consequence of the principle of passive obedience and discipline. Now-a-days even "bayonets think," as I have often told; but not all bayonets think. The Russo–Austrian advisers of Louis Napoleon did very well know that to strike the first lever of attack against a despised, chattering Assembly, often hated soldiers – and never with more reason than now in France – that to such a purpose of attack, even that army will submit to the iron rule of disciplines which, when the people strike the first blow, becomes a citizen, and lowers his thinking bayonet before his fellow-citizen. An army which would not support a government attacked by the people, obeys of course its leaders when led to attack an Assembly despised by the people itself. *There* is one key to Louis Napoleon's first day's success. Further, some men did so much talk about the spring of 1852 as the appointed moment of action, that it became quite natural for the people not to be prepared to act in December, 1851. And you know he who is not prepared to defend himself is easily taken by surprise. Since rescued by your generous aid from captivity, I am free to judge circumstances by myself; I often foretold this surprise, because beating the drum is not the best means for catching fowl. This is the second key to Louis Napoleon's momentary success. The third is the prestige of centralization in France. They were wont to look to Paris as all-in-all; now, when we know that our enemy has only one camp, and that that camp is neither prepared nor watched, that camp is easily taken on a fair night. All this, of course, is very natural.

The blow will not be sent where mankind's enemy is prepared to meet it; but where he is not prepared. Everywhere he cannot be prepared. Would he be so, he would be beaten everywhere, of course, with one single blow. Soldiers well know the axiom, "that he who guards everything, guards nothing." Revolution in Europe has no Paris more – one single city is no more the key of success. Freedom has no extensive metropolis. What I have shown in Hungary, that a nation is then invincible, when it does not depend upon its metropolis – that has now become a truth for all the European continent – Centralization is replaced by federative harmony. I thank Louis Napoleon for it. There are yet several other things providential in his sacrilegious blow.

And that ground gained is the more important because it has assured community of the action and interest of the French nation with the oppressed nations of the continent. It has enlisted France into the ranks of those who are ranged against the despots of the continent, without subjecting the oppressed nations to the necessity of accepting the initiative of Paris.

Peace in France is impossible; that is clear, because every political party is against Louis Napoleon, and he has nobody to support him but his personal friends. You will soon see the consequences of this fact. But two things only are possible – either a protracted civil war; or a sudden victory of the not centralized, but national republicanism in France.

Civil war in France is a largely diffused war in Europe, in which not only the other nations, but France itself becomes engaged. Whereas, on the other hand, a sudden victory of Republicanism in France won by arms against the tool of absolutistical plots, is a consolidation of the Republican principles, and not only a pledge of success to European Revolution, but an indispensable alliance with the other nations aiming at freedom and independence.

And one great gain there yet is in all this matter. The principle of centralization is struck down morally in France. Louis Napoleon has convinced the French nation that to give centralized power into the hands of one man is as much as to give to his mercy freedom, constitution, and all sovereign rights. Louis Napoleon's stroke threw at once the whole continent to that spot where your republic stands. Your principies have conquered the world. God the Almighty be blessed for it.

In this triumph of your principles, there is yet another great victory for humanity. The French Republic triumphant, but centralized, would have conserved the great standing armies – this comsumptive sickness of Europe, and this dangerous instrument of ambitious men. The nations of the European continent re-constructing their freedom and independence upon the basis of your principles, delivered mankind from that consumptive sickness, and that dangerous curse – great standing armies.

But why have I chosen this topic for this occasion, which your kindness has offened to me? Why have I dwelt so largely upon it? The motive, gentlemen, is – firstly, to show that there is nothing in the news from France of such a nature as to arrest that attention which public opinion of the people of the United States has been pleased to bestow to the question. What course your country has to adopt in its foreign policy in respect to European countries – but that the news from France transforming my prophesy of being on the very eve of a crisis in Europe into an accomplished fact, brings that question of foreign policy home to your immediate decision, which you cannot more postpone, cannot more delay; because even the very delay of it would be more than a delay; it would be a positise answer given to the expectations of the world, an answer which not only I but all the oppressed nations of the European continent would exactly understand to be so much as to say: *the people of the United States, in its private capacity has good wishes for the freedom of the European continent; but in its public capacity as a power on earth, it declares not to care about it if the public laws of nations are respected or violated by the interference of the strong arm of a foreign power, oppressing the spirit of freedom in whatever country.*

Well, gentlemen, may be that if it is the will of the sovereign people of the United States to give such an answer to the expresions and hopes of the world, you will see a mournful tear in the eye of humanity, and its heart heaving with a sorrowful sigh; but the answer must be accepted, of course; you are mighty and powerful enough not to care about the laws of nations, the expression of my down-trodden land, and about the farewell of freedom on the European continent. You may answer thus, if you please. I have said that by declining to be willing now to allow (speaking in the very terms of your President) *that the strong arm of a foreign power should repress the spirit of freedom* in any country, by declining to be willing now to allow that the laws of nations in which you have the same interest as a private individual in the laws of his own country, should be violated by the armed interference of foreign powers with the sovereign right of every man to dispose of his own domestic concerns. Well, you may answer me, that you don't believe me, that you are not conscious of your power, that you fear Russia, that you know that Russia does not fear you and will not respect your word; that you will rather be on friendly terms with the Czar, than rejoice in the liberty and independence of Hungary, Italy, Germany, France.

I am on my way to Washington. If the Congress adjourns its decision in respect to your policy pointed out to its consideration by the President of the United States – if your National Government delays to answer my humble request, I will understand it – it is a negative.

So much is done. History had seconded my humble requests, and history is recording the answer of the people, Congress and Government of the United States. No answer at all will be also recorded. It is an answer too clear to be misunderstood.

My task here is nearly done. It was a duty imposed upon me by Providence, by the confidence of nations, by the voice of peoples from Sweden down to Italy; and from Hungary across to Portugal, by the expectations caused on my liberation by your gracious aid. The confidence may fail – the voice of Europe die like the sound of the wanderer's step in the desert, and the expectations turn out to have been in vain. I am in the hands of God, and no man is too humble to become an instrument in the hands of Providence, if it be God's will. So I have done what it was my duty to do. So much at least nobody can lay to my charge, that I have not dealt fairly, and openly, or left any doubt as to what I wish, request, and humbly ask. I am in Philadelphia, the city of Brotherly Love, the city founded by William Penn, whose likeness I saw this day in a history of your city, with this motto under it, "Si vis Pacem para bellum," (prepare for war if thou wilt have peace.)

A weighty memento indeed, joined to the name of William Penn; and I am in that city which is the cradle of your independence; where, in the hour of need, the appeal was proclaimed to the laws of nature and of nature's God, and the appeal for help from Europe, which was granted to you. I stood in the Independence Hall, whence the spirit of freedom is whispering eternal words of history to the secret recesses of your hearts. Man may well be silent when from such a place history so speaks. So my task is done – with me the pain, with you the decision, and, let me add with the poet, "the moral of the strain."

When Kossuth finished his speech, the whole company rose spontaneously, and gave him the most prolonged and enthusiastic cheering.

Kossuth's Speech at Baltimore

He arrived at Baltimore on Saturday afternoon; and, after his public reception; addressed the citizens. The following is a synopsis of the speech, embracing all that is new or of interest.

After some expressions of thanks – as Kossuth only can thank – to the authorities and citizens of Baltimore, for their generous sympathy and encouraging promises, he proceeded to speak of the foreign policy of nations, and argued that the neutrality policy which some uphold as the peculiar foreign policy of the United States is no policy at all – because a foreign policy is not to have no *concern* with other nations, but to have some *concern*.

But a nation must have a foreign policy, unless it is content to cease to exist as a powerful nation – and that policy can be neither indifference nor neutrality. A great nation cannot seclude itself from intercourse, and from being interested in the concerns of other nations. You cannot help, said Kossuth, the United States cannot help, feeling the influence of the condition of Europe at home. The peace or the war, the civilization or the barbarism, the freedom or the oppression, the happiness or the distress, the progress or the stagnation of Europe, cannot fail to react upon you – as your freedom or oppression, your civilization or your barbarism, your stagnation or your progress, must of course react upon the European continent. There is a link in destinies of mankind from which no man in the world can separate himself. You therefore cannot remain indifferent to the condition of that Europe.

Kossuth proceeded to speak of the present condition of Europe, and of Louis Napoleon's treason, as prompted by the despotic powers of Austria and Russia. The Revolution in Europe is already broken out – the first blow of revolution is struck, and no man in the world has power to stop its progress. Its vibration will be felt throughout Europe, and nowhere with more resolution than in my poor down-trodden fatherland. (Applause.)

Gov. K. then entered into an explanation of the reasons Hungary had for renewing the contest for freedom. Civil and religious freedom is destroyed in Hungary by Austria. There is no freedom of the Press – no Press at all now. We have had freedom: we established freedom – entire religious liberty – equal protection to whatever religion, to whatever cause. Now there is equal oppression for all. The Protestant Church had its own self government for its own Churches and schools, now it is taken from it. The Catholic Church had its own power to dispose of its temporary affairs – now that is taken from it, and day by day the nearly bankrupt Austrian Government is encroaching upon the property of the Catholic Church, which is considered as the best means to get up a new loan. That is the condition of the Catholic Church, of which it is with high gratification that I, a Protestant not only by birth but also by conviction, declare that when we struggled for a lifetime for religious liberty in Hungary, we had that church in the foremost rank of the struggle for the rights of our Protestant religion. (Great applause.)

So much do we value the freedom of conscience, that the single thought that a Protestant has lost his religious liberty equally with the Catholic, or that those who profess the faith of Moses are excluded from the rights of citizenship, because of their religion – this very circumstance will be sufficient for us Hungarians or Magyars to carry on the war as long as there is a single drop of blood in our veins. (Applause.)

I have succeeded in my efforts to make the agriculture in Hungary free, and to transform the peasants into entirely free proprietors of the soil which they cultivate. Now the government of Austria is again introducing feudal rights, under different pretexts, in several parts of Hungary, and when we freed the people and the peasants of Hungary, we did not touch any material right of whatever class; but we declared that the nation would give indemnification to landlords who lost by the reform laws any of the rights – any of the oppressive rights – which they held upon the peasantry. Now Austria, by heavy taxation, takes from the people its very life's sweat, and out of this the people's treasure itself. It is giving the indemnification which we promised, not out of the people's pocket, because we all know that freedom is a right for which the people have nothing to pay. The nation has other treasures out of which to make such indemnification. Now Austria takes it out of the pockets of the people, and the landlords will not collect the indemnification, except only a few of them who are most faithful to the oppression of the Austrian despot. (Applause.) Therefore, you see, the Protestants and Catholics, every religious party, and the peasantry and landlords, are equally interested not to endure the present condition of Austrian oppression.

We have in Hungary large property of the State itself which we declared by law, we would divide among the peasantry, because we considered no government to be a good agriculturist, mechanic or tradesman. That is no business of the government. It must be left to private individuals, to private industry; therefore we declared that we would divide the property among those who had no landed property, who should pay a moderate price for it, by-and-by, through facilities offered them by a banking system, and that out of that price we would pay the landlords for their lost rights. Now, of course this landed property cannot be given by the Austrian Government to those who have nothing, because Austria wants every foot of land to support its existence by means of loans.

Again you have a class interested in the revolution of Hungary. We had to provide for the necessity of our past struggles by an issue of paper money – the Kossuth Bank Notes, as it was called. It was some $33,000,000. Now, out of these thirty-three millions, twenty millions are yet in sacred trust by the people, who will in no case let it pass out of their hands. All these twenty millions can be of no value except in a new revolution and new independence, because Austria will not recognize its establishment.

Kossuth spoke further on the taxation of Hungary. Before Russia interfered to enslave it, the taxation was only four and a half millions of dollars; now it is sixteen millions. Then there were no duties on tobacco, now Austria has taken a monopoly of the trade, and the people of Hungary, with whom, heretofore, smoking was almost indispensable, have abandoned smoking. It has burned its tobacco as your fathers formerly threw in the water the tea which was imposed upon them by taxation, (laughter and applause,) and will neither produce tobacco nor buy it from the oppressor. There is a heavy taxation laid upon the production of wine, amounting to twenty millions of dollars annually. Now the people prefer to cut down its vines than to endure the heavy taxation. Even our fruitful trees are cut down rather than endure the taxation. Such is the condition of Hungary. The Magyars love freedom. We have a heart in our breast, and we have armies ready to shed the last blood of that heart for the freedom and independence of our fatherland. (Applause.) Therefore you see that a revolution in Hungary is unavoidable.

He then went on to say that without freedom in Hungary there could be no freedom in Europe – Hungary oppressed, the Continent becomes Cossack. Catholics and Protestants are alike oppressed under the hands of Russia.

Kossuth then wound up by submitting his three great propositions. First, that the U. States should uphold the doctrine of non-interference, and show Hungary fair play. Second, that it should protect the freedom of commerce to its citizens with all parts of the world, so that this commerce might not suffer at the will of despots who may be at war with their subjects, or with each other. And third, that it should recognize the Hungarian Declaration of Independence as a legitimate thing, and the right of the people to exist and act as an Independent nation.

On the subject of material aid, Kossuth thus spoke: – I pray that the generosity of the American citizens will furnish me with the means to be somewhat better prepared for that war which we will fight, even if forced to fight with only our nails. (Great laughter.) But, suppose that your private generosity provides me with the means to furnish some preparation to my nation for that indispensable war, may I not be permitted to buy with this money, which you give for the benefit of Hungary, some ships built here in Baltimore, and put upon these ships some cannon, cast here, or some hundred weight of powder from Wilmington, to blow up the despots in the air, (great cheers,) or some cotton to guard our breasts against the chill wintry campaign? Why may I not be permitted to buy this, if you are willing to sell to me and I am willing and have the means to pay?

Now it is not permitted to make this commerce with me. The Emperor of Austria may come and buy ships, powder, cannon, muskets, everything; but oppressed nations have not the right, even for ready money, to buy these means, for their self defense. (Applause.) I would humbly ask, is such a commerce founded upon the principle of the eternal rights of men? I answer, No. Freedom of commerce is, that when you find any market in the world ready to accept your merchandise, you should not be excluded from that market to sell what you have. Commerce must be restored to the basis of those principles which are your rights because you may dispose of your own domestic concerns, and nobody in the world has a right to interfere with them, and the intercourse of nations with you. That is a common right of Hungary.

I have spoken of ships, and muskets, and cannon, and powder of Wilmington. I beg leave not to be misunderstood. I am told it would not be lawful for me to buy these things. Of course I will obey; because, the law has to command, and I will not only respect it, but will not evade it, and I only want humbly to entreat the people of the United States to be pleased to look to those laws, and perhaps if you should find them not quite convenient to your own interest, to make with constitutional means – with the same means by which you make other laws – such changes as will allow the Emperor of Austria to buy what he pleases and also to allow the oppressed nations to buy what they require. You are ready to sell them. (Applause.) For this purpose, I humbly entreat that the people of the United States may be pleased to restore the word sovereignty to that place where it must stand. You must recognize that the word sovereignty can only rest in the people of whatever country, and that there is no other sovereignty than the people's will. That is the principle upon which you stand; and therefore you must recognize it also with respect to other nations, for it is a logical consequence of your own existence.

My humble wish is that public opinion may pronounce whether it is willing or not willing to bestow anything upon the cause of Hungary. The question cannot be delayed, because delay is a negative. But if you are willing to do something for Hungary, then do not delay, because, if you do, your help will come too late.

Kossuth then averted to the adoption of resolutions by the citizens of Harrisburgh and Philadelphia, endorsing and supporting his three requests. I received more, said he, in Philadelphia – I was told that when war breaks out for Hungary's freedom and independence, I will find brave hearts and stout arms among the twenty-four millions of the people of the United States to go over to Europe and fight side by side in the great battle for the freedom and independence of the European continent. (Great applause.) I was told that it was not possible, when the battle for mankind's liberty is fought; for the sword of Washington to rest in its scabbard. That sword, which struck the first blow here on this continent for the Republican freedom of this great country, must be present there, where the last stroke for all humanity will be given. (Great cheering.)

I will only say, that should this be the generous will of the people of the United States, in the name of the honor of my nation, I can give the assurance that the Hungarians will be found worthy to fight side by side with you, for civil and political freedom on the European continent. And now may the ladies who have honored me with their presence, graciously allow me to express to them my most humble thanks and one humble prayer. The destinies of mankind – the future of humanity repose in the hands of womankind. Ladies of the United States, when the wandering exile passes away from your presence, take to your kind care the great cause of the liberty of the world with the tenderness with which a mother takes care of her child; and when you take care of this great cause, the sympathy of the people of the United States will not vanish like the passing emotion of the heart, but will become substantial, active and operative.

The speaker then took his seat, with three times three from the audience.

Kossuth at the Capital of the United States

This great chieftain and philanthropist reached the City of Washington about the last of December, 1851; and notwithstanding the strong influence against him, caused by the Austrian and Russian ministers; was received with great enthusiasm. He was soon waited upon by Hon. Daniel Webster and other dignitaries.

Kossuth's Introduction to President Fillmore

Hon. Daniel Webster, Secretary of State, presented the great Magyar Statesman to the President, Jan. 3, 1852, and Kossuth made the following address:

Kossuth's Speech to President Fillmore

Mr. President – Enlightened by the spirit of your country's institutions, when we succeeded to consolidate our natural and historical State's right of self government, by placing it upon the broad foundation of democratic liberty:

Inspired by your history when we had to fight for independence against annihilation by centrailzed absolutism:

Consoled by your people's sympathy when a victim of Russian interference with the laws of Nature and of Nature's God:

Protected in exile by the government of the United States supporting the Sultan of Turkey in his noble resolution to undergo the very danger of a war, rather than leave unprotected the rights of humanity against Russo–Austrian despotism:

Restored by the United States to life because restored to freedom, and by freedom to activity in behalf of those duties which, by my nation's unanimous confidence and sovereign will, devolved upon me:

Raised in the eyes of many oppressed nations to the standard of a harbinger of hope, because the star-spangled banner was seen casting protection around me, announcing to the world that there is a nation, alike powerful as free, ready to protect the laws of nations, even in distant parts of the earth:

Cheered by your people's sympathy, so as freemen cheer – not a man whatever, but a principle:

I now bow before you, sir, in the proud position of your great nation's guest, generously welcomed by a resolution of the Congress af the United States, with equal generosity approved and executed by your Excellency.

I beg leave to express my fervent thanks, in my name, and in the name of my associates; who, after having shared my misfortunes, have now the reward to share the honor and the benefit which the great republic of the United States was pleased to bestow upon Hungary, by bestowing it upon its freely chosen chief when he became a persecuted victim of despotic violence.

I beg leave to express my fervent thanks in my country's name also, which, amidst the sorrows of its desolation, feels cheered by your country's generosity, and looks with resolution to the impending future, because it is confident that the time draws near when the eternal code of the law of nations will become a reality.

President! I stand before your Excellency a living protestation against the violence of foreign interference oppressing the sovereign right of nations to regulate their own domestic concerns.

I stand before your Excellency a living protestation against centralization oppressing the State right of self-government.

May I be allowed to take it for an augury of better times, that in landing on the happy shores of this glorious republic I landed in a free and powerful country, whose honored Chief Magistrate proclaims to the world that this country cannot remain indifferent when the strong arm of a foreign power is invoked to stifle public sentiment, and repress the spirit of freedom in any country.

I thank God that He deemed me not unworthy to act and to suffer for my fatherland.

I thank God that the fate of my country became so intimately connected with the fate of liberty and independence of nations in Europe, as formerly it was intimately connected with the security of Christendom.

I thank God that my country's unmerited woe, and my personal sufferings, became an opportunity to seek a manifestation of the spirit and principles of your Republic.

May God the Almighty bless you with a long life, that you may long enjoy the happiness to see your country great, glorious, and free, the corner-stone of international justice, and the column of freedom on the earth, as it is already an asylum to the oppressed.

Sir, I pledge to your country the everlasting gratitude of Hungary.

President Fillmore's Reply to Kossuth

I am happy, Governor Kossuth, to welcome you to this land of freedom; and it gives me pleasure to congratulate you upon your release from a long confinement in Turkey, and your safe arrival here. As an individual, I sympathized deeply with you; in your brave struggle for the independence and freedom of your native land. The American people can never be indifferent to such a contest, but our policy as a nation in this respect has been uniform from the commencement of our government; and my own views as the Chief Executive magistrate of this nation, are fully and freely expressed in my recent message to Congress, to which you have been pleased to allude. They are the same, whether speaking to Congress here, or to the nations of Europe.

Should your country be restored to independence and freedom, I should then wish you – as the greatest blessing you could enjoy – a restoration to your native land; but should that never happen, I can only repeat my welcome to you and your companions here, and pray that God's blessing may rest upon you wherever your lot may be cast.

The same day, (Jan. 3,) by previous invitation, L. Kossuth dined with the President.

Kossuth's Reception by Congress

Both Houses of Congress having almost unanimously voted to give the Governor a public reception, Jan 5th was fixed upon for the ceremony, in the Senate.

Long before 10 o'clock, every avenue leading to the Senate chamber was thronged with persons anxious to witness the reception.

At 11 the galleries were open, and, amidst great tumult and confusion, were immediately filled to their utmost capacity.

Mr. Mangum moved that the rules be suspended so far as to admit ladies behind the bar of the Senate, which was agreed to.

Madame Kossuth here, entered, leaning on Mr. Gwinn's arm; and M. Pulszky led in the other ladies of the suite.

At one o'clock, Messrs. Shields, Seward, and Cass entered with Kossuth, who was leaning on the arm of Mr. Shields.

Mr. Shields said – Mr. President, we have the honor to announce Louis Kossuth to the Senate of the United States.

The Chair invited Kossuth to a seat placed in front of the secretary's desk. The Senators then rose, and Kossuth advanced to the seat, and sat down.

Mr. Mangum – In order that Senators and all others may have an opportunity of paying their respects to our illustrious guest, I move that the senate now adjourn. Agreed to, and the Senate adjourned.

A crowd then advanced and were introduced to Kossuth by Messrs. Seward and Shields.

On Jan. 7th, Kossuth was received in a similar manner by the House of Representatives.

Kossuth's Speech in the House of Representatives of the U. States

The following are Kossuth's remarks in reply to Speaker Boyd, in the House of Representatives, when introduced to that body on Wednesday.

"Sir: It is a remarkable fact in the history of mankind, that while through all the past, honors were bestowed upon glory, and glory was attached only to success, the Legislative Authorities of this great Republic bestowed honors upon a persecuted exile, not conspicious by glory, not favored by success, but engaged in a just cause. There is a triumph of Republican principles in this fact. Sir, I thank, in my own and my country's name, the House of Representatives of the United States, for the honor of this cordial welcome."

Congressional Banquet to Kossuth at Washington

About 300 persons were present in the National Hotel. The dining Hall was handsomely decorated with flags, etc.

A raised table in the centre of the room was appropriated to the Hon. W.R. King, (President of the Senate,) who presided – with Kossuth and Speaker Boyd at the right, and the Hon. Daniel Webster on the left. Secretaries Corwin and Stuart, Judge Wayne, General Houston, Mr. Seward and other distinguished men occupied seats in the vicinity of the chair.

The first toast was – The President of the United States.

After the fifth toast was given, by Hon. W. R. King, Kossuth replied as follows.

Kossuth's Great Speech before the Congressional Banquet

SIR: As once Cyneas, the Epirote, stood among the Senators of Rome, who, with an earnest word of self conscious majesty, controlled the condition of the world and arrested the mighty kings in their ambitious march, thus full of admiration and of reverence, I stand before you, Legislators of the new capital – that glorious hall of your people's collective majesty. The Capitol of old yet stands, but the spirit has departed from it and come over to yours, purified by the air of liberty. The old stands a mournful monument of the fragility of human things – yours as a sanctuary of eternal rights. The old beamed with the red lustre of conquest; now darkened by oppression's gloomy night – yours beams with freedom's bright ray. The old absorbed the world by its own centralized glory – yours protects your own nation against absorption, even by itself. The old was awful with irrestricted power – yours is glorious with having restricted it. At the view of the old, nations trembled – at the view of yours, humanity hopes. To the old, misfortune was only introduced with fettered hands to kneel at the triumphant conqueror's heels – to yours, the triumph of introduction is granted to unfortunate exiles, invited to the honor of a seat, and where kings and caesars never are hailed for their powers, might, and wealth, there the persecuted chief of a down-trodden nation is welcomed as your great Republic's guest, precisely because he is persecuted helpless, and poor.

In the old, the terrible vae victis was the rule – in yours, protection to the oppressed, malediction to ambitious oppressors, and consolation to the vanquished in a just cause. And while, out of the old, a conquered world was ruled, you in yours provide for the common confederative interests of a territory larger than the conquered world of the old, there sat men boasting their will to be the sovereign of the world: here sit men whose glory is to acknowledge the laws of Nature and of Nature's God, and to do what their sovereign, the people, wills. Sir, there is history in these parallels. History of past ages, and history of future centuries may be often recorded in few words. The small particulars to which the passion of living men cling with fervent zeal – as if the fragile fingers of men could arrest the rotation of destiny's wheel; these particulars die away. It is the issue which makes history, and that issue is always logical. There is a necessity of consequences wherever the necessity of position exists. Principles are the Alpha; they must finish with Omega, and they will. Thus history may be told often in few words. Before yet the heroic struggle of Greece first engaged your country's sympathy for the fate of freedom in Europe, then so far distrant, and now so near, Chateaubriand happened to be in Athens, and he heard from a minaret raised upon the Propylaean ruins, a Turkish priest, in Arabic language, announcing the lapse of hours to the Christians of Minerva's town. What immense history in the small fact of a Turkish Imaum crying out, "Pray, man, the hour is running fast, and the judgment draws near."

Sir, there is equally a history of future ages written in the honor bestowed by you to my humble self. The first Governor of independent Hungary, driven from his native land by Russian violence, an exile on Turkish soil, protected by a Mohammedan Sultan against the blood-thirst of Christian tyrants, cast back a prisoner to far Asia, by diplomacy, rescued from his Asiatic prison by America, crossing the Atlantic, charged with the hopes of Europe's oppressed nations, pleading, a poor exile, before the people of this great Republic, his down-trodden country's wrongs, and its intimate connection with the fate of the European continent, and with the boldness of a just cause, claiming the principles of the Christian religion to be raised to a law of nations; and to see not only the boldness of the poor exile forgiven, but to see him consoled by the sympathy of millions. Encouraged by individuals, associations, meetings, cities and states, supported by operative aid, and greeted by Congress and by the Government as the Nation's guest, honored out of generosity, with that honor which only one man before him received – and that man received then out of gratitude – with honors such as no potentate ever can receive, and this banquet here, and the toast which I have to thank for – oh, indeed, sir, there is a history of future ages in all these facts. Sir, though I have the noble pride of my principles, and though I have the inspiration of a just cause, still I have also the conscience of my personal humility. Never will I forget what is due from me to the sovereign source of my public capacity. This I owe to my nation's dignity, and, therefore, respectfully thanking this highly distinguished assembly, in my country's name, I have the boldness to say that Hungary well deserves your sympathy – that Hungary has a claim to protection, because it has a claim to justice. But as to myself, permit me humbly to express that I am well aware not to have in all these honors any personal share. Nay, I know that even that which might seem to be personal in your toast, is only an acknowledgment of a historical fact, very instructively connected with a principle valuable and dear to every republican heart in the United States of America.

Sir, you were pleased to mention in your toast that I am unconquered by misfortune and unseduced by ambition. Now, it is a providential fact; that misfortune has the privilege to ennoble man's mind, and to strengthen man's character. There is a sort of natural instinct of human dignity in the heart of man, which steels his very nerves not to bend beneath the heavy blows of a great adversity. The palm tree grows best beneath a ponderous weight – even so the character of man. There is no merit in it. It is a law of psychology. The petty pangs of small daily cares have often bent the character of men, but great misfortunes seldom. There is less danger in this than in great good luck; and as to ambition, I, indeed, never was able to understand how anybody can more love ambition than liberty. But I am glad to state a historical fact as a principal demonstration of that influence which institutions exercise upon the character of nations. We Hungarians are very fond of the principle of self-government, and we have a natural horror against the principle of centralization. That fond attachment to municipal self-government, without which there is no providential freedom possible, is a fundamental feature of our national character. We brought it with us from far Asia, a thousand years ago, and we conserved it throughout the vicissitudes of ten centuries. No nation has perhaps so much struggled and suffered from the civilized Christian world as ours. We do not complain of this lot. It may be heavy, but it is not inglorious. Where the cradle of our Saviour stood, and where his divine doctrine was founded, there another faith now rules, and the whole of Europe's armed pilgrimage could not avert this fate from that sacred spot, nor stop the rushing waves of Islamism absorbing the Christian Empire of Constantine. We stopped those rushing waves. The breast of my nation proved a breakwater to them. We guarded Christendom, that Luthers or Calvins might reform it. It was a dangerous time and the danger of the time often placed the confidence of all my nation into one man's hand, and their confidence gave power into his hands to become ambitious. But there was not a single instance in history where a man, honored by his people's confidence, had deceived his people by becoming ambitious.

The man out of whom Russian diplomacy succeeded in making the murderer of his nation's confidence – he never had it, but was rather regarded always with distrust. But he gained some victories when victories were the moment's chief necessity. At the head of an army, circumstances placed him in the capacity to ruin his country. But he never had the people's confidence. So, he is even no contradiction to the historical truth, that no Hungarian whom his nation honored with its confidence, was ever seduced by ambition to become dangerous to his country's liberty. That is a remarkable fact, and yet it is not accidental. It is the logical consequence of the influence of institutions upon the national character. Our nation, through all its history, was educated in the school of municipal self government, and in such a country, ambition having no field, has also no place in man's character. The truth of this doctrine becomes yet more illustrated by a quite contrary historical fact in France. Whatever have been the changes of Government in that great country – and many they have been to be sure – we have seen a Convention; a Directorate of Consuls, and one Consul, and an Emperor and the restoration – the fundamental tone of the Constitution of France was power always centralized. Omnipotence always vested somewhere – and remarkable, indeed, France has never yet raised the single man to the seat of power who has not sacrificed his country's freedom to his personal ambition. It is sorrowful, indeed; but it is natural. It is in the garden of centralization where the venemous plant of ambition thrives. I dare confidently affirm that in your great country there exists not a single man through whose brains has ever passed the thought that he would wish to raise the seat of his ambition upon the ruins of your country's liberty. If he could, such a wish is impossible in the United States. Institutions react upon the character of nations.

He who sows the wind will reap the storm. History is the revelation of Providence. The Almighty rules by eternal laws not only the material but the moral world, and every law is a principle, and every principle is a law. Men, as well as nations, are endowed with free will to choose a principle, but that once chosen, the consequences must be abided. With self government is a freedom, and with freedom is justice and patriotism. With centralization is ambition, and with ambition dwells despotism. Happy your great country, sir, for being so warmly addicted to the great principle of self-government. Upon this foundation your father raised a home to freedom more glorious than the world has ever seen. Upon this foundation you have developed it to a living wonder of the world. Happy your great country, sir, that it was selected, by the blessing of the Lord, to prove the glorious practicability of a federative Union of many sovereign States all conserving their State rights and their self government, and yet united in one. Every star beaming with its own lustre; but all together one constellation on mankind's canopy.

Upon this foundation your free country has grown to a prodigious power in a surprisingly brief period. You have attracted power in that. Your fundamental principles have conquered more in seventy-five years than Rome by arms in centuries. Your principles will conquer the world. By the glorious example of your freedom, welfare and security, mankind is about to become conscious of its aim. The lesson you give to humanity will not be lost, and the respect of the State rights in the Federal Government of America and in its several states, will become an instructive example for universal toleration, forbearance of justice, to the future States and Republics of Europe. Upon this basis will be got rid of the mysterious question of language, and nationalities raised by the cunning despotisms in Europe to murder Liberty, and the smaller states will find security in the principles of federative union, while they will conserve their national freedom by the principles of sovereign self-government, and while larger states, abdicating the principles of centralization, will cease to be a bloodfield to sanguinary usurpation and a tool to the ambition of wicked men; municipal institutions will insure the development of local particular elements.

Freedom, formerly an abstract political theory, will become the household benefit to municipalities, and out of the welfare and contentment of all parts will flow happiness, peace and security for the whole. That is my confident hope. There will at once subside the fluctuations of Germany's fate. It will become the heart of Europe, not by melting North Germany into a Southern frame, or the South into a Northern; not by absorbing historical peculiarities by centralized omnipotence; not by mixing in one State, but by federating several sovereign States into a Union like yours, upon a similar basis, will take place the national regeneration of the Slavonic States, and not upon the sacrilegious idea of Panslavism, equivalent to the omnipotence of the Czar. Upon a similar basis will we see fair Italy independent and free. Not Unity, but Union, will and must become the watchword of national bodies, severed into desecrated limbs by provincial rivalries, out of which a flock of despots and common servitude arose. To be sure, it will be a noble joy to this your great Republic, to feel that the moral influence of your glorious example has operated in producing this happy developmnent in mankind's destiny; and I have not the slightest doubt of the efficacy of your example's influence. But there is one thing indispensable to it; without which there is no hope for this happy issue. This indipensable thing is, that the oppressed nations of

Europe become the masters of their future, free to regulate their own domestic concerns; and to secure this, nothing is wanted but to have that fair play to all, and for all, which you, sir, in your toast were pleased to pronounce as a right of my nation, alike sanctioned by the law of nations as by the dictates of eternal justice. Without this fair play, there is no hope for Europe – no hope of seeing your principles spread. Yours is a happy country, gentlemen. You had more than fair play. You had active, operative aid from Europe in your struggle for independence, which, once achieved, you so wisely used as to become a prodigy of freedom and welfare, and a Book of Life to nations. But we, in Europe – we, unhappily, have no such fair play with us, against every palpitation of Liberty.

All despots are united in a common league, and you may be sure despots will never yield the moral influence of your great example. They hate the very existence of this example. It is the sorrow of their thoughts and the incubus of their dreams. To stop its moral influence abroad and to check its spreading development at home, is what they wish instead of yielding to its influence. We will have no fair play. The Cossack already rules by Louis Napoleon's usurpation, to the very borders of the Atlantic Ocean. One of your great statesmen – now to my sorrow bound to the sick bed of advanced age – alas, that I am deprived of the advice which his wisdom could have imparted to me! – your great statesman told the world thirty years ago that Paris was transferred to St. Petersburg. What would he now say, when St. Petersburg is transferred to Paris, and Europe is but an appendix to Russia? Alas! Europe can no longer secure to Europe fair play. Albion only remains, but even Albion casts a sorrowful glance over the waves. Still we will stand our place, sink or swim, live or die. You know the word. It is your own. We will follow it. It will be a bloody path to tread. Despots have conspired against the world. Terror spreads over Europe, and anticipating persecution rules from Paris to Pesth. There is a gloomy silence like the silence of nature before the terrors of a hurricane. It is a sensible silence, only disturbed by the thousand-fold rattling of the muskets by which Napoleon murders the people which gave him a home when he was an exile, and by the groans of new martyrs in Sicily, Milan, Vienna and Pesth. The very sympathy which I met in England, and was expected to meet here, throws my sisters into the dungeons of Austria. Well, God's will be done. The heart may break, but duty will be done. We will stand in our place, though to us in Europe there will be no fair play. But so much I hope, that no just man on earth can charge me with unbecoming arrogance, when here, on this sod of freedom, I kneel down and raise my prayer to God – "Almighty Father of Humanity, will thy merciful arm not raise a power on earth to protect the law of nations, when there are so many to violate it?" It is a prayer, and nothing else. What would remain to the oppressed if they were not permitted to pray. The rest is in the hand of God.

Gentlemen, I know where I stand. No honor, no encouraging generosity will make me ever forget where I stand, and what is due from me to you. Here my duty is silently to await what you or your wisdom will be pleased to pronounce about that which public opinion knows to be my prayer and my aim; and be it your will to pronounce, or be it your will not to take notice of it, I will understand your will, and bow before it with devotion – hopeless, perhaps, but my heart full of admiration, love and gratitude to your generous people, to your glorious land. But one single word, even here, I may be permitted to say – only such a word as may secure me from being misunderstood. I came to the noble-minded people of the United States to claim its generous, operative sympathy for the impending struggle of oppressed freedom on the European Continent, and I freely interpreted the hopes and wishes which these oppressed nations entertain; but as to your great Republic, as a State, as a power on earth, I stand before the Statesmen, Senators and Legislators of that Republic, only to ascertain from their wisdom and experience what is there judgment upon a question of national law and international right. I hoped and now hope that they will, by the foreboding events on the other great continent, feel induced to pronounce in time their vote about that law and those rights, and I hoped and hope that pronouncing their vote, it will be in favor of the broad principles of international justice, and consonant with their republican institutions and their democratic life.

That is all I know and Europe knows: – the immense weight of such a pronunciation from such a place. But never had I the impious wish to try to entangle this great Republic into difficulties inconsistent with its own welfare; its own security, its own interest. I rather repeatedly and earnestly declared, that a war on this account, by your country, is utterly impossible, and a mere phantom. I always declared that the United States remained masters of their actions, and under every circumstance will act as they judge consistent with the supreme duties to themselves. But I said and say that such a declaring of just principles would insure the nations of Europe fair play in the struggle for freedom and independence, because the declaration of such power as your Republic will be respected even where it is not liked: and Europe's oppressed nations will feel cheered in resolution and doubled in strength, to maintain the decision of their American brethren on their own behalf with their own lives. There is an immense power in the idea to be right, when this idea is sanctioned by a nation like yours, and when the foreboding future will become present; there is an immense field for private benevolence and sympathy, upon the basis of the broad principles of international justice pronounced in the sanctuary of your people's collective majority. So much to guard me against misunderstanding.

Sir, I most fervently thank you for the acknowledgment that my country has proved worthy to be free. Yes, gentlemen, I feel proud of my nation's character, heroism, love of freedom and vitality, and I bow with reverential awe before the decree of Providence which placed my country into a position, that without its restoration to independence, there is no possibility for freedom and the independence of nations on the European continent. Even what now in France is about to pass, proves the truth of this. Every disappointed hope with which Europe looked towards France is a degree more added to the importance of Hungary to the world. Upon our plains were fought the decisive battles for Christendom. There will be fought the decisive battle for the independence of nations, for state rights, for international law, and for Democratic liberty. We will live free, or die like men; but should my people be doomed to die, it will be the first whose death will not be recorded as a suicide, but as a martydom for the world; and future ages will mourn over the sad fate of the Magyar race, doomed to perish; not because we deserved it, but because, in the nineteenth century, there was nobody to protect the laws of nature and of nature's God; but to look to the future with confidence and with hope. Adversities, manifold, of a tempest-tossed life, could, of course, not fail to import a mark of cheerfulness upon my heart; which if not a source of joy, is at least a guaranty against sanguine illusions. I, for myself would not want the hope of success for doing what is right to me. The sense of duty would suffice. Therefore, when I hope, it has nothing in common with that desperate instinct of a drowning man, who, half sunk, is still grasping at a straw for help. No; when I hope, there is motive for that hope. I have a steady faith in principles. I dare say that experience taught me the logic of events, in connection with principles. I have fathomed the entire bottom of this mystery, and was, I perceive, right in my calculations there, about once in my life. I supposed a principle to exist in a certain quarter, where, indeed, no principle proves to exist. It was a horrible mistake, and resulted in a horrible issue.

The present condition of Europe is a very consequence of it; but precisely this condition of Europe proves I did not wantonly suppose a principle to exist there, where I found none would have existed. The consequences could not have failed to arrive as I have contemplated them well. There is a providence in every fact. Without this mistake, the principles of American republicanism would, for a long time yet, find a sterile soil on that continent where it was considered wisdom to belong to the French school. Now matters stand thus: That either the continent of Europe has no future at all, or this future is American Republicanism. And who could believe that three hundred millions of that continent, which is the mother of civilization, are not to have any future at all? Such a doubt would be almost blasphemy against Providence. But there is a Providence indeed – a just a bountiful Providence – I trust, with the piety of my religion, in it; I dare say my very humble self was a continual instrument of it. How could I be else in such a condition as I was – born not conspicious by any prominent abilities? Having nothing in me, more than an iron will which nothing can bend, and the consciousness of being right – how could I, under the most arduous circumstances, accomplish many a thing which my sense of honest duty prompted me to undertake?

Oh, there is indeed a Providence which rules, even in my being here, when four months ago I was yet a prisoner of the league of European despots, in far Asia, and the sympathy which your glorious people honor me with, and the high benefit of the welcome of your Congress, and the honor to be your guest – to be the guest of your great Republic – I, the poor, humble, unpretending exile – is there not – a very intelligible manifestation of Providence in it? The more when I remember that the name of your humble, but thankful guest, is, by the furious rage of the Austrian tyrant to the gallows nailed.

Your generosity is great; and loud your patriotism of republican principles against despotism. I firmly trust to those principles; and relying upon this very fact of your generosity, I may be permitted to say that that respectable organ of the free press may be mistaken, which announced that I considered my coming hither to be a failure. I confidently trust that the nations of Europe have a future. I am aware that the future is contradicted. Bayonets may support, but afford no chair to sit upon. I trust to the future of my native land, because I know that it is worthy to have it;

and it is necessary to the destinies of humanity. I trust to the principles of republicanism, whatever may be my personal fate. So much I know, that my country will remember you and your glorious land with everlasting gratitude.

Hon. Daniel Webster's able Speech at the Congressional Banquet

Mr. Granger gave the following toast:
The Secretary of State – "His sympathies are as broad as his intellect is profound."
Mr. Webster rose and responded as follows:
I have great pleasure in participating in this festival. It is a remarkable occasion. He who is your honored guest tonight has led thus far a life of events that are viewed as highly important here, and still more important to his own country. Educated, spirited, full of feeling, of liberty and independence, he entered early into the public councils of his native country, and he is here today, fresh from acting his part in the great struggle for Hungarian national independence. That is not all this distinction. He was brought to these shores by the authority of Congress. He has been welcomed to the capital of the United States by the votes of the two Houses of Congress.
Mr. Seward. (interrupting) "He is welcome!" and there were loud cries of "Welcome! Welcome!" from various parts of the room.
Mr. Webster, (resuming) – I agree, as I am not connected with either branch of the Legislature, in joining, and I do join in my loudest tone, in that welcome pronounced by them to him. (Great applause.) The House of Representatives – the immediate representatives of the people – full themselves of an ardent love of liberty, have joined in that welcome; the wisdom and sobriety of the Senate have joined in it; and the head of the Republic, with the utmost cordiality, has approved of whatsoever official act was necessary to bid him welcome to these shores, and he stands here to-night in the midst of an assembly of both Houses of Congress, and others of us met here in our individual capacity, to join the general acclaim, and signify to him with what pleasure we receive him to the shores of this free land – this asylum of oppressed humanity.
Gentlemen, the effect of the reception thus given him cannot but be felt. It cannot but have its influence beyond the ocean, and among

countries where our principles and our sentiments are either generally unknown or generally disliked. Let them go forth; let it be borne on all the winds of heaven, that the sympathies of the Government of the United States, and all the people of the United States, have been attracted toward a nation struggling for national independence, and toward those of her sons who have most distinguished themselves in that struggles (Great applause.) I have said that this cannot be without its effect. We are too much inclined to underrate the power of moral influence, and the influence of public opinion, and the influence of principles, to which great men, the lights of the world and of the age, have given their sanction.

Who doubts that, in our own struggle for liberty and independence, the majestic eloquence of Chatham, the profound reasoning of Burke, the burning satire and irony of Colonel Barre, had influence upon our fortunes here in America? They had influence both ways. They tended, in the first place, somewhat to diminish the confidence of the British Ministry in their hopes of success in attempting to subjugate an injured people. They had influence another way, because all along the coasts of the country – and all our people in that day lived upon the coast there was not a reading man who did not feel stronger, bolder, and more determined in the assertion of his rights, when these exhilarating accounts from the two Houses of Parliament reached him from beyond the seas. He felt that those who held and controlled public opinion elsewhere were with us; that their words of eloquence might produce an effect in the region where they were uttered; and, above all, they assured them that, in the judgment of the just, and the wise, and the impartial, their cause was just, and they were right; and therefore they said, we will fight it out to the last. (Applause.)

Now, gentlemen, another great mistake is sometimes made. We think that nothing is powerful enough to stand before autocratic, monarchical or despotic power. There is something strong enough, quite strong enough, and if properly exerted, will prove itself so; and that is the power of intelligent public opinion in all the nations of the earth. There is not a monarch on earth whose throne is not liable to be shaken by the progress of opinion, and the sentiment of the just and intelligent part of the people. It becomes us, in the station which we hold, to let that public opinion, so far as we form it, have a free course. (Bravo, bravo.) Let it go out; let it be pronounced in thunder tones; let it unstop the ears of the deaf; let it open the eyes of the blind; and let it everywhere be proclaimed what we of this great Republic think of the general principle of human liberty, and of that oppression which all abhor. (Applause.)

Depend upon it, gentlemen, that between these two rival powers, the autocratic power maintained by arms and force, and the popular power maintained by opinion, the former is constantly decreasing, and, thank God, the latter is constantly increasing. (Applause.) Real human liberty and human rights are gaining the ascendent; and the part which we have to act in all this great drama is to show ourselves in favor of those rights, to uphold our ascendency and to carry it on until we shall see it culminate in the highest heaven over our heads. (Applause.) On topics, gentlemen, which this occasion seems to invite, I have nothing to say, because, in the course of my political life – not now a short one – I have said all that I wish to say, and all that I wish to transmit to, posterity connected with my own name and history. What I said of Greece twenty-five years ago, when our friend was too young to be in political life, I repeat tonight, *verbum Post verbum*, exactly what I said then. (Great applause.)

What I said of Spain at a later period, when the power of the restored Bourbons was exerted to impose upon Spain a dynasty not wished by the people of Spain, that I repeat in English and Spanish, and French, and in every other language, if they choose to translate it. (Applause.) May I be so egotistical as to say that I have nothing new to say upon the Subject of Hungary? Gentlemen, in the autumn of the before last, out of health, and retired to my paternal home among the mountains of New Hampshire, I was, by reason of my physical condition, confined to my house; but I was among the mountains, whose native air I was born to inspire. Nothing saluted my senses, nothing saluted my mind or my sentiments, but freedom, full and entire, (Applause,) and there, gentlemen, near the graves of my ancestors, I wrote a letter, which most of you have seen, addressed to the Austrian charge d'affaires. (Great applause, which was continued for some time.)

I can say nothing of the ability displayed in that letter; but as to its principles, while the sun and moon endure, and while I can see the light of the sun and the moon, I stand by them. (Great applause.) In a letter, dated February last, moved by those considerations which have influenced all the Christian world, making no particular merit of it, I addressed a letter to the American Minister at Constantinople, at the Court of the Sublime Porte, for the release of M. Kossuth and his companions in exile; and I happen to know that the letter was not without some effect. At any rate, it is proper for me here to say, that this letter, and that one to which I have before alluded, were despatched with the cordial-approbation of the President, of the United States. It was, therefore, so far the act of the Government of the United States in its executive capacity. Now, I shall not further advert to these topics tonight, nor shall I go back to ancient times, and discuss the provisions of the Holy Alliance; but I say that, in the sentiments avowed by me, I think in the year 1823 and 1824, in the cause of Greece, and in the more subsequent declarations of opinion, there is that which I can never part from without departing from myself. I should cease to be what I am if I were to retract a single sentiment which has been espressed on those several occasions.

Now, gentlemen, I do not propose, at this hour of the night, to entertain you, or to attempt to entertain you by any general disquisition upon the value of human freedom, upon the inalienable rights of man, or upon any general topic of that kind; but I wish to say a few words upon the precise question as I understand it, that exists before the civilized world, between Hungary and the Austrian Government. I wish to arrange the thoughts to which I desire to give utterance under two or three general heads.

And, in the first place, I say that wherever there is in the Christian and civilized world a nationality of character – wherever there exists a nation of sufficient knowledge, and wealth, and population, to constitute a Government – then a national Government is a necessary and proper result of a nationality of character. We may talk of it as we please, but there is nothing that satisfies the human mind in an enlightened age, unless man is governed by his own country and the institutions of his own Government. No matter how easy may be the yoke of a foreign power – no matter how lightly it sits upon the shoulders, if it is not imposed by the voice of his own nation and of his own country, he will not, he cannot, and he means not to be happy under its burden. (Applause.)

There is gentlemen, the great element of human happiness mixed up with others. We have our social affections, our family affections; but then we have this sentiment of our country, which imbues all our hearts and enters into all our other feelings; and this sentiment of country is an affection not only for the soil on which we were born, it not only appertains to our parents, and sisters, and brothers, and friends, but our habits and institutions, and to the government of that country in all respects. There is not a civilized and intelligent man on earth, that enjoys entire satisfaction in this condition, if he does not live under the government of his own nation – his own country, whose volitions, and sentiments, and sympathies, are like his own. Hence he cannot say, "This is not my country; it is the country of another power; it is a country belonging to somebody else." Therefore, I say, that wherever there is a nation of sufficient intelligence, and numbers, and wealth to maintain a government, distinguished in its character, and its history, and its institutions, that nation cannot be happy but under a government of its own choice. (Applause.)

Then, sir, the next question is whether Hungary, as she exists in our ideas, as we see her, and as we know her, is distinct in her nationality, is competent in her knowledge and devotion to correct sentiment, is competent in her national capacity for liberty and independence; to maintain a government that shall be Hungary out and out? Upon that subject, gentlemen, I have no manner of doubt. Let us look a little at the position in which this matter stands. What is Hungary? I am not, gentleman, about to fatigue you with a long statistical statement; but I wish to say that, as I understand the matter, and I have taken some pains to look at it, Hungary contains a sufficient population to constitute a nation.

The following enumeration of the races that constitute the population of Hungary is taken from one of the latest and most authoritative publications of Austrian statistics, that of Haefler.

Magyars 4,231,500
Slowacks 2,200,000
Russniacks 350,000
Servians 740,000
Croatians 660,000
Sclavonians (Styrians) 50,000
Bulgarians and others 12,000

Sclavonians, total 4,012,800
Germans 986,000
Wallachians 930,000
Jews 250,000
Greeks and others 62,500

                                                        10,522,800

TRANSYLVANIA

Magyars 260,170
Szeklers 260,000
Germans 250,000
Wallachians 1,287,840
Others 60,400

                                                      2,117,910

MILITARY FRONTIERS

Magyars 54,000
Croatians 692,960
Servians 203,000

Sclavonians total 875,960
Germans 185,500
Wallachians 100,000

                                                      1,235,400

Magyars	4,605,670
Sclavonians	4,905,760
Germans	1,421,560
Wallachians	2,317,840
Szeklers	250,000
Jews and others	372,900
Grand total	13,876,170

By a still more recent account, taken from the official statistics of Austria, it appears that Hungary including Transylvania and military frontiers, has 122,000 square miles, with 14,400,000 inhabitants, and contains:

Jews and others	372,900
Cities	75
Towns	88
Villages	16,000
Roman Catholics	9,000,000
Greeks	4,000,000
Protestants	3,250,000
Jews	260,000

Hungary is about the size of Great Britain, and comprehends nearly half of the territory of Austria.

It is stated by another authority that the population of Hungary is nearly 14,000,000; that of England (in 1841) nearly 15,000,000; that of Prussia, about 16,000,000.

Thus it is evident that, in power, so far as power depends upon population, Hungary possesses as much power as England proper, or even as the Kingdom of Prussia. Well, then, there is population enough – there are people enough. Who, then, are they? They are distinct from the nations that surround them. They are distinct from the Austrians on the west and the Turks on the east, and I will say in the next place that they are an *enlightened* nation. They have their history; they have their traditions; they are attached to their own institutions – institutions which have existed for more than a thousand years.

Gentlemen, it is remarkable that on the western coasts of Europe political light exists. There is a sun in the political firmament, and that sun sheds his light on those who are able to enjoy it. But in Eastern Europe, generally speaking, and on the confines between Eastern Europe and Asia, there is no political sun in the heavens. It is all an arctic zone of political life. (Applause.) The luminary that enlightened the world in general, seldom rises there above the horizon. The light which they possess is at best crepuscular, a kind of twilight, and they are under the necessity of groping about to catch, as they may, any stray gleam of the light of day. (Hear, hear.) Gentlemen, the country of which your guest tonight is a native, is a remarkable exception. She has shown through her whole history, for many hundreds of years, an attachment to the principles of civil liberty, and of law out of order, and obedience to the constitution which the will of the great majority has established. That is the fact; and it ought to be known wherever the question of the practicability of Hungarian liberty and independence is discussed. It ought to be known that Hungary stands out from it above her neighbors in all that respects free institutions, constitutional government, and a hereditary love of liberty. (Applause.)

Gentlemen, I have taken the pains to prepare some facts from an intelligent writer, and that writer is a lady. She must, of course, he great authority. She says:

"The Hungarian nation has been distinguished from its first appearance in history, for uniting to a passionate love of liberty a scrupulous reverence for law. The Magyars did not enter the plains of Dacia an undisciplined rabble. From the first, they possessed a fixed form of Government and were distinguished for their subordination to their leaders and their laws. To these habits of discipline, in which the Magyars were trained, to their love of order and regard for law, it is to be ascribed that they did not pass away, like the common hordes of barbarian adventurers, but established a permanent kingdom in the country they invaded. To these qualities, not less than to the courage is to be ascribed their successful maintenance of their constitutional rights against all the attacks of a power before which the liberties of so many other nations have fallen.

"The ancient institutions of the Magyars were eminently democratic. Their chief ruler was elected by the votes of the people. For the first century after their establishment in the country he received only the title of *Vezér*, or leader. In the year 1000, they bestowed the title of King on

Stephen, of the family of Arpad, the leader under whose guidance they had entered Pannonia. The power of the king was, however, strictly limited. The consent of the people was necessary to give efficacy to every royal act. The excellent prince who first filled the throne of Hungary had no disposition to infringe the liberties of the people. On the contrary, he endeavored to guard them against the encroachment of future sovereigns. He framed a code of law, founded on the ancient institutions of the Magyars, which have ever since been regarded as of the highest authority, these statutes were drawn up for the guidance of his sun Emeric, whom he educated as his successor in the kingdom. The enlightened and humane spirit in which these decrees are composed gives a very high idea of the civilization and political advancement of Hungary at that period. We find in them an express recognition of the principles of universal equality – *'Omnes homines unius sunt conditiones'.*

It is in the following terms that he prescribes the duty of a king towards his subjects.

"Let them be to thee, my son, as brothers and fathers; reduce none of them to servitude, neither call them thy servants. Let them fight for thee, not serve thee. Govern them without violence and without pride – peacefully, humbly, humanely, remembering that nothing elevates but humility; that nothing abases but pride and an evil will.

"My son, I pray thee. I command thee, to show thyself propitious, not only to thy kindred, not only to princes, to leaders, to the rich, nor only to thy country people, but likewise to strangers, and to all that come unto thee. Be patient with all, not only with the powerful, but with those lacking power. Bear ever in mind this precept of the Lord, 'I will have mercy and not sacrifice'."

He recognizes the right of the people to depose an unworthy prince:

"If thou art mild and just, then thou shalt be called a king, and the son of a king; but if thou art proud and violent, they will deliver thy kingdom to another."

The princes of this dynasty, (the house of Arpad,) with few exceptions, were just and patriotic kings, who understood the origin and true objects of government, and held their power for the benefit of the people, not for their own selfish aggrandizement. There are traits recorded of many of them, which prove them to have been worthy successors of St. Stephen. "The Republic is not mine," said Gezza II.; "It is I who belong to the Republic. God had raised me to the throne in order that I might maintain

155

the laws. " In 1222 Andrew II. issued the celebrated statutes know by the name of the "Golden Bull", by which the decrees of St. Stephen were confirmed, and some new laws added to them, designed to secure yet further the liberties of the people. The Golden Bull has been termed a charter of aristocratic privilege. It was so in the same sense that the great charter of English liberties may be called so. The Golden Bull corresponds very closely to the Magna Charta of King John, both in its provisions and as regards the class of persons whose liberties it was designed to protect.

As to St. Stephen, I will not say how he ought to stand as a Christian, but will say that on the political and especially the Royal Calendar, he ought to he regarded as a saint, and to have a day strongly marked in red letters.

Mr. Seward (interposing.) "Three cheers for St. Stephen." The cheers were accordingly given.

Mr. Webster, (continuing.) Gentlemen, my sentiments in regard to this effort made by Hungary; are here sufficiently well expressed. In a memorial addressed to Lord John Russel and Lord Palmerston – said to have been written by Lord Fitz William, and signed by him and several other peers and members of Parliament, the following language is used, the object of the memorial being to ask the mediation of England in favor of Hungary:

"While so many of the nations of Europe have engaged in revolutionary movements, and have embarked in schemes of doubtful policy, and still more doubtful success, it is gratifying to the undersigned to be able to assure your lordships that the Hungarians, demand nothing but the recognition of ancient rights, and the stability and integrity of their ancient constitution. To your lordships it cannot be unknown that that constitution bears a striking family resemblance to that of our own country".

Gentlemen, I have one other reference to make, and then I shall take leave of you.

You know, gentlemen, that in "Measure for Measure," Shakespeare, speaking of the Duke of Vienna, says: "If the Duke, with other dukes, comes not to composition with the King of Hungary, why then all the dukes fall upon the King." "Heaven grant us peace," says another character; thou concludest, says the first speaker, "like the sanctimonions pirate that went to sea with the ten commandments, but scrapes one out of the table – thou shalt not steal! – Aye, that he razed," "Why, 'twas a commandemant to command the captain and all the rest from their functions; there is not a soldier of us all that, in the thanksgiving before meat, doth relish the petition well that prays for peace."

Now, I am afraid that, like the Dukes of Austria in former times, the Emperor of Austria in our times doth not relish the petition for peace, unless it be founded on the utter extermination of the nationality of Hungary.

Gentlemen, I have said that a national Government, where there is a distinct nationality, is essential to human happiness. I have said, that in my opinion, Hungary is thus capable of human hapiness; I have said that she possesses that distinct nationality, that power of population, and that wealth, which entitle her to have a government of her own; and I have now to add what I am sure will not sound well upon the Upper Danube – and that is, that, in my humble judgment, the imposition of foreign yoke upon a people capable of self-government, while it oppresses and depresses that people, adds nothing to the strength of those who impose that yoke. (Great applause.) In my opinion, Austria would be a better and a stronger government tomorrow, if she confined the limits of her power to her hereditary and German dominions.

Mr. Seward. – True, true.

Mr. Webster, (continuing.) Especially if she saw in Hungary a strong, sensible independent neighboring nation; because I think the cost of keeping Hungary quiet is not repaid by any benefit derived from Hungarian levies of tributes. And then, again, good neigborhood, and the good will and generous sympathies of mankind, and the generosity of character that ought to pervade the minds of governments as well as those of individuals, are vastly more prompted by living in a state of friendship and amity with those who differ from us in modes of government than by any attempt to consolidate power in the hands of one over all the rest.

Gentlemen, the progress of things is unquestionably onward. It is onward with respect to Hungary. It is onward everywhere. Public opinion in my estimation at least, is making great progress. It will penetrate all resources; it will come more or less to animate all minds; and in respect to that country for which our sympathies tonight have been so strongly invoked, I cannot but say that I think the people of Hungary are an enlightened, industrious, sober, and well-inclined community; and I wish only to add, that I do not now enter into any discussion of the form of government which may be proper for Hungary. Of course, all of you, like myself, would be glad to see her, when she becomes independent; embrace that system of government which is most acceptable to ourselves.

We shall rejoice to see our American model upon the Lower Danube, and on the mountains of Hungary. But that is not the first step. It is not that which will be our first prayer for Hungary. The first prayer shall be that Hungary may become independent of all foreign power, (great applause;) that her destinies may be entrusted to her own hands and to her own discretion. (Renewed applause.)

I do not profess to understand the social relations and connections of races, and of twenty other things that may affect the public institutions of Hungary. All I say is, that Hungary can regulate these matters for herself infinitely better than they can be regulated for her by Austria – (applause) – and therefore I limit my aspirations for Hungary, for the present, to that single and simple point – Hungarian independence.

Mr. Seward – Hungarian independence! (Applause.)

Mr. Webster – Hungarian self-government; Hungarian control of Hungarian destinies. (Renewed applause.) These are the aspirations which I entertain; and I give them to you therefore gentlemen as a toast:

"Hungarian independence; Hungarian control of her own destinies; and Hungary as a distinct nationality among the nations of Europe."

The toast was received with enthuiastic applause.

Kossuth's Speech before the Senate of Maryland

At half past twelve o'clock; Gov. Kossuth and suite were conducted to the State House by Gov. Lowe. At the door of the Senate chamber they were met by the Committee appointed by the Senate to receive them, when Mr. Down, the Chairman, addressed Gov. K. in an eloquent manner.

Kossuth's Reply

Mr. President – The stormy current of my life has offered several moments to me when the importance of the occasion, connected with associations of historical interest, impressed a deep emotion upon my mind; but perhaps never yet in my life has the memory of the past made such a gloomy impression upon me as here.

I bow with reverential awe before history, in bowing before you, senators of Maryland, in this glorious a hall – the sanctuary of immortal deeds, hallowed by the memories of immortal names.

Before I thank the living, let me look to those dead whose immortal spirits dwell within these walls, (looking at the portraits that adorn the walls,) living in an unimperishable life, in the glory, freedom and happiness of your great united Republic, destined, as I confidently hope, to become the corner stone of the future of humanity.

Yes, there they are – the glorious architects of the Independence of this Republic, grown up to such a giant in such a short time.

There is Thomas Stone; there your Demosthenes, Samuel Chase; there Charles Carrol of Carrolton, who designedly added that epithet to the significance of his name, that nobody should be mistaken about who was the Carrol who dared the noble deed, and was rewarded by his being the last of his illustrious companions whom God called to the heavenly Paradise, after he had long enjoyd the paradise of freedom on earth; and here William Paca; – all of them signers of the Declaration of American Independence, that noblest, that happiest page in manhood's history.

How happy that man must have been (pointing to the portrait of Governor Paca,) having to govern this sovereign state on that happy day, when within these very walls was ratified the act, which, by the recognition of your very enemy, raised your country to the seat of an independent nation on earth!

Ye spirits of the departed! cast a ray of consolation by the thundering voice of your nation, over that down-trodden land, whose elect chief, a wandering exile, for having dared to imitate the inspiration of your manly hearts, lays the trembling hopes of an oppressed continent before the generous heart of your people – now not only an independent nation but also a mighty, glorious power on earth.

Alas! what a difference in the success of two like deeds! Have I not done what ye did? Yes, I have. Was the cause for which I did it not alike sacred and just as yours. It was. Or have we not fought to sustain it with equal resolution as your brethren did? Bold though it be to claim a glory such as America has, I am bold to claim it, and say, yes, we did. And yet what a difference in the result! And where this difference? Only out of that single circumstance that while you in your struggle met with assistance, we in ours met not even "fair play", because when we fought, there was nobody on earth to maintain the laws of nature's God.

America was silent, and England did not stir; and while you were assisted by a French *King*, we were forsaken by the French *Republic* – itself now trodden down because it has forsaken us!

Well we are not broken yet. There is hope for us, because there is a God in Heaven and an America on earth. (Applause.) May be that our nameless woes were necessary, that the glorious destiny of America be fulfilled – that after it was all asylum for the oppressed, it became, by regenerating Europe, the pillar of manhood's liberty.

Oh, it is not a mere capricious change of fate that the exiled Governor of that land whose name four years ago was scarcely known on your glorious shores, and which now (oh let me have the blessings of this faith) is near the generous heart of America – it is not a mere chance that Hungary's exiled chief thanks the Senators of Maryland for the high honor of a public welcome in that very Hall where the first Continental Congress met, where your great Republic's Glorious Constitution was framed, where the treaty of acknowledged independence was ratified, and where you, Senators, guard with steady hand the sovereign States' Rights of your own States, united to thirty else, not to make you less free, but to make you more mighty – to make you a power on earth.

I believe there is the hand of God in history. You assigned a place in this hall of freedom to the memory of Chatham, for having been just to America by opposing the stamp-act, which awoke your nation to resistance.

Now the people of England think, as once Pitt the elder thought, and honor with deep reverence the memory of your Washington.

But suppose the England of Lord Chatham, time had thought as Chatham did; and his burning words had moved the English aristocracy to be just towards the colonies: those four men there (pointing to the portraits) had not signed your country's independence; Washington were perhaps a name "unknown, unhonored and unsung", and this proud constellation of your glorious stars had perhaps not yet risen on mankind's sky – instead of being now about to become the sun of freedom. (Applause.) It is thus Providence acts.

Let me hope, Sir, that Hungary's unmerited fate was necessary in order that your stars should become such a sun.

Sir, I stand perhaps upon the very spot where your Washington stood, a second Cincinnatus, consummating the greatest act of his life. The walls which now listen to my humble words, listened once to the words of his Republic virtue, immortal by their very modesty. Let me upon this sacred spot express my confident belief that if he stood here now, he would tell you that his prophecy is fulfilled, that you are mighty enough to defy any power on earth in a just cause, and he would tell you that there never was and never will be a cause more just than the cause of Hungary, being as it is the cause of oppressed humanity.

Sir, I thank the Senate of Maryland in my country's name for the honor of your genorous welcome. Sir, I entreat the Senate kindly to remember my down-trodden fatherland.

I bid you farewell, feeling heart and soul purified, and the readoption of my desires strenghthened by the very air of this ancient city of Providence. (Applause.) On motion the Senate adjourned.

The Committee, on the part of the House of Delegates, received Kossuth at the door of their chamber, and presented him to the Speaker; who briefly addressed him.

KOSSUTH REPLIED –

Sir – I most humbly thank the House of delegates of Maryland for the honor of the public reception. If to be an invited and welcomed guest of his exellency, the noble minded and warm hearted Governor of the State, was already a source of high gratification to my heart and a valuable benefit to the cause which I represent – the generous welcome of the Legislature has raised this benefit to the level of a principle.

I cannot forbear to believe that in this concurence of the Legislature with the Executive Government of this sovereign state in bestowing upon my humble self the high honor of a solemn welcome, there is a more than kindness so congenial to true American hearts, and in itself so dear to me; there is a political revelation of the public opinion of the people from whom both the Legislature and the Executive desire the autority of their high position.

And whenever a people, by its elect, pronounces in such a solemn way, there is in that pronunciation more than civility to a stranger, more than generous hospitality to a homeless wanderer, more than compassion for the misfortune, even though it be connected with noble and just cause –

there is a principle in it. Public opinion can never be moved to a great extent but by a principle.

May it be a whim of mysterious destiny, or, as I believe, something providential, it is no merit of mine that my arrival in the United States became an opportunity for the manifestation of a principle pre-existing in the heart of your people, which, besides the glory of being mighty, intelligent and free, possesses also that of being especially practical, as the prodigious independence of your great Republic in such a brief period shows. And that pre-existing principle is, that the people of the U. S. are aware of having to take the high position of a power on earth, weighing, with all the importance of this position in that scope where the great interests of the world are weighed.

Sir, the rays of generous sympathy with which the people of the United States brighten my sad brow, came upon me only because the light of your country's fundamental principles is reflected from the mirror of your country's position. (Applause.) Sir (pointing towards a full-length portrait of Lafayette), that very picture is a principle! If Washington's likeness teaches the world that "Who will be free, themselves must strike the blow," Lafayette's presence there tells the world what Europe's oppressed nations expect from the gallant sons of Republican America.

And besides this glorious personification of patriotic duty and private generosity, there is the great idea in that picture there, that if America was not too far from Europe to see, as Lafayette said in Annapolis – "French and American standards united in the cause of mankind" when your country was in need, Europe should not be considered too far to see the powerful Republic of the U.S., when Europe is in need of seeing protected the laws of nations in which every nation is interested, just as every citizen is in the laws of his country.

America received from Europe private generosity and public assistance. Europe expects from America only private generosity and the assurance of "fair play." Sir, let me hope that in this Hall, where history thus speaks, principles will rule.

Upon this appeal rest my hopes; and it is with the consolation of hope that I beg you, Sir, and the House of delegates of the State of Maryland, to accept the warmest acknowledgments of this distinction they were pleased to honor me with, and the assurance of my own and my country's sincere gratitude.

Kossuth's Speech before the Legislature of Pennsylvania

(This speech was in reply to the address of welcome tendered to him by Gov. Johnson, in the hall of the capital at Harrisburg.)

Senators and Representatives of Pennsylvania: I came with confidence, I come with hope to the United States – with the confidence of a man who trusts with burning faith to the logic of principles, knowing that where freedom is sown, there generosity grows – with the hope of a man who knows that there is life in his cause, and that where there is life there must be a future yet. And still the hope of man is only an instinctive throb of the heart with which nature's motherly care counteracts the sad impression of adversity. We often hope without knowing why, and like a lonely wanderer on a stormy night, direct our weary steps towards the first glimmering window light, without knowing whether we are about to knock at the door of a philantropist or a heartless egotist.

But that hope and that confidence with which I came to the United States was not such a one. There was a knowledge of facts in it. I did not know whom it may be fate to meet, but I knew that meet I will with two living principles – with that of *freedom* and that of *national hospitality*. Both are political principles here.

Freedom is expansive like the light; it likes to spread; and hospitality here in this happy land, is raised out of the narrow circle of private virtue to a principle of political states wisdom.

Just as you, gentlemen, are the representatives of your people, so the people of the United States at large is the representatives of European humanity – a congregation of nations assembled in the hospitable Hall of American liberty. Your people is linked to Europe not only by the common tie of humanity – not only by the communicative spirit of liberty – not even only by commercial intercourse; but by the sacred ties of blood. The people of the United States is Europe transplanted to America. You are not one national tribe, like the retreating Indians, who retire before the white man to be with nature alone. You came over not like the migrative people of the middle ages seeking a home in one compact national mass.

I said by design the people of the United States is Europe transplanted to America. And it is not Hungary's woes alone, it is the cause of that Europe which I came to plead. Where was ever a son who, even in his happiest days, could indifferently look at the sufferings of his mother, whose heart blood is running in his very veins? And Europe is the mother of the United States.

Oh, I hope to God that the people of this glorious land is, and will ever be, fervently attached to this their free, great and happy home. I hope to God that whatever tongue they speak, they are and will ever be American, and nothing but American. And so they must be, if they will be free – if they desire their adopted home's greatness and continued existence.

But while I hope that all the people of the United States will never become anything but Americans, and even its youngest adopted sons, though fresh with sweet home recollections, will know here no South, no North, no East, and no West – nothing but the whole country, the common nationality of freedom – in a word, America; still I also know, that blood is blood – that the heart of the son must beat at the contemplation of his mother's sufferings.

Sir, it is a gratifying view to see how the generous sympathy of your people for the cause which I respectfully plead, is rising, in natural process, to the elevation of public opinion. But nowhere had I the happy lot to see this rising process more clearly expressed than in the great commonwealth of Pennsylvania, this mighty key-stone State of the Union. (Applause.)

First the people of Harrisburg spoke, and no city before had so distinctly articulated the public sympathy into acknowledged principles. It has framed the sympathy of generous instinct into a political shape. I forever will remember it with fervent gratitude. Then came the metropolis – a hope and consolation by its very name to the oppressed – the sanctuary of American Independence, where the very bells speak prophecy – which now, sheltering more inhabitants than all Pennsylvania did, when, 75 years ago the prophetic bell of Independence Hall announced to the world that free America is born; which now with the voice of thunder will, I hope, tell the world that the doubtful life of that child has developed into a mighty power on earth. (Applause.)

Yes, after Harrisburg, the metropolis came, a flourishing example of freedom's developing power, as the metropolis of the west is the proof of freedom's creative power; and after the metropolis, now the first personification of your great Republic's manufacturing interests, that mighty link of nations and this natural ally of international law – then came Pittsburgh, the immense manufacturing workshop, alike memorable for its moral power and its natural advantages, which made it a link with the great

164

valley of the west, that cradle of a new world, linked in its turn to the old world by boundless agricultural interests.

And after the people of Pennsyvania thus spoke, now here I stand in the temple of this people's sovereignty, with joyful gratitude acknowledging the inestimable benefit of this public reception, where with the elect of Pennsyvania, entrusted with the Legislative and Executive power of the sovereign people, gather into one garland the flower of the people's public opinion, and with the authority of their high position announce loudly to the world, the principles, the resolution, and the will of the the millions of this great Commonwealth. (Applause.)

Sir: the words your Excellency honored me with will have their weight throughout the world. The jeering smile of the despots, which accompanied the poor exile's wandering steps, may turn, at the report of these proceedings, into a frown which may yet cast mourning over families, as it has over mine, but which will look for consolation at the drawn of public happiness. The words your Excellency spoke will have their weight with the nations who, under the encouraging auspices of such principles, will feel redoubled in resolution to shake off the yoke of despotism.

The proceedings of today will have their weight in the development of public opinion in other States of your united Republic; and when Congress and the National Government bestow the cares of their patriotic wisdom to the question of foreign policy, now so pre-eminent by the condition of the world and the position of this Republic, will feel inclined to pronounce what shall be the common law of nations, as true republics can acknowledge (as I have full reason to hope that they will feel inclined to pronounce) the corresponding transactions of State legislatures, and manifestations like this, and words full of principles and generosity like yours, will give the practical weight to the pronunciation of the highest federative authorities.

And if, in addition to this, the sympathy of the people, registered by establishing associations of friends of Hungary to support European liberty, proves itself practical "by material aid", then allow me confidently to state, the resolute attitude of your great Republic will be sufficient to raise it to that glorious seat amongst the powers on earth, the glory of which no nation on earth has yet ever reached.

And if, connected with that, you establish the right of commercial intercourse – which only under the protection of the star-spangled banner can be restored to humanity, and which now is only a toy in the arbitrary hands of ambitious despots – then may your Excellency, and the Senate and the Representatives of this glorious commonwealth, be sure that the oppressed nations of Europe will find "fair play" to settle the terrible account with their oppressors – (applause); and America the son of Europe, will save Europe regenerated by the gigantic glory, the gigantic spirit of freedom which rules in this place. (Applause.)

Governor! I plead no dead cause. Oh! what happiness would it be for me to enjoy, on the evening of my tempest-tossed life, a tranquility for which I so fervently long, and which I never yet enjoyed – if duty would not press me on with the confidence of success. Sir, Europe is no corpse; it has a future yet; because it will. There is no difficulty to him who wills!

Sir, from the window of your room, which your hospitality opened to me, I saw suspended a musket and a powder horn, and this motto – "Material Aid!" And I believe that the Speaker of the House of Representatives of Pennsylvania is seated in that chair whence the Declaration of American Independence was signed. The first is what Europe wants in order to have the success of the second. (Applause.)

Permit me to take this for a happy augury; and allow me, with the plain words of an earnest mind, to give you the assurance of my country's warm, everlasting gratitude, in which, upon the basis of our restored independence, a wide field will be opened to mutual benefit, by friendly-commercial intercourse, ennobled by the consciousness of imparted benefit from your side, and by the pleasant duty of gratitude on the side of my people, so well deserving your generous sympathy. (Great applause.)

Kossuth's Great Banquet Speech at Harrisburg, Pa.

GENTLEMEN – The daily opportunity of addressing public assemblies, affords me scarcely a moment for reflection. The continual exertion of my days and the cares of my sleepless nights have worn out my strength. The restless excitement of my soul has shaken my frame, like as the captured lion shakes his iron frame; and domestic griefs have troubled the serenity of my mind, peculiar to the resolute conviction of martyrs, but also indispenable to orators. I want some time to recover from the new blow which makes the heart of the son bleed, while the tongue of the patriot has to plead where the approbation of the listening tribunal is the condition of success. Indeed, my case is hard. I never had any eloquence but that of principles, so simple because so true; and that of sincere feelings, finding their way to the heart, because they come from the heart, and meeting an echo in virtuous hearts, like the simple whispers of a limpid well in the breast of nature's happy son. But the limpid well of my feelings is troubled by an impious tyrant's hands. Excuse me for sharing the common frailty of men, and do not expect eloquence from me. I cannot – indeed, I cannot be eloquent; and to what purpose is eloquence here? Have you not anticipated my wishes? You have. Have you not sanctioned my principles? You have. Are you not going on to action as generous men do who are conscious of their power and of their aim? You are. Well, to what purpose, then, is eloquence here? I have nothing to ask from you. I have nothing but to thank; and that is more eloquently to told by a warm grasp of the hand, than by all the skilful arrangement of words. Well, I beg therefore your indulgence for the dry combination of some facts, which perhaps may contribute to strengthen that conviction in the public opinion, that the people of the United States in bestowing its sympathy upon my cause, does not support a dead cause, but one which has a life, and whose success is rationally sure. Let me before all cast a glance at the enemy; and let those imposed upon by the attitude of despotism, in 1852, consider how much stronger it was in 1848. France was lulled by Louis Philippe's politics of peace at any price into apathy. There was a faith in the firm solidity of his government. No heart-revolting cruelty of bloody persecution stirred the public mind. No universal indignation of offended national self-esteem prevailed. The faith of insured security encouraged the circulation of capital and by that circulation, large masses of industrious poor found, if not contentment, at least daily bread. The King was taken for a prudent man, and the private morality of his family cast a sort of halo around his house. The spirit of revolution was reluced to play the scanty part of secret associations. Not seconded by any movement of universal interest, the stirring spirit of radical innovation was restrained into scientific polemics, read by few and understood by less. There was a faith in the patriotic authority of certain men whose reputatian was that of being liberal; and one part of the nation lived on from day to day; without any stirring passion, in entire passiveness; the other believed in gradual improvement and progress, because it had confidence in the watchful care of party leading men. The combat of parliamentary eloquence was considered to be a storm in a glass of water; and the highest aspiration of parties was to oust the ministry and to get in; and yet an interdict of a public banquet blew asunder the whole compound, like mere void chaff. Germany was tranquil, because the honest pretentions or the ambition of her statesmen were highly satisfied by the opened lists of parliamentary eloquence. The public life of the nation had a field opened in legislative debates – a benefit which had not been enjoyed for centuries. The professors being transferred to the tribune and the college to the Parliament, the nation was gratified by legislative improvements, and flattered by the oratory of her renowned men, who never failed to flatter the national vanity. It believed itself to be really in full speed train of greatness, and listened contented and quiet – like an intelligent audience to an interesting lecture – even in respect to the unity of great Germany. The Custom Association (Zollverein) became an idol of satisfied national vanity and of cheerful hopes; science and art developed fast; speculative researches of political economy met an open field in social life, and men conscious of higher aims, took the walking-stick of the wanderer in their hands and sought a new home, despairing; to find a field of action in their native land. Materialism was the ruling word, and the lofty spirit of freedom became withering between the blasting fingers of small interests; and yet a prohibited banquet at Paris shook the very foundation of this artificial tranquility, and the princely thrones of Germany trembled before the rising spirit of freedom, though groping in darkness, because unconscious of its aim. Italy, fair unfortunate Italy, looking into the mirror of its ancient glory, beamed with gloomy grief; but the sky of the heaven was clear and blue above as it ever was since creation's dawn, and it sung like a bird in a cage placed upon a bough of a blooming orange tree. And then Pius IX., placing himself at the head of Italian regeneration became popular as no man in Rome since Rienzi's time. Even in 1848, men may have heard in surprise, on the coast of the Adriatic, my name coupled in Evviva's with the name of Pius IX. The sarcasm of Madame de Stael "that in Italy men became women," was considered true; and Carlo Alberto became the hero of Italian independence, because he fought against Austria, and the hatred against Anstria was a national inheritance; but the spirit of Italy was divided between Charles Albert, Mazzini, and the Pope. Austria did not for centuries, and Prussia never yet has, experienced what sort of thing a revolution is; and the falling of the vault of the sky would have been considered less improbable than a popular revolution in Berlin or Vienna, where Metternich ruled in triumphant, proud security. The House of Austria was considered as a migty power on earth – respected, because thought necessary to Europe against the preponderance of Russia. No people under the dominion of this dynasty had a national army, and all were divided by the controversies of false language rivalries, entertained by Metternich's satanic Machiavelism. The nations divided, none of them was conscious of his strength; but all were conscious of the united strength of a disciplined and large imperial army, the regiments of which never fought one against an other, and never yet shook the prestige of the black and yellow flag, by tearing it to pieces by its own hands. And yet Paris stirred, and I made a plain, unpretending speech in the Hungarian Parliament, and the House of Austria was at the mercy of the people of Vienna, and Metternich was driven away, and his absolutism replaced by a promise of constitutional life. In Gallicia, the odiosity connected with the despotic Austrian rule, was, by satanic craft, thrown upon those classes which represent the ancient Polish nationality, and the well deserved hatred of aristocratic oppression, through living only in traditional remembrances, prevailed in the sentiments of the people, even over the hatred against Austria, though despotic and a stranger, so much, that to triumph over the ill-advised, untimely revolution of 1846, Austria had nothing to do but to open the field to murder by granting a two dollar reward for every head of a Polish land proprietor.

And in Hungary, the people of everyrace was equally excluded from all political right – from any share of constitutional life. The endeavors of myself and my friends for internal improvements, for emancipation of the peasantry, for the peoples restoration to its natural rights in civil, political, social and religious respects, was cramped by the government. But the odium of this cramping was thrown upon the conservative party: and thus the national force was divided into antagonistical elements. Besides the idea of panslavism and of national rivalries, raised by Russia, and fostered by Austria, gave to the excitement of the public mind a diversion inimical to the development of common political freedom. And Hungary had no national army. Its regiments were filled with foreign elements and scattered over foreign countries, while our own country was guarded with well disciplined foreign troops.

And what was far more than all this – Hungary, by long oppression, poisoned in its character, deprived of its ancient heroic stamp – gormandized in its saloons – demolished in its cottages and huts – impressed with the unavoidable fatality of Austria's sovereignty, and the knowledge of Austria's power, secluded from tho attention of the world, which was

169

scarcely aware of its existence, Hungary had no lope in its national future, because it had no consciousness of its strength, and was highly monarchical in its inclinations, and generous in its allegiance to the king. No man dreamed of the possibility of a Revolution there, and he who would have suggested it, would only have gained the reputation of a madman.

Such was the condition of Europe in the first part of February, 1848. Never yet seemed the power of despots more steady, more sure. And one month later every throne on the Continent trembled, except the Czar's. The existence of dynasties depended upon the magnanimity of their peoples, and Europe was fire and flame.

And in what condition is Europe now? Every man on earth is aware that things cannot endure as they are. Formerly millions believed that a peaceful development of constitutional monarchy was the only future reserved to Europe by destiny. Now nobody more believes that constitutional monarchy can have yet a future on the European Continent.

Absolutistical reaction goes with all that arrogance which revolts every sentiment and makes furious the very baby in its mother's arms. The promise, the word, the oath of a king became equivalent to a lie and to perjury. Faith in the morality of kings was plucked out, even to the last root from the people's heart. The experiment of constitutional concessions proved dangerous to the absolutistical tendency of the dynasties, because they became aware the people of Europe is no imbecile child which takes the moon for a cheese – that it cannot be lulled to sleep by mockery, but that it will have reality. Thus the kings on the greatest part of the Continent, throwing away the mask of liberal affectations, deceived every expectation, broke every oath and embarked with a full gale upon the open bark of irrestrained despotism. They know that loved they cannot now be, so they told the world openly, that they will not have love, but money to keep large armies with which to keep the world in servitude. On the other hand, the nations so assailed in their moral dignity and material welfare, raging at the idea of being degraded to the condition of a flock of sheep, kept only to be shorn – these nations equally detest the working of constitutional royalty, which proved so prejudicial to them. Royalty has lost its prestige in France, Germany, Italy, Austria and Hungary. Both parties equally recognize that the time has come when the struggle of principles must be decided. Absolutism or republicanism – the Czar or the principles of America – there is no more transaction, no more truce possible. The two antagonist principles meet upon the narrow bridge of a *knife-edge* breadth, cast across the deep gulf, ready to swallow him who falls. There is no giving way – there is no turning round possible. He who would give way to his enemy would fall into the yawning gulf himself. He who would turn round, would be pushed down by his enemy pressing on his rear – it is a struggle for life and death.

That is the condition of the European continent in general. A great, terrible, bloody revolution is unavoidable! That is known and felt by everyone. And every sound man knows equally well that the temporary success of Louis Napoleon's usurpation made but the terrible crisis more unavoidable yet.

Ye men of "peace at any price," do not shut willingly your eyes before the finger of God pointing to the *mene tekel upharsin*, written with gigantic letters upon the sky of Europe. Despots never yield to justice, and mankind inspired with love's freedom will not yield to annihilation cowardly. Peace is impossible. Nobody can stop the wheels of destiny.

It would be a mistake, terrible in its consequences, to believe that if I should fail in my mission here, and if the U. S. Should remain indifferent, then no revolution would break out on the European continent. That is an udavoidable necessity, which no power on earth can avert. Should even the U. S. not only remain indifferent, but with all their immense power even side with the despots of the world, that the churchyard peace of Europe may not be disturbed, (which the U. S., of course, would never do,) even that could not prevent a revolution in Europe. Hungary, Austria, Italy, Germany, would fight, be it against the combined power of the world. They would fight even with the certainty of death; because there is a condition in the life of nations, when oppression is more hated than death is feared.

No, Gentlemen, the success of my mission here can insure the victory of freedom, can prevent torrents of martyr's blood; can shorten the earthquake of impending war, and bring nearer the restoration to solid peace. But be sure, the certainty of the European revolution is not in the slightest manner depending upon my good luck here, and your Governor's support; as also my failure here, would not for a single week retard the outbreak of that hurricane, the scent of which is already preceived in the very air.

Well, the question rushes instinctively to the mind, "but has Hungary – have the other oppressed nations of Europe a chance of success." Revolution being unavoidable, even were there no chance of success, that question is in my opinion pretty indifferent in respect to what course this your great Republic may be pleased to adopt, because the greater the means and chances of absolutism were, the greater claims had the cause of humanity to your operative sympathy. A just cause, sufficiently strong in itself, requires no support. We may well dispense from feeling interested in the struggle of a man, of whom we have no doubt that he is by his own means sure of victory. To want sympathy and support in a just cause, is precisely a claim to more sympathy and support.

Should we, meeting with no support here such as your glorious Republic in its public capacity, and your generous citizens in their private capacity, can afford, without jeopardizing your own welfare and your own interest, (and to be sure it never came to my mind to desire more) – should we, meeting with no support here be crushed again, and absolutism consolidate its powers upon the ruins of murdered nations, I indeed, gentlemen, cannot forbear to believe that it would become a historical reproach of conscience, lying like an incubus upon the breast of the people of the United States, from generation to generation. I mean that idea, that had you not withheld that support which you were able to afford in time consistently with your own interest, Hungary perhaps would be a free, flourishing country, instead of being blotted out from the earth, and Europe were perhaps free, and the absolutistical tyranny of the despots were swept from the earth – you then would shed a tear of compassion upon our sad fate, and mourn over the grave of nations. You would do so, I know, because I know your generous hearts. But believe me, gentlemen, the tear of compassion could not fall to partake somewhat of a bitter self reproach. Forgive me, gentlemen; the word was perhaps too bold; but it is true. It is the more true, because the victory of absolutism could not fall to be felt, even here in your mighty and blessed home. You would first resent it in your commercial intercourse, and were long you would become inevitably entangled; because all the power in Europe concentrated in absolutism and obeying the orders of the Czar, would not look indifferently upon the development of your power, that personification of Republican principles in America.

But I am not afraid to answer the question as to what are our means and chances of success, though, of course, prudence commands me to be discreet on that subject. I am not willing to imitate those who spoke so much about 1852 in France, that they were anticipated in 1851. There is no fowling by beating the bush. Still, some considerations I may suggest.

The prestige of Austria's power is broken. It is known that the power of the Austrian dynasty though disciplined, well provided and supported by deluded races, roused to the fury of extermination against us – it is known that all this satanically; well combined power could not withstand the power of Hungary, though we were surprised and unprepared, and had no army and no arms, no communication, no money, no friends, and were secluded and forsaken by the whole world. It is moreover proved that Austria could not conquer us when we were unprepared; who can believe that we do not match her now we are prepared. Yes, we are prepared, because resolved not to endure cowardly our national annihilation, we have learned by experience what is required for our success.

In former times Hungary was the strength of Austria. Now, Austria is weak because it possesses Hungary. It was strong by the unity of its army, the power of which was founded upon the Confidence in this unity. That confidence is broken since one part of that army raised the tri-colored flag, and with it beat down the double-headed Eagles, the black and yellow flag – the emblem of the army's unity.

Formerly the army believed that it was strong enough to uphold Austria's throne; now it knows that it is nothing by itself, and rests only upon the support of the Czar. That spirit-depressing sentiment in the Austrian army, even the most attached part of it (if such there be), is so universally diffused, that only take the reliance upon Russia away, or weaken it only so as to make it doubtful whether Russia will interfere or not, and the Austrian Army will disperse and fall asunder almost without any fight; because it knows that the Austrian army has its most dangerous enemies within its own ranks, and it is so far from having any cement, that no man, if he be attached to that perjured dynasty, can trust the man next in rank to him, but watches every movement of his arm. In such an army there is no hope for tyrants.

The old soldiers feel humiliated by the issue of our struggle.

They feel offended by having no share in the reward thrown away on despised court favorites. The old Croatian regiments feel outraged in their national honor, by being deceived in their national expectations. The recruits brought with them recollections of their bombarded cities, and of the oppression of their families; and in that army are 140,000 Hungarians who fought under our tricolor flag against Austria, and whose burning feelings of national wrong are inspired by the glorious memory of their victories. Oh! had we in 1848 such an army of disciplined soldiers as

Austria itself keeps now for us, never had one Cossack trod the soil of Hungary, and Europe were free. Or, let Austria dismiss them, and they will be disciplined soldiers at home. The trumpet of national resurrection would reach them wherever they are. Hungary has the conviction of her strength. The formerly hostile races, all oppressed like us, and besides deceived, unite with us. I have no opposite party in the nation. Some ambitious men there are, perhaps – but these are no party; they always turn towards the sun, and they melt like snow in March.

And besides Hungary, the people also in Austria, in Italy, in Prussia, in all Germany, is conscious of its strength. Every large city on the continent has been in the power of the people, and kept down by bombardings and by martial law. Italy has redeemed its heroic character at Milan, Venice, Brescia and Rome – all of them immortal pages in Italian history, glorious sources of inspiration, heroism and self conscious strength; and now they know their aim, and are united in their aim, and burning to show to the world that the spirit of ancient Rome inspired them. And then take into consideration the financial part. Without money there is no war. Now the nations, once engaged in the war, find money enough at home for the expenses of the war, in the rich resources of their own land; whereas, the despots lose the disposition of these resources by the first outbreak of the war, and are reduced entirely to loans, which no Emperor of Austria will find again in any market in the world. And mark well, gentlemen, every operative friendly step, by which your great Republic and its generous people testifies its lively interest for our just cause, adding to the certainty of success, diminishes the credit of the despots. They can find no more money, and this circumstance alone is of decisive weight in the issue. Though absolutism was much more favorable in 1847 than in 1851, it was overtaken by the events of 1848, when, but for the want of unity and concert, the liberal party must have triumphed everywhere. That unity and concert is attained.

Why should not absolutism in 1852 be as easily shaken as in 1848? The liberal cause is stronger everywhere because conscious of its aim and prepared. Absolutism has no more bayonets now than in '48; but scarcely can it depend less upon them. Whitout the interference of Russia our success is not only probable, but is almost sure. And as to Russia, it is not the military power it is taken for. It has never since 1815, succeeded in sending more than 250,000 men across the frontier, or in making one campaign without a loan. Where would she have had credit for a second campaign before her? And be sure she can never send more troops across her frontier so long as she has Poland to occupy, Finland to guard, Turkey to watch, and Circassia to fight. Herein is the reason why I confidently state that if the United States declare that a new intervention of Russia will be considered by your glorious Republic a violation of the law of nations, that declaration will be respected, and Russia will not dare to interfere. Be pleased to consider the consequences of such a renewed interference, after the passive acceptance of the first has proved so fatal to Europe, and so dangerous even to England herself.

The most unavoidable consequence of it would be, at least, that England could not forbear to encourage Turkey not to lose again the favorable opportunity to shake off the preponderance of Russia. I have lived in Turkey. I know what enthusiasm exists there for that idea, and how popular such a war would be. Well, Turkey alone is a match for Russia on the continent. The weak point of Turkey is from the neighborhood of Sebastopol to Constantinople and the Black Sea. Well, an English fleet, or an American fleet, or both joined, stationed at the mouth of the Bosphorus, may easily prevent this danger without one cannon shot; and this prevented, Turkey alone is a match for Russia. And Turkey would not stand alone. The brave Circassians, triumphant through a war of twenty years, would send down eighty thousand of their unconquerable horsemen to the plains of Moscow. And Poland would rise, and Sweden would remember Finland and Charles the XII., and Hungary in the rear, delivered by this very circumstance from the invaders, and Austria fallen to pieces for want of foreign support. Oh! by the Almighty God, Russia *must* respect your protestation in behalf of international law, or else she will fall never rise again.

But, suppose your protection should not be respected by Russia, is it indeed true that the United States could not make it respected without having to go to war? Are there no other means of giving practical meaning to your protestation than a war? Let me only suggest one hint. Suppose the United States declare that in regard to any power which, by armed intervention in the domestic concerns of any nation violates the laws of nations, that act of the Congress which we might term the "Neutrality law" is not to be considered to exist; suppose this single sanction added to your protestation, and judge by your own generous feelings if I am wrong confidently to hope that the people of the United States, in its private capacity, would soon settle the account of all oppressed nations with all the Czars of the world. That is my confident belief, and I have indeed good reason for it. And think only of the Black Sea and of the Land – of Odessa, Sevastopol, Cronstadt, Petersburg! No! Russia will not dare to interfere in your protest. And if she should, only help me, generous people of America, to have some money to provide for my brave countrymen, that they may have something better to fight with than their own nails, and you will soon see 400,000 Hungarians ranged in resolute attitude, calmly shouting out, "Russia, come on!" Oh! had I possessed arms to arm the hundred thousands of volunteers eager to fight for freedom and father-land, not even the surrender of Gorgey would have broken our brave Hungary. But we were secluded from the world. Races then hostile to us stood between us and the Adriatic; and the hesitation of Turkey admitted the Danube to be locked up from us. Where hostile Races then stood, friends now stand; and if your generous encouragement help only a little on the way, friendly resolution will be found where wavering hesitation ruled.

Gentlemen – I, in my condition, am induced to value everything, even money, by the muskets and swords it will procure. That is my test as the camel is to the Arab. Well, there are in Pennsylvania probably 400,000 homesteads. If only half of the families inhabiting them would sacrifice one dollar each, that alone would give from fifty to seventy thousand muskets. Generous people of America! help me to this legitimate com-merce – for I am told that it is lawful to buy arms here – and be assured that no stately intervention will be required to enforce nonintervention as a law of nations. Gentlemen! I am not an idle man here; be pleased to believe that I have not been idle in other quarters, not even during my captivity. I never speak a word in vain when I speak of facts and of hopes. The man who controlled the finances of Hungary, created armies out of nothing, and led on the people of Hungary in the glorious contest, may perhaps claim so much credit as not to be taken for an untried theorist, but for something of a practical man.

And one thing even I may be permitted to say, and that is, that my whole life attests, if nothing else, at least the honesty of my intentions. Therefore, when I humbly beg leave to say that I have strong prospects of success, if I had material means conveniently to utilize the short time which yet remains before the hour of decisive strife – when I humbly beg leave to say, that I have strong prospects, even independent of fortunate accidents – I may perhaps not be considered too bold when I say that there is reality in my prospects and in my hopes.

Gentlemen, I most profoundly thank you for the generous patience with which you have listened to this exposition of dry facts – long and tedious, because I had no time to be brief. And begging leave to assure you of my lasting gratitude for all the generous favors you were and will yet be pleased to bestow upon my cause, let me proclaim my fervent wishes in this sentiment:

"Pennsylvania – The Keystone State of the Union – may it, by its legitimate influence upon the destinies of this mighty power on earth, and by the substantial generosity of its citizens, soon become the Keystone of European Independence."

PAGE

Kossuth's Speech in Pittsburgh

The Hungarian Chief came out upon the balcony of the St. Charles Hotel, and was presented by Col. Black, the orator of the day, who delivered a most eloquent address.

Kossuth's Speech from the Balcony

Gentlemen – I believe your warm-hearted and eloquent orator will be best contented with an answer addressed not to him, but to you, people of Pittsburgh, and of the country of Alleghany. (Cheers.)

In crossing the mountains of Pennsylvania, gentlemen, I found confirmed that Switzer proverb – that "the spirit of freedom likes in the mountains to dwell." The weather was chill, but the hearts were warm. (Applause.) And upon the very snow grew up around me flowers of sympathy, benevolent as nature itself. (Applause.)

Since I breathed the air of your great Republic, the bounty of Providence has thrown many a flower of consolation and of hope in my thorny way. But though bright be the lustre of sympathy which the stars of your great nation casts over me from nigh and from far, never was the sympathy of this people more decidedly and more universally manifested than in Pennsylvania. (Cheers.) Citizens of Pittsburgh and Alleghany, with your friendly hands you have bound the flowers of Pennsylvania in a garland full of blossoms, and I hope full of fruit like the orange tree (Cheers.)

177

Sir, (turning to Colonel Black,) you have told me that the peculiar character of this people is industry. Well, where one finds industry, he sees a working people – and that word, "working people," is noble title on earth. I am proud to have belonged to it. (Cheers.) Gentlemen, amongst all the testimonials of sympathy, those of working men are dearest to my heart; because there is not only a touching, high-minded fact, but also a true revelation of the power of principles, when we see those who have no other capital than their time, and no other treasure than the honest hard work of their hands, sacrifice their time, and stop in their work not only, but also sacrificing a part of what they have earned by their hard honest labor, for the support of the cause of liberty.

Oh, indeed such a manifestation reveals mankind's divine origin! It is dear to the heart, and cannot fail to be attended with the blessings of God. Surely, I have met with such sympathy here, and I thank you for it, gentlemen, with the most sincere feelings of a warm heart, in the name of my poor country. (Cheers.) My country! That very word brings home to the heart the sorrows of my days and nights, which I had almost forgotten, in looking at your warm and generous reception here. Well may my country rejoice at the honors which the people of America is pleased to bestow upon Hungary's exiled chief; and God knows, even one moment's rejoicing is even now a great benefit to poor Hungary.

But you are too practical a people not to excuse my country when it looks over to yours with the inquiry beaming from its weeping eyes – after all what is, what will be the result of all these demonstrations – all these honors – all these sympathies? – Indeed, I cannot answer it yet, urgent though the necessity may be for it. Fear and hope alternate in my breast; and then the irreparable value of swiftly passing time makes my heart beat with new sorrows. But, considering where I am, and casting my looks over the scene around me, I may confidently say that hope prevails.

Yes, Gentlemen, it is impossible that such a manifestation, in such a place, from such a people, as I received in the United States, should be nothing else than mere applause to the melancholy part which we had to act in the sad tragedy in mankind's history? No! these principles which you express, Sir, fully answer me, that in this manifestation there is the upbearing of the heart of the people of the United States, telling the world that the great Republic of the West is becoming concious of its position and of its glorious destiny – such is to become the rock upon which the

Hall of Freedom shall be raised, extending its lofty walls all over the earth. (Great cheering.)

And indeed, either that Hall must so extend, or, let me tell you, gentlemen, that soon you will have to fight for your own position on earth, on which your own freedom depends; because the victorious despots in Europe will not endure to see such a Republic as yours a great power on earth. You will be attacked in your most vital interest – in those interests which are nowhere in the nation so conspicuously personified as here in Pittsburgh: – Pittsburgh being as it is the very threshold of the West, the link between the New World of the West and the East – linking the interests of the Gulf of Mexico and the Atlantic, and thus personifying the agricultural, manufacturing and commercial interests of your great Republic.

STEVEN BÉLA VÁRDY[1]

Epilogue

KOSSUTH AND MID-NINETEENTH-CENTURY AMERICA In the course of the past century and a half no Hungarian could rival Louis Kossuth's name and fame in America and in the English-speaking World. Since Kossuth's tour of the United States in 1851–1852, old empires have fallen and new states have come into being by the scores. During the same period hundreds of thousands of Hungarians have left their homeland to emigrate to America. Others have come to the New World only to look around and then to return to Hungary. This large mass of Hungarians – whether coming permanently or temporarily – included a good number of internationally known statesmen, scholars, scientists, artists, musicians, and sportsmen – particularly since the mid-1930s. Some of them were even able to increase their fame through their exploits and achievements in the United States. Yet, none of them could come close to matching Kossuth's popularity among Americans. As put by Gyula Szekfű (1877–1955), one of Hungary's greatest twentieth-century historians, "Kossuth alone did more for the popularization of Hungary and for arousing sympathy for the Hungarians than all the efforts of all the successive generations since. This success was the direct result of his personality."[2]

Kossuth's brief presence in the United States impacted upon the whole of American society and politics, and even upon the very age which embraced it. And this was true even though the period of his coming coincided with the emergence of the expansionist "Young America" on the American political scene, as well as with the rise of the anti-immigrant "Know Nothing Party," spawned by the massive Irish-Catholic and German immigration of the 1840s and 1850s. (If asked about their movement, the members were instructed to answer: "I know nothing.") Moreover, the same period also served as the preamble to the great Civil War, which pitted the anti-slavery North against the slave-owning South.

The human magnetism, brilliant oratorical skills, and the very presence of Hungary's revolutionary "Governor-President" [kormányzó-elnök] was so overpowering that millions of Americans fell under his spell. The ranks of his fans included many who prior to their encounter with Kossuth had never even heard of Hungary and the Hungarians. Yet, following his appearance, most of them became fervent supporters of the Hungarian cause – although they were unable to translate their enthusiasm into concrete help for Kossuth and his struggling nation across the Atlantic.

Kossuth's appearance in the United States was followed by the publication of dozens of books, hundreds of pamphlets, and thousands of articles and essays, as well as nearly two hundred poems written to or about him.[3] The authors of many of these literary pieces included some of America's greatest intellectual figures, including Ralph Waldo Emerson (1803–1882), Henry Wadsworth Longfellow (1807–1892), John Greenleaf Whittier (1807–1892), Horace Greeley (1811–1872), James Russel Lowell (1819–1891), Harriet Beecher Stowe (1811–1896), and many others.[4]

Kossuth's name resounded everywhere, and his cult spread far and wide. Counties, cities, towns, streets, town squares, and even babies born during his American tour were named after him.[5] The latter usually took the form of middle names, such as in the case of Melvil Louis Kossuth Dewey (1851–1931), the originator of the so-called Dewey Decimal System of Classification, and Joseph Kossuth Dixon (?–1926), the author of the once influential work, The Vanishing Race.[6] But the ranks of these Kossuth-enthusiasts also included E. K. Wilcox of Cleveland, Ohio, whose initials allegedly were derived from the Hungarian phrase "Éljen Kossuth" – meaning " Long Live Kossuth."[7]

Although the political payout for the Hungarian cause after Kossuth's "triumphal tour" of the United States was minimal, his influence continued to shine for many decades after his return to the old continent. His name and fame remained in America, and he himself became a beacon and guiding light to the average American, as well as to some of America's great national leaders. He likewise inspired the hundreds of thousands of Hungarian economic immigrants who had entered the United States in the four decades prior to World War II, and he continued to serve as a source of inspiration to their second, third, and fourth generational descendants.

Beyond serving as a beacon for human freedom and national self-assertion, Kossuth even influenced American fashion during his stay in the United States. The most visible of this fashion-craze was the appearance of the so-called "Kossuth-hat," which was a tall black hat decorated with feather plumes in the front. Almost as popular as the Kossuth-hat were the

"Kossuth-jacket" (braided Hungarian nobleman's jacket), the "Kossuth-trousers" (Hungarian cavalry or hussar trousers), and the "Kossuth-beard" that surrounded the individual's face in a horseshoe fashion.[8] The combination of these items, particularly as worn by Kossuth with his elegant noble demeanor, presented an overpowering spectacle to the mid-nineteenth-century celebrity-hungry Americans.

During World War II one of America's "liberty ships" – built with the financial support of Hungarian Americans – was also named after Kossuth.[9] Even as recently as June 1999, when President Árpád Göncz of Hungary made his first official state visit to the United States, President Clinton began his welcome speech with a quotation from one of Kossuth's orations that he had delivered a century and a half ago.[10] But above and beyond this, Kossuth is the only Hungarian, whose name is generally known to most Americans, and who is represented in the United States by three life size standing statues, a life size bust, and about half a dozen bronze plaques.[11]

KOSSUTH'S HOLD UPON THE AMERICAN MIND   The best example of Kossuth's hold upon the American mind is the case of his input upon the wording of President Lincoln's "Gettysburg Address." In his speech delivered on February 7, 1852 in the Ohio's state capitol in Columbus, Kossuth characterized his age as the age of democracy, and did so with the following words: "The spirit of our age is democracy. – All for the people, and all by the people. Nothing about the people, without the people. That is democracy, and that is the ruling tendency of the spirit of our age."[12] This Kossuthian definition of democracy is startlingly similar to that of Abraham Lincoln's in his memorable speech that he delivered after the Battle of Gettysburg: "We here resolve... that this nation, under God, shall have a new birth of freedom; and that, government of the people, by the people, for the people, shall not perish from the earth."[13]

The similarity of these two definitions leaves no doubt in our mind that Lincoln, as a young lawyer and legislator, had followed Kossuth's every move while in America and he too fell under the influence of the great Hungarian statesman. Of course, these expressions by these two great leaders contain words that are part and parcel of the basic definition of American Democracy, stated in spirit – if not in exact words – in the Constitution of the United States of America (1788). But the resemblance between Kossuth's and Lincoln's definitions of democracy – more specifically the expression "for the people, by the people" – still makes us think about the influence that Kossuth's words had upon President Lincoln, when engaged in writing his brief, but most significant address in wake of that bloodiest encounter of the Civil War.[14]

Kossuth's eloquent orations, delivered in an elegant if somewhat archaic English, mesmerized his American audiences. Naturally, he did have his critics and enemies on both sides of the Atlantic, but even the latter were overawed by his oratorical abilities. "What suggestive power lies in his supernaturally beautiful voice!" exclaimed the turncoat actor Gábor Egressy (1808–1864) in one of his secret reports to the Austrian Imperial Government. And then he continued: "Against his [Kossuth's] magic, like Ulysses [three thousand years ago], we have to tie ourselves to the mast, so that unknowingly we do not run after him."[15] Most Americans agreed with this assessment, including the greatest contemporary American orator, Daniel Webster (1782–1852), who was unable to divine the secret of Kossuth's powerful influence. Some people found the source of his hypnotic powers in the Latin construction of his sentences, others attributed it to his frequent use of archaic words, and still others to the accented but elegant English in which he delivered his orations.[16]

Whatever the reasons for Kossuth's phenomenal influence, the reverberations of his visit to America were still very much alive eleven years later in 1863, when President Lincoln brooded over the content of his proposed speech at Gettysburg – which turned out to be "the most memorable of all American [presidential] addresses."[17] In that hour of sorrow, he undoubtedly remembered Kossuth's uniquely phrased expression about the nature of democracy.

When Kossuth arrived in America in December 1851, after two and a half years of exile in the Ottoman Turkish Empire, he came to ask for American help in rekindling Hungary's struggle for independence against monarchical absolutism. Welcomed by most Americans as a hero, he gained some private financial support, but he was never able to persuade the U.S. Government to abandon its path of neutrality. That policy had been set down by George Washington in his "Farewell Address" (September 17, 1796), where the first President of the newly formed American Republic warned his nation against "entangling foreign alliances."[18] This policy of nonintervention made Kossuth's American tour far less successful than anticipated. He returned to Europe somewhat disenchanted and disillusioned. But his disillusionment was not with American democracy, only with the noninterventionist and isolationist policy of the U.S. Government.

THE AGE OF REFORM IN HUNGARY AND THE HUNGARIAN REVOLUTION It is perhaps appropriate to recall a few things about Hungary and Louis [Lajos] Kossuth (1802–1894) in the period before the eruption of the Hungarian Revolution of 1848. This, in spite of the fact that the work reprinted here does contain two – although somewhat error-filled – essays about Kossuth and Hungarian Revolution of 1848–1849.[19]

Like much of Central Europe, following the post-Napoleonic age and the Congress of Vienna (1814–1815), Hungary was also suffering under the oppressive "Metternich System."[20] This system had been shaped by, and named after the arch-conservative Chancellor of the Austrian Empire, Prince Klemens von Metternich (1773–1859). It was Prince Metternich, who was the chief architect of the post-Vienna conservative alliance system that had been established for the sole purpose of keeping the powerful new ideologies of nationalism and liberalism in check. Metternich feared these ideologies like a plague, and he did everything in his power to hinder their development and their spread. But as we all know, it is next to impossible to keep the dominant ideologies of an age from asserting and perpetuating themselves. This was also true for the ideas of nationalism and liberalism as applied to Hungary of those days. The fact was that Hungary's leaders – the progressive members of the common nobility, and even aristocracy – began to reshape the country's social and political life soon after the Congress of Vienna. This process of change continued throughout the second quarter of the nineteenth century. It culminated partially in the reforms of the last feudal Diet of 1847–1848 (November 12, 1847–April 11, 1848), and then continued with the social and political reforms of the Revolution and the War of Independence of 1848–1849. The most important achievement of the last feudal Diet was the abolishment of all vestiges of feudalism, while those of the Revolution included the promulgated the so-called April Laws[21] and a number of other progressive legislations through the War of Independence. The April Laws transformed Hungary from a near-feudal and politically dependent province of the Habsburg Empire into a modern and independent parliamentary democracy, with an elected government that was responsible to a broadly based elected legislature.[22]

Ever since the late 1830s Kossuth had been in the forefront of this struggle for Hungary's modernization. He did not assume the country's political leadership until early October 1848, when he did so as the President of the newly created National Defense Committee [Országos

Honvédelmi Bizottmány]. Formed to deal with the crisis created by the increasingly violent relationship between Hungary and the Habsburg Imperial Court – the latter being supported by some of the artificially aroused non-Magyar nationalities of Hungary –, the Committee served as the country's chief executive organ until Hungary's declaration of independence on April 14, 1849. Thereafter, Kossuth remained in charge of this struggle to the very end. He was the driving force behind Hungary's military efforts to defend the achievement of the Revolution, as well as behind the dethronement of the Habsburg dynasty on April 14, 1849.[23] This last deed did not abolish the monarchy but declared the throne vacant and made Kossuth the Regent, or "Governing President." Sadly enough, however, it also brought about the Russian military intervention (June 15–18, 1849) that ultimately sealed Hungary's fate and forced Kossuth to choose the life of a political exile.

KOSSUTH AND AMERICAN DEMOCRACY   Kossuth was a man of great political dedication, unusual linguistic ability, and phenomenal oratorical flare, who had idealized American democracy already in his youth. He did this largely on the basis of the works of Benjamin Franklin (1706–1790), Thomas Jefferson (1743–1826), Alexis de Tocqueville (1805–1859),[24] and the Hungarian Alexander Bölöni Farkas (1795–1842). The latter had traveled in the United States in the same year as de Tocqueville (1831) and then published an equally sophisticated, but lesser known work on the nature of American democracy.[25] These works had wetted Kossuth's appetite for the American way of life and urged him on to try to implement these ideas and practices in his own country, once freed from Vienna's stifling control.

While in the United States, Kossuth had visited all of the major centers of American culture, learning and politics – as well as scores of minor settlements – east of the Mississippi. Wherever he went he made speeches, hammering repeatedly on need to enlist American support for the Hungarian cause.

During his stay in America, Kossuth made about 400 official addresses and perhaps close to a thousand short, impromptu speeches.[26] Some of his longest, most memorable, and most detailed speeches were delivered on the east coast between New York and Washington, where he also addressed the U.S. Congress. Most of these early speeches are incorporated in the work that is here being reprinted – the last being the one Kossuth made in Pittsburgh on January 28, 1852. His speeches in Cleveland,

Columbus, Indianapolis, St. Louis, and numerous others are to be found in other contemporary publications. Unavoidably, he often repeated many of his main points, but at the same time he also introduced new elements – either in the way he phrased and rephrased his references to his main ideas and goals, or by introducing elements of local history into his speeches. Notwithstanding these repetitions, Kossuth himself regarded about fifty of his addresses to have been so significant that he agreed to their publication in a separate volume under the editorship of Francis W. Newman.[27]

One of the most memorable of these speeches – which is not included in this reprinted collection – was delivered in Columbus, Ohio, on February 7, 1852. It is the same speech, where he defined democracy as "All for the people, and all by the people. Nothing about the people, without the people."[28]

In Columbus, Kossuth was received with great enthusiasm and much generosity by Governor Wood, Lieutenant Governor Medill, the members of the Ohio Legislature, as well as by the local chapter of the "Association of the Friends of Hungary." The latter was a group which had branches in cities and towns throughout America, and which had been established even before Kossuth's arrival to the New World. In their enthusiasm the members of the Ohio State Senate went so far as to pass a resolution which authorized the Governor of Ohio "to deliver to Louis Kossuth, constitutional Governor of Hungary, on loan, all the public arms and ammunitions of war belonging to the state…, to be returned in good order upon the achievement of Hungarian Liberty."[29] This, of course, was a well-meaning, but naive act on the part of the Ohio Legislature, which could never have been implemented without the approval of the U.S. Government. Even the Ohio legislators realized their folly after Kossuth's departure, for subsequently they tabled this resolution and then conveniently forgot about it.

Kossuth returned to Europe shattered and disappointed by the lack of American willingness to intervene in the affairs of Hungary and the Austrian Empire.[30] But like many others before and after him, he too was unable to crack America's attachment to the policy of nonintervention that had dominated American thinking for over a century, right up to World War I; and then also through much of the interwar years. Yet, his disappointment with American foreign policy never altered Kossuth's admiration for American democracy, nor for American society – with the exception of the institution of slavery, which he could never fathom. (The anti-slavery forces tried to enlist him into their ranks, but Kossuth fought desperately to avoid being dragged into the quagmire of American domestic politics, which could have hurt his cause considerably.)[31] His admiration for American democracy is amply demonstrated by his continued praise of the American political system and the American way of life through much of his long and lonely years as an increasingly sidelined political exile.[32] His disdain for slavery, however, is crouched in obtuse sentences, for fear that his remarks during those emotional antebellum times would turn half of the United States against him and thus hurt his hope for American support for the Hungarian cause.

For a short period in the middle of the nineteenth century, Kossuth's influence in the New World was so persuasive that his presence and views impacted even American domestic party politics. Following his arrival to America both political parties consciously sought his favors and his support. These included the Democratic Party, which, while saturated with the ideas of Jacksonian democracy, supported the institution of slavery; as well as the Whig Party, which supported federalism, but opposed slavery.

KOSSUTH AND "YOUNG AMERICA"   Kossuth had an especially close relationship with the Young America movement, which climaxed precisely at the time of his arrival to the United States. They supported America's rise to a great power position, and for the same reason advocated a "policy of intervention" – favored also by Kossuth. And because Kossuth's only hope for the continuation of his struggle against the Habsburgs lay in the triumph of Young America, he consciously built a close relationship with that movement,[33] as well as with all politicians who espoused anti-isolationist sentiments. Among them were Senator Lewis Cass (1782–1866) of Michigan, Senator Henry Foote (1804–1880) of Mississippi, and the French-born Senator Pierre Soulé of Louisiana. There were also others who sympathized with the policy of intervention, but they were generally more careful and less outspoken than the above. Moreover, they always viewed intervention from the vantage point of American foreign policy interests, and tended to disregard ethically and emotionally based arguments, which generally characterized Kossuth's speeches. Among the latter was President Zachary Taylor (1782–1850), who died unexpectedly on July 9, 1850; the noted orator and Secretary of State Daniel Webster (1782–1852); and Senator Stephen Arnold Douglas (1813–1861) from

Illinois, known as the "little giant," who in 1860 was Abraham Lincoln's rival for the presidency of the United States.[34]

The proof of Kossuth's unparalleled influence in contemporary America can be found in the multitudes of writings that have appeared about him and about his struggle for an independent Hungary. No other Hungarian has received as much attention as the former governor-president of Hungary during the early 1850s.[35] Never has any event connected with Hungary – not even the anti-Soviet and anti-communist Hungarian Revolution of 1956 – ever impacted upon American society as did Kossuth and the Hungarian cause that he represented. And no Hungarian name has ever shone as brightly and as impressively as did that of Kossuth during his American tour.[36]

Kossuth's arrival in New York aboard the ocean liner Humboldt was almost like a national holiday. This festive atmosphere persisted for several months, notwithstanding the Hungarian governor's growing realization that he would not be able to alter American foreign policy in the direction of intervention, and that George Washington's dictum about avoiding "entangling alliances" was still the law of the land.

Triumph of Nonintervention To the outside world, Kossuth's nearly eight months tour of the United States appeared like a "triumphal tour." Outside the deep South, with its attachment to the institution of slavery, he was received with great ovations everywhere.[37] Yet, because of his inability to nudge the U.S. Government in the direction of intervention, from the political point of view his tour was less than successful. This became evident already in January 1852, when he paid a visit to President Millard Fillmore (1800–1874), who left no doubt in Kossuth's mind that no cause of any sort could make him break with the Washingtonian policy of nonintervention. When speaking to Kossuth, Fillmore basically pointed to the essence of his State of the Union message, delivered a bit earlier, where he asserted that "no individuals have the right to hazard the peace of the country, or to violate its laws upon vague notions of altering or reforming governments in other states... Friendly relations with all, but entangling alliances with none, has long been a maxim with us. Our true mission is not to propagate our opinions, or impose upon other countries our form of government by artifice or force; but to teach by example, and show by our success, moderation and justice, the blessings of self-government and the advantages of free institution."[38]

189

Although initially more flexible on the idea of intervention, by the end of 1851 Daniel Webster was also of this opinion. Even before Kossuth's arrival to the capital, Webster wrote to his friend Richard Milford Blatchford (1798–1875) that he would "treat him [Kossuth] with respect, but shall give him no encouragement that the established policy of the country will be from any degree departed from… If he should speak to me of the policy of intervention, I shall have ears more deaf than adders."[39]

This view was generally shared by most Americans, and it gained even more currency when Kossuth began to question – however slightly – the Washingtonian policy of neutrality. It was precisely Kossuth's repeated subtle criticism of this policy, which made the general public aware of its existence and its significance. As a result, some of them began to view Kossuth's questioning of his politics as an uncalled-for personal attack by a foreigner against the "father" of the American nation.

One of the typical examples of this new phenomenon was the attitude expressed by the Boston Unitarian clergyman, Rev. Francis Parkman, the father of the noted historian Francis Parkman (1823–1993), who, in November 1852, made the following statement about Kossuth's efforts to undermine the Washingtonian principle of nonintervention: "No one respects the talents of Louis Kossuth more than I do. But if the Archangel Gabriel and his brother Michael were to quit their celestial homes and come to Boston, clothed in white robes and bearing palms in their hands, and should undertake to teach the doctrines of Washington's Farewell Address – so help me heaven, not meaning to be profane, I should pluck them by their robes and say to them, go back where you came from, praise God, and mind your own business."[40]

The ever more widely held view that the policy of intervention was unacceptable to the United States gradually made Kossuth's American tour progressively more and more difficult. Thus, notwithstanding the repeated public adulation that surrounded him, he was forced to realize that his hopes for an American intervention have been built on a cloud. Consequently, by the end of his American tour, his early optimism all but evaporated, and he returned to the old continent incognito – under the name of Alexander Smith[41] – in full realization that for the time being the New World will not intervene in the affairs of the Old World. He, therefore, decided to pursue his goals for Hungarian independence with the help of European powers. Those hopes, however, eventually also gave way to hopelessness as the Austro–Hungarian Compromise of 1867 made that goal both unattainable and perhaps also undesirable.

Kossuth departed the United States – the scene of his great triumphs and bitter disappointments – on July 14, 1852. Although he left never to return, his memory remained in the New World, and so did the memory of his "triumphal tour." He continued to be viewed by most Americans as one of the most important representatives and exponents of human freedom and political independence. His captivating speeches, his lofty ideas, and his creative expressions continued to circulate in American society, and he himself continued to serve as a source of inspiration for all Americans.

To the Hungarian economic immigrants, who had inundated this land at the turn of the century, Kossuth was even more. He was the exponent of all of their human and individual wishes, desires, and aspirations, as well as the primary source of their national pride. In their eyes, Kossuth "was a giant among the giants of world history, whose name can only be said and written without qualifying adjectives. He was a comet, which – although falling out of the firmament – left behind an eternal luminance that shines upon the past and throws continuous rays of glory upon all Hungarians."[42] This was a definition of Kossuth's role in history that all Hungarian immigrants believed in. As put by a chronicler of the Hungarian–American past – the immigrants were convinced that Kossuth had been "Sent by God! The God of the Hungarians! So that as the Messiah of universal freedom… he should journey through America, exact tears with his melodious voice, create enthusiasm, strengthen millions in their belief in the sanctity of human rights, and make the Hungarian name immortal throughout America."[43]

Today, on the 150th anniversary of Kossuth's visit to the United States, we remember with affection and respect the achievements of the Hungarian Revolution of 1848, as well as the deeds and sacrifices of men associated with that Revolution. Among the latter no one was more significant than Kossuth, who is perhaps the only Hungarian who had captured the attention of all Americans for a brief moment in history, and who had also left an almost indelible mark upon mid-nineteenth-century American history. This fact is another important link between Hungary and the United States, the country which Kossuth and most other Hungarians have always called – and continue to call even today – "the land of liberty."

COMMENTS ON THE REPRINTED WORK The work reprinted here contains some of the major speeches that Kossuth had delivered in the course of December 1851 and January 1852 in New York City, Philadelphia, Baltimore, Washington, DC, and Pittsburgh. They were collected and edited by someone who identifies himself as "An Officer of the Hungarian Army." The speeches themselves are reprinted faithfully, but because the work had been put together hurriedly under adverse circumstance, the two appended essays – on Kossuth's life and on the military history of the War of Independence – contain a number of inaccuracies and errors in judgment.

Thus, Kossuth's biographical essay incorporates several factual errors. For example, Kossuth was not a "general;" he did not even serve in the armed forces. He was not born on April 27, 1806, but on September 18 or 19, 1802. His father did not serve in the Austrian Army during the Napoleonic wars. At most, the elder Kossuth may have participated in the "last Hungarian nobles' uprising" in 1809, when Napoleon invaded Western Hungary. Moreover, the assertion that "during the wars which occurred in Austria from 1527 to 1715, seventeen of the family of Kossuth had been attained for high treason against Austria" is pure myth. Certainly, Kossuth himself did not know anything about these alleged high treasons when he composed his unfinished family history and autobiography in 1844, where he wrote about his family's origins going back to the 13th century. The only victim of Habsburg aggression within his family – and that only on his mother's side – appears to have been a certain Andreas Weber, a Protestant Zipzer-German from Zemplén County in Upper Hungary, who had been "exiled" by the Habsburg Imperial General Antonio Caraffa (d. 1693) during the Kurucz-wars and the simultaneous anti-Protestant crusade (1686–1688) for his Lutheran beliefs.[44] There are a good number of other mistakes as well, including the misspelling of Hungarian names and titles (e.g., Mezlenyi = Meszlényi, Batthyanyi = Batthyány, Pesti Hirlap = Pesti Hírlap, Debreczin = Debreczen or Debrecen, etc.).

The second essay entitled "Battles of Hungary" – which should have been a brief history of the Hungarian Revolution – is a collection of brief descriptions of each of the military encounters the author judged to be significant in the Hungarians' struggle against the Austrians, Russians, and the country's rebellious non-Magyar nationalities. The worst problem from the vantage point of a modern reader is the confusing use of place names. Hungarian, more-or-less Hungarian, and archaic German names are used and mixed without any system or pattern. Thus, nowadays it takes a historian to tell that Waitzen is Vác, Gran is Esztergom, Comorn is Komárom, Ofen is Buda (Budapest), and Raab is Győr. A number of the places mentioned are no longer part of Hungary, and their official name today is a Slovak, Romanian or Serb version. The dates given for the various battles are often wrong. Ozora took place on October 7, Friedau on November 8, Mór on December 30, Tétény on January 3, Egerfarmos on March 1, the Czibakháza crossing was on March 16–17, Isaszeg on April 6, Vác on April 10. Figures on the participants and their losses are often exaggerated.

Even more meaningful is the author's strong bias against General Artúr Görgey (1818–1916), the commander-in-chief of the Hungarian Revolutionary Army, whom he describes as a traitor – as was customary in those days among Kossuth's followers. This bias is demonstrated by the very title of the section dealing with the end of the War of Independence: "The Traitor Gorgey's Shameful Surrender to the Russians" (pp. 48–52). In contrast to this statement, however, Görgey's decision to surrender at Világos on August 13, 1849, was a well-reasoned pragmatic act, and his alleged treachery is a myth rooted in the personal rivalry among Hungary's revolutionary leaders. This has been amply demonstrated time and again by some of the country's best historians.[45]

Given the above, the reader should pay more attention to the content of Kossuth's speeches, than to the commentary by the unidentified author of these essays. As we know, Kossuth was not only a marvelous speaker, but he was also a man filled with ideas. His speeches have much to offer on the revolutionary ideas of liberty, equality, and fraternity, as well as on the dominant ideologies of his age: nationalism (national sovereignty), political liberalism (parliamentary government), and economic liberalism (capitalism or free economic system).[46]

NOTES

[1] When writing in Hungarian, the author publishes under the name "Várdy Béla."

[2] Bálint Hóman and Gyula Szekfű, Magyar történet [Hungarian History], 5. vols. Budapest: Király Magyar Egyetemi Nyomda, 1943, vol. 5, p. 453; hereafter Hóman–Szekfű, Magyar történet.

[3] See Joseph Széplaki, Louis Kossuth: "The Nation's Guest". Ligonier, Pennsylvania: Bethlen Press, Inc., 1976, p. 11. Széplaki lists over 1600 mostly contemporary publications that deal with Kossuth, among them 189 poems addressed to the Hungarian statesman. The definitive work on Kossuth's tour is Dénes Jánossy, A Kossuth-emigráció Angliában és Amerikában. 1851–1852 [The Story of the Hungarian Exiles Led by Kossuth in England and America] 2 vols. Budapest, 1940–1948.

[4] Greeley's, Whittier's, Emerson's, and Lowell's tributes to Kossuth are reprinted in Endre Sebestyén, Kossuth. A Magyar Apostle of World Democracy. Pittsburgh: Expert Printing Company, 1950, pp. 207–218.

[5] Concerning this Kossuth-cult, in addition to Széplaki's above-cited work, see Kende Géza, Magyarok Amerikában. Az amerikai magyarság története [Hungarians in America. The History of Hungarian Americans], 2. vols. Cleveland: A Szabadság Kiadása, 1927, I, pp. 77–115; István Gál, "Az amerikai Kossuth-kultusz" [American Kossuth Cult], in István Gál, Magyarország, Anglia és Amerika [Hungary, England, and Amerika]. Budapest: Officina, 1944, pp. 187–194; Donald S. Spencer, Louis Kossuth and Young America. A Study in Sectionalism and Foreign Policy, 1848–1852. Columbia and London: University of Missouri Press, 1977, pp. 29–81; Sebestyén, Kossuth, pp. 205–218; and John H. Komlós, Kossuth in America, 1851–1852. Buffalo: East European Institute, State University of New York College at Buffalo, 1973, pp. 75–94.

[6] Judit and Lajos Koncz, "Kossuth, Amerika történelmének része" [Kossuth is Part of America's History], in Amerikai Magyar Népszava/Szabadság, vol. 111, no. 9 (March 9, 2001), pp. 13–14. It should be noted here that this type of information is often based on hearsay, which then is adopted from one work to another. Generally, these middle names are seldom mentioned in major biographical dictionaries, partially because they were hardly ever used, and partially because they were generally dropped later in life. In the case of Dewey, for example, one of the major sources has this to say: "His baptismal name was Melville Louis Kossuth, but he discarded the Louis when he was in his teens and Kossuth when he was in his twenties, at the same time shortening Melville to Melvil." Cf. Dictionary of American Biography, vol. 9 (Supplement vol. 1). New York: Scribners, 1944, pp. 241.

[7] Kende, Magyarok Amerikában, vol. 1, p. 84.

[8] See Spencer, Louis Kossuth and Young America, pp. 60–63.

[9] Béla Várdy, Magyarok az Újvilágban [Hungarians in the New World]. Budapest: Magyar Nyelv és Kultúra Nemzetközi Társasága, 2000, p. 384.

[10] The author and his wife, Dr. Agnes Huszár Várdy, were invited guests at this White House reception for President Göncz on June 8, 1999.

[11] These include the full standing Kossuth-statues of Cleveland (1902), New York City (1929), Algona, Kossuth County, Iowa (2001), and the Kossuth-bust in the U.S. Capitol (1990). Bronze plaques can be found in Washington, D.C., Pittsburgh, Columbus, St.Louis, Los Angeles, and perhaps a few other cities.

[12] See the article "Ohio Legislature," in Ohio State Journal, February 7, 1852. See also Széplaki, Louis Kossuth, p. 10; Sebestyén, Kossuth, p. 130; and Selected Speeches of Kossuth. Condensed and Abridged with Kossuth's Express Sanction, by Francis W. Newman. London: Trübner # Co., 1853, p. 185. See also Steven Béla Várdy, "Louis Kossuth's Words in Abraham Lincoln's Gettysburg Address", in Eurasian Studies Yearbook, 71. évf., 1999, pp. 27–32; and Béla Várdy, "Kossuth és az amerikai demokrácia" [Kossuth and American Democracy], in Emlékkönyv L. Nagy Zsuzsa 70. születésnapjára [Memorial Volume for the Occasion of the 70th Birthday of Zsuzsa L. Nagy], ed. János Angi and János Barta. Debrecen: Multiplex Media – DUP, 2000, pp. 173–182.

[13] Lincoln's "Gettysburg Address" has been reprinted in thousands of books and in many languages. The first to point out the likely influence of Kossuth on Lincoln's Gettysburg Adress was György Szabad, "Kossuth on the Political System of the United States of America" Etudes historiques hongroises …Budapest, 1975, also in the series Studia Historica Academiae Scientiarum Hungaricae 106.

[14] On Kossuth's impact on contemporary American society and political life, see Spencer, Louis Kossuth and Young America, cited above. For a map of Kossuth's tour through the United States, see Széplaki, Louis Kossuth, p. 22.

[15] Gábor Egressy (1808–1866), as quoted in Andor M. Leffler, The Kossuth Episode in America. Ph.D. dissertation, Western Reserve University, Cleveland, Ohio, 1949, p. 95; and in Spencer, Louis Kossuth and Young America, pp. 54–55.

[16] Spencer, Louis Kossuth and Young America, p. 55.

[17] Richard B. Morris, Encyclopedia of American History. New York: Harper # Brothers, 1953, p. 242.

[18] Ibid., p. 123. Morris asserts that Washington used the term "permanent alliances," and that the term "entangling alliances" was used by Thomas Jefferson in his first inaugural speech on March 4, 1801: "Peace, commerce, and honest friendship with all nations, entangling alliances with none." Cf. ibid., p. 131.

[19] For the essay on Kossuth's life, see the reprinted work below: The Life of Gov. Louis Kossuth with his Public Speeches, pp. 11–25; and for the summary of the history of the Hungarian Revolution see pp. 27–57.

20 On the Metternich System, see Heinrich Ritter von Srbik, Metternich: Der Staatsmann und der Mensch. 3 vols. Gratz: Akademische Druck- und Verlagsanstalt, 1925–1954; and the excellent short analytical essay by Arthur May, The Age of Metternich. New York: Holt, Rinehart and Winston, 1933. See also the relevant sections of the following popular works: A.J.P. Taylor, The Habsburg Monarchy, 1809–1918. London: Hamish Hamilton, 1948, pp. 33–70 (and several later editions); C.A. Macartney, The Habsburg Empire, 1790–1918. New York: Macmillan Co., 1969, pp. 199–425; and Robert A. Kann, A History of the Habsburg Empire, 1526–1918. Berkeley-Los Angeles: University of California Press, 1974, pp. 243–318.

21 The April Laws, which were signed by King Ferdinand V [Emperor Ferdinand I] on April 11, 1848, included 31 paragraphs, among them the following: 3) the establishment of an independent Hungarian Government responsible to Parliament, 4) annual Parliament in Pest [Budapest], 5) voting rights extended to the peasants who owned at least one-quarter "peasant plots," to independent artisans and tradesmen, and to the members of the intelligentsia, 7) reunification of Hungary and Transylvania, 8) uniform and proportional taxation, 9) abolishment of all feudal obligations of the peasantry to the nobility, 11) abolishment of the feudal courts, 12) establishment of a banking system for credit purposes, 13) abolishment of the tithe paid to the church, 15) abolishment of the entail system, 17) establishment of a new elected governmental system for the counties, 18) establishment of a jury system to deal with freedom of expression in journalism, 19) establishment of a new Hungarian university, 20) proclamation of the equality of all religions, 21) standardization of Hungarian national colors and national coat of arms, 22) establishment of a Hungarian National Guard, 23) establishment of city governments and elected city councils, 24) establishment of a new elected governmental system for the villages. Concerning the April Laws, see Az 1847/8-iki évi országgyűlési törvényczikkek [Legislative Acts of the Diet of 1847–1848]. Pest: Landerer and Heckenast, 1848; reprinted 1998. See also Hóman–Szekfű, Magyar történet, vol. 5, pp. 389–394; and Magyarország története, 1848–1890 [History of Hungary, 1848–1890], eds. Endre Kovács and László Katus. Budapest: Akadémiai Kiadó, 1979, pp. 107–117. The author of the relevant chapter is György Spira. The most up-to-date study on the April Laws is András Gergely, "A magyar polgári államrendszer 1848-ban" [The Hungarian Constitutional System in 1848] in Tanulmányok Magyarország és Közép-Európa 1848–49-es történetéből [Studies on the History of Hungary and Central Europe in 1848–49] Budapest, 2001. pp. 93–136.

22 For a good and balanced English language account of the Hungarian Revolution of 1848–1849, see István Deák, The Lawful Revolution: Louis Kossuth and the Hungarians, 1848–1849. New York: Columbia University Press, 1979. See also The Hungarian Revolution and War of Independence, 1848–1849. A Military

History. Ed. Gábor Bona. War and Society in East Central Europe. Vol. XXXV. New York: Columbia University Press, 1999. Bonn.

[23] The text of the Hungarian Declaration of Independence has just been published in an annotated reprint edition in four languages: Hungarian, German, French, and English, with a postscript about the conditions of its issuance. See Függetlenségi Nyilatkozat 1849 Debreczen, ed. János Angi, Botond G. Szabó, and Béla Tóth. Debrecen: Multiplex Media – Debrecen University Press, 1999. For an assessment of this work see Béla Várdy, "Az 1849-es magyar függetlenségi nyilatkozat" [The Hungarian Declaration of Independence of 1849], in Debreceni Szemle [Debrecen Review], New Series, vol. 7, no. 3 (September, 2000), pp. 464–468.

[24] Alexis de Tocqueville, La démocratie en Amérique, 2 vols., Paris, 1835–1840; English translation: Democracy in America, 4 vols., 1835–1840, and many editions since; Hungarian translation: A demokratia Amerikában, 4. vols., Pest, 1841–1843.

[25] Sándor Bölöni Farkas, Utazás Éjszak-Amerikában. Kolozsvár, 1834. For English translations of this work, see Journey in North America by Alexander Bölöni Farkas, trans. and ed. by Theodore Schoenman and Helen Benedek Schoenman. Philadelphia: American Philosophical Society, 1977; and Sándor Bölöni Farkas, Journey in North America, 1831, trans. and ed. by Árpád Kadarkay. Santa Barbara, CA: ABC-Clio, Inc., 1978.

[26] See Leffler, The Kossuth Episode in America, p. 31.

[27] See Selected Speeches of Kossuth. Condensed and abridged, with Kossuth's Express Sanction, ed. Francis W. Newman. London: Trübner and Co., 1853. The speech delivered in Cleveland and Columbus respectively was printed in "Report of the Special Committee appointed by the Common Council of the City of New York to make Arrangements for the Reception of Gov. Louis Kossuth, the Distinguished Hungarian Patriot," New York, 1852. pp. 527–563. Many of the drafts of Kossuth's speeches are deposited in the Hungarian National Archives, R 90. 28. See note #12 above.

[29] Quoted in Komlós, Louis Kossuth, p. 119.

[30] Kossuth's lack of success in gaining American military and political support for the Hungarian cause is discussed by this author in his "Kossuth amerikai 'diadalútja' 1851–1852-ben" [Kossuth's American 'Triumphal Tour' of 1851–1852], in Debreceni Szemle, New Series, vol. 6., no. 3. (September 1998), pp. 331–339.

[31] On Kossuth and the slavery question, see Várdy, "Kossuth és az amerikai demokrácia," especially pp. 178–180 (note #12 above).

[32] See Gyula Szekfű, "Az öreg Kossuth, 1867–1894" [Old Kossuth, 1867–1894], in Emlékkönyv Kossuth Lajos születésének 150. évfordulójára, [Memorial Vol-

ume on the Occasion of the 150th Anniversary of Louis Kossuth's Birth], 2 vols. Budapest: Akadémiai Kiadó, 1952, vol. 2, pp. 341–433.

³³ The most important leader of the Young America movement was the publicist George Nicholas Sanders from Kentucky, who, as the editor-in-chief of the influential The Democratic Review, became a fanatical advocate of the policy of American expansionism and interventionism. See Spencer, Louis Kossuth and Young America, pp. 116–120.

³⁴ Ibid., pp. 18–27, 37–47, 112–116, 137–140.

³⁵ To prove this point, it is enough to point out that the huge documentary collection assembled by Rev. Edmund [Ödön] Vasváry about the Hungarians in the United States, nearly 10 per cent of which (34 of the 436 boxes) is about Kossuth. Concerning Kossuth's contemporary influence on American politics and society, see András Csillag, "The Edmund Vasváry Collection", in Hungarian Studies, vol. 1., no. 1 (1985), pp. 123–130. Concerning Rev. Vasváry, see Steven Béla Várdy, "Reverend Edmund Vasváry: Personal Reminiscences about a Chronicler of the Hungarian-American Past", in Eurasian Studies Yearbook, vol. 71 (1999), pp. 207–212; and its earlier Hungarian version, Béla Várdy, "Vasváry Ödön, az amerikai-magyar múlt krónikása," in Vasváry Collection Newsletter, no. 19 (1998/1), pp. 3–4.

³⁶ On the changing image of Hungarians in the United States, see "Change in Social Standing in Polls Taken in 1964 and 1989", in The New York Times, 1992. január 8, p. A-12. See also Béla Várdy, "A magyarság változó képe Amerikában az elmúlt másfél évszázadban," in Valóság, vol. 43, no. 9 (September, 2000), pp. 70–89; and its slightly revised English version, Steven Béla Várdy, "Image and Self-Image among Hungarian-Americans since the Mid-Nineteenth Century," in East European Quarterly, vol. 35, no. 3 (September 2001), pp. 309–342.

³⁷ Concerning the main stops on Kossuth's tour of the United States, see Joseph Széplaki, Louis Kossuth, pp. 22–24.

³⁸ Congressional Globe, 31st Congress, 1st Session, p. 15; quoted by Komlós, Louis Kossuth, p. 103.

³⁹ Webster to Blatchford, December 30, 1851, in The Writings and Speeches of Daniel Webster. Boston: Little, Brown and Co., 1903, vol. 18, pp. 501–502; also quoted by Komlós, Kossuth, p. 100.

⁴⁰ Quoted in Richard Henry Dana, Jr., The Journal of Richard Henry Dana, ed. Robert F. Lucid, 3 vols. Cambridge: Cambridge University Press, 1968, vol. II, p. 52; and Spencer, Louis Kossuth, p. 172.

⁴¹ The New York Tribune, July 15, 1852.

⁴² Kende, Magyarok Amerikában, vol. 1, p. 56.

⁴³ Ibid., pp. 77–79.

⁴⁴ This officer was most probably not an actual Hungarian officer but someone

who made a compilation based on the memoirs of Lt-Colonel János Prágay, the aide de camp of General Klapka. The relatively most accurate battle descriptions all refer to the campaign of Klapka, while the erroneous dates and the inflated figures all appear in the volume by Prágay. (Johann Prágay, The Hungarian revolution. Outlines of the Prominent Circumstances attending the Hungarian Struggle for Freedom together with Brief Biographical Sketches of the Leading Statesmen and Generals who took Part in it. New York–London, 1850.)

45 Kossuth's short, unfinished autobiographical family history has been reprinted by György Gracza, Kossuth Lajos élete, működése és halála, 3rd ed. Budapest: Lampel Róbert, R.T., 1902, pp. 4–7.

46 See for example Domokos Kosáry, A Görgey-kérdés és története [The Görgey-Question and its History]. Budapest: Királyi Magyar Egyetemi Nyomda, 1936; and its much enlarged recent version: A Görgey-kérdés története [The History of the Görgey-Question], 2 vols. Budapest: Akadémiai Kiadó, 1994. Cf. László Pusztaszeri, "General Görgey's Military and Political Role. Civil-Military Relations during the Hungarian Revolution. In Béla K. Király (ed.), East European Society and War in the Era of Revolution, 1775–1856. War and Society in East Central Europe. Vol. IV. New York: Columbia University Press, 1984. pp. 472–518.

Pictures

Louis Kossuth, Cincinnati, 1852.
Daguerreotype by Thomas Faris

Louis Kossuth and Archduke Stephen
arrives at Vienna to put forward the
reform claims of the Pozsony Diet to
the Emperor, March 14, 1848.
Lithograph

Louis Kossuth arrives from Pozsony to Pesth, April 6, 1848. (?)
Engraving by Joseph Tyroler

Louis Kossuth makes a speech at Cegled, the first station of his recruiting tour of the Hungarian lowlands, September 24, 1848.
Lithograph by Franz Kollarz

Battle of Isaszeg, April 6, 1848. ► Painting by Mór Than
National Museum, Galery of Historical Paintings

Battle of Comorn, February 24, 1849. ► Lithograph by Vinzenz Katzler

After a lost battle Louis Kossuth says a prayer for the souls of the dead on the Kapolna battlefield, February 27, 1849. ➤ Lithograph by Pál Böhm

Battle of Waitzen. Hungarian hussars and Russian cavalry fight on the High Square of the town, in front of the Cathedral, July 17, 1849.

Surrender at Vilagos, August 13, 1849.

Farewell of Louis Kossuth from Hungary, August 16, 1849.
Lithograph by an Austrian artist

Reception in the harbour of Southampton, October 23, 1851. ➤ Wood-print

The Vanderbilt ship, with Kossuth and his family on the deck, makes port in front of Covent Garden on 6 December, 1851. ➤ Reprinted in Vasárnapi Újság, 1894.

Louis Kossuth enters the city of New York on the Broadway, December 6, 1851. ➤ Colour

Banquet given to honour Louis Kossuth at Astorhouse, New York, December, 1851.
Reprinted in Vasárnapi Újság, 1894.

Reception at Central Park, New York, December, 1851.
Reprinted by John H. Komlós in *Louis Kossuth in America* 1851–1852. Buffalo, New York, 1973.

Artillery parade held to honour Louis Kossuth, New York, December, 1851.
Reprinted in Vasárnapi Újság, 1894

Portrait of Louis Kossuth published
in New York, showing four episodes
of his life, 1851–1852.
Steel-engraving by Watermen Lilly

Louis Kossuth in Philadelphia, 1851.
Reprinted by John H. Komlós in *Louis Kossuth in America* 1851–1852. Buffalo, New York, 1973.

Silver envelope-file with a welcoming speech in it to Governor Kossuth, presented to him by the citizens of Baltimore, December, 1851.

Silver goblet presented to Louis Kossuth in Philadelphia. Engraved inscriprions are: To Louis Kossuth, the revered and well-beloved freedom fighter from the women and maidens of Philadelphia, as a token of their deepest respect. In the year of 1851. Those like you, consumed with a passionate love for liberty live on in the hearts of many.

An allegory displaying the figure of Kossuth
accompanied by the spirit of Freedom, History
and Hungary. On the front-page of a Boston
journal, December 27, 1851.

Louis Kossuth in America, 1851.
This portrait was displayed on
the so-called Kossuth dollars
issued in the USA.
Steel-engraving by Thomas
Philibrown

The 1, 5, 10 and 50 dollar notes of the Kossuth dollar issued by the Hungarian Fund. Kossuth dollars and public contribution helped to raise a hundred thousand dollars intended to cover the cost of a renewed fight for the freedom of Hungary.

Louis Kossuth, Boston, 1852.
Photograph of a J. J. Hawes daguerreotype

Celebration at the Kossuth monument
in New York, 1937.
Photograph by John Albok

Osiris Publisher
H–1053 Budapest, Egyetem tér 5
www.osiriskiado.hu

On the Cover: *Louis Kossuth in America, 1851*
(Steel-engraving by Thomas Philibrown)

Printed in Hungary by Szekszárdi Nyomda Kft., 2001

ISBN 963 389 188 4

		DATE DUE